SHIFT
AHEAD

▼

ALLEN ADAMSON
AND JOEL STECKEL

SHIFT AHEAD

HOW THE BEST COMPANIES
STAY RELEVANT IN A
FAST-CHANGING WORLD

AMACOM

AMERICAN MANAGEMENT ASSOCIATION

New York • Atlanta • Brussels • Chicago • Mexico City • San Francisco
Shanghai • Tokyo • Toronto • Washington, D.C.

Bulk discounts available. For details visit:
www.amacombooks.org/go/specialsales
Or contact special sales:
Phone: 800-250-5308
Email: specialsls@amanet.org
View all the AMACOM titles at: www.amacombooks.org
American Management Association: www.amanet.org

This publication is designed to provide accurate and authoritative information in regard to the subject matter covered. It is sold with the understanding that the publisher is not engaged in rendering legal, accounting, or other professional service. If legal advice or other expert assistance is required, the services of a competent professional person should be sought.

Library of Congress Cataloging-in-Publication Data

Names: Adamson, Allen P., author. | Steckel, Joel H., author.
Title: Shift ahead : how the best companies stay relevant in a fast-changing
   world / Allen Adamson and Joel Steckel.
Description: New York : AMACOM, [2018] | Includes index.
Identifiers: LCCN 2017027507 (print) | LCCN 2017038895 (ebook) | ISBN
   9780814438343 (ebook) | ISBN 9780814438336 (hardcover)
Subjects: LCSH: Strategic planning. | Diffusion of innovations–Management. |
   New products. | Marketing.
Classification: LCC HD30.28 (ebook) | LCC HD30.28 .A3113 2018 (print) | DDC
   658.4/06–dc23
LC record available at https://lccn.loc.gov/2017027507

About AMA

American Management Association (www.amanet.org) is a world leader in talent development, advancing the skills of individuals to drive business success. Our mission is to support the goals of individuals and organizations through a complete range of products and services, including classroom and virtual seminars, webcasts, webinars, podcasts, conferences, corporate and government solutions, business books, and research. AMA's approach to improving performance combines experiential learning—learning through doing—with opportunities for ongoing professional growth at every step of one's career journey.

10 9 8 7 6 5 4 3 2 1

CONTENTS

ACKNOWLEDGMENTS

There's a belief that the busier you are, the better you are. And, there was no doubt, I *was* busy. Busy-ness syndrome was taking over my life. I was going from meeting to meeting, texting and answering emails along the way, in cabs (and Ubers), on the subway, and walking down city streets (not smart). I realized that all this busy-ness was keeping me occupied, certainly, but was it really making me better at my job, which is to help my clients build and manage brands?

The world was moving at warp speed, and I was getting caught in the maelstrom. I needed to get out of my busy-ness bubble — to pick up my head and take out my earbuds. It was time for a fresh look and a fresh perspective. After a bit of looking and learning, I realized it was time for a new book. This one about how the best marketers are *dealing* with a world in which everyone seems to be pedaling as fast as they can to keep up.

I knew I didn't want this book to be another "brand" book. It had to have a wider scope. To brainstorm possible directions, I called my long-time partner, Betsy Karp.

We were tossing around a few ideas when, one day, she asked: "How about *Shift Focus* or *Shift Ahead*? How *do* the best brands shift ahead in the face of accelerating change while keeping a focus on what they mean to consumers?" Bingo! Over the course of the next year, Betsy worked her magic, zeroing in on the "aha" points in more than 100 transcripts of interviews with some of the best marketing experts in the industry. Without Betsy, I wouldn't have been able to shift my focus, let alone shift ahead. So, thank you to this partner!

An enormous thank-you, as well, to my newest partner, Joel Steckel, who expanded and pressure-tested my thinking. Joel and I met when I was guest-lecturing in his class at New York University's Stern School of Business. After a few slides, Joel started to build on my remarks, and I started to build on his comments. After class, we kept talking, and the conversation moved on to the topic of this book. Within a few weeks, we were spending hours together in conference rooms, adding to each other's thoughts on whiteboards, creating a framework for *Shift Ahead*. His input and fresh perspectives on every topic were greatly appreciated.

Warm thanks are very well deserved by three others who helped make *Shift Ahead* possible: Emily Ambrose, my intern, who did copious research and assisted in developing the subject matter; Susan Velazquez, my assistant, who helped transcribe and organize interviews, and who fact-checked and researched additional material for the stories; and Chuck Routhier, my creative partner for the cover design. Thanks, too, to my many, many friends and colleagues in the marketing business who gave generously of their time and talent for this book.

Busy-ness syndrome aside, the real inspiration for this book may have been generated when I was looking over some photos on my iPhone and came across a picture of my son, Josh, and my daughter, Elissa, taken during a family trip to Oxford, England. They had discovered my first book, *BrandSimple*, in a bookstore there and, for about fifteen seconds, were interested in what their dad did for a living. Thanks, kids, for your interest—and for your love!

Thanks most of all to my wife, Maddie, who has always encouraged me to push further, to be better, and to never take the easy "this is good enough" route.

Finally, a note to my mom and dad, Ruth and Joe Adamson, who both escaped Nazi Germany with only the shirts on their backs. Because of their drive to shift ahead in the face of intense challenges, I was given the opportunity to live the life I do, for which I am very grateful.

Allen Adamson

I want to thank Allen Adamson for inviting me on this ride to *Shift Ahead*. I remember that first day he came to speak to my class. I said to myself, "This guy thinks like I do." Allen had a world of experience, experience that I couldn't touch. However, I had something that he didn't. I had the ability to apply rigor and generalize across specific cases. That's what academics do. I'm grateful to Allen for all that he taught me and for the opportunity to participate in the conversations that form the core of this book.

Beyond Allen, I want to thank those who helped me develop the ability to apply rigor and generalize across specific cases. In the last chapter, you will read about my mentors in graduate school: Len Lodish, Abba Krieger, and Jerry Wind. I have also benefitted from having offices next to or near world-class academics at various institutions. The opportunities to bounce ideas off and write with people like Don Lehmann and Vithala Rao have helped make me the academic I am today. Their contributions to my way of thinking cannot be underestimated.

Allen's team became my team. I, too, am grateful to Betsy, Emily, and Susan.

Part of what I have learned about shifting ahead, I have observed from watching my two wonderful children grow. Ben and Phil have provided me with the North Star, the direction that I have used to guide all the major decisions I have made since they were born.

My wife, Felice, could not have been more supportive. She is my greatest supporter, my biggest cheerleader, and the person whom I could always turn to when I was having a block in thinking. It's her inspiration that drives me.

Joel Steckel

1

WHY THIS BOOK?

SHIFT AHEAD

It's a good question. And a good part of the answer resides in the word
relevant. To say something is "relevant" is to say that it matters. Being
relevant has always been a critical factor for success in all walks of life.
Writers and artists want their work to be relevant. Musicians want their
music to be relevant. Filmmakers want their movies to be relevant to
viewers. Scientists and researchers want their discoveries to be relevant.
Teachers want their lessons to be relevant. We all want to believe we are
relevant to our employers and to our partners. But, more germane to
this book, businesses must continually ensure that they are relevant to
their customers if they want to continue to *stay* in business. A central
premise of this book is that to remain relevant, businesses must indis-
putably know *why* they matter to their customers.

That said, maintaining relevance in a world that is changing so very,
very fast is very, very challenging. (Lest you doubt that the world is
changing fast, when was the last time you got late-breaking news from

an actual newspaper versus a media app or Twitter feed, took a picture
with a camera instead of a phone, thought there was no possibility for a
self-driving car, sent your resume through the mail rather than posting
it on the cloud, or watched a television show at the time it actually
aired?)

The ability to stay relevant is being significantly challenged by the
accelerating pace of change—and new ways of doing things—that are
emerging with every passing day.

As Thomas L. Friedman, award-winning author and columnist for
the *New York Times* told us, the planet's three largest forces—Moore's
Law (technology), the Market (globalization), and Mother Nature (climate change and biodiversity loss)—are accelerating all at once, transforming five key realms: the workplace, politics, geopolitics, ethics, and
community.

"When change is happening at five miles per hour, if you get off
track it's not that big a deal, because how far off track can you get? But
when change is happening at 500 miles per hour, a small error in navigation can have a huge effect. If you don't start every day by asking,
What world am I living in? What are the biggest drivers in the world?
What are the biggest drivers shaping more things and places?, you won't
get the proper diagnoses. This really matters more than ever," Friedman
told us when we spoke. "These three forces aren't just changing the
world; they're fundamentally reshaping everything. And I would say
that, as such, they require massive innovation in both business and
society. Change is happening at a compound rate and innovation has
to happen at a compound rate in these other realms. That's the main
argument in my book [*Thank You for Being Late*]. Either we align ourselves with these drivers to shape the world to get the most out of them
or not. That said, I would also say you need to build off that solid foundation."

Breakthroughs in science, data analysis, healthcare, media, and education *are* occurring at compounded rates of speed. The way we bank,
secure our homes, get our entertainment, measure the effect of our
exercise regimens, acquire information, share information, buy our
food, use energy to run our households, and perform almost every other

daily activity is changing literally before our eyes and during our lifetimes. The ongoing transformations in the way technology works, businesses work, and almost everything else in the world works is having a major impact on how *we* work, plan, decide, think, and live.

It was with this idea in mind that we set out to write *Shift Ahead*. It is based on our hands-on experience, our academic research, and most significant, our more than 100 interviews with senior management and category experts from a wide spectrum of applicable fields. We wrote *Shift Ahead* to document *how* the smartest companies and organizations shift their strategies in order to stay relevant in the face of the swift and exponential changes in everything from technology to the forces of globalization, from politics to culture, from consumer tastes to human behavior. We wanted to find out *how* they shift ahead—how they stayed ahead of the curve, the competition, and the evolving requirements of their customers—given the barrage of evolving challenges.

We also wanted to clarify how businesses and organizations shifted the focus of their endeavors *without* losing focus on what they stand for in the minds of consumers. As marketing professionals, we know that in a world as transparent and skeptical as this one, authenticity has taken on far greater significance. We found in case after case that staying connected to your organizational DNA, staying true to your "true north" as you shift ahead is critical for credibility. Firms that shift ahead, but without maintaining a focus on who they are, do so at their own peril.

One goal of this book is to distill the experiences of over 100 companies through the lenses of our diverse practical and academic backgrounds to provide usable and, yes, relevant lessons learned on how to stay relevant in this frenetic world. We want these lessons to be as applicable to small start-ups and nonprofits as they are to multinational organizations. We want them to be as beneficial for brick-and-mortar establishments as they are for online enterprises. With a minimal amount of buzzwords and jargon, and with a wealth of, again, relevant examples, *Shift Ahead* demonstrates how organizations across a wide range of categories effectively and efficiently shift gears, shift direction, but always with the intention of shifting *ahead,* so as to continue to matter in a meaningfully different way to those they serve.

As marketing professionals, we'd like to share a quick lesson in one of the fundamentals of marketing having to do with relevance, what we call being "meaningfully different." Marketers know it's not enough to be merely relevant to be worthy of a customer's admiration and loyalty. Something must be relevantly different to attain this status. This is not an emerging business school concept, especially as it relates to organizational, brand, or even personal success. It has always been a factor in whether a business succeeds or doesn't, success being quantified as being able to solve a problem that is important to a customer better than anyone else can. How to most efficiently get from point A to point B. How to get clothes cleaner. How to give children a healthy start to the day. How to quench thirst. How to get better gas mileage. How to alleviate a headache. How to feed a puppy as opposed to an older dog. How to save money on airfare. How to store and share photographs. How to find a reputable plumber, electrician, or spouse. The best businesses, the best brands, achieved their positions because they found a gap in the marketplace that needed filling, or identified a problem that needed solving, and they did it better than their competition at a cost that makes it worthwhile doing. That is the essence of the *market-based firm*.[1]

About twenty-five years ago the global communications firm Young & Rubicam (Y&R) developed one of the most respected proprietary tools in the advertising industry for figuring out how a brand is performing relative to others in its category. Brand Asset Valuator (BAV) is a diagnostic tool that not only indicates how a brand is performing, but provides insight into what must be done to keep the brand healthy and strong (i.e., relevant) going forward.

The BAV is the world's largest database on how consumers see brands. It purports to provide insight on how brands grow, get into trouble, and can recover. BAV collects consumer perceptions of approximately 43,000 brands along seventy-two dimensions. It reports the percentile for each of these measured brand dimensions for each of the brands compared to the entire database. For example, a single United States Postal Service (USPS) brand characteristic might score a 90, meaning survey respondents rated that characteristic higher for the USPS than for 90 percent of the other brands in the database.

As a result of extensive statistical analyses of the underlying data, BAV has found it effective to aggregate these seventy-two dimensions into four fundamental measures underlying the brand asset. These measures, referred to as "pillars," are:

1. Energized Differentiation (a brand's unique meaning with motion and direction)
2. Relevance (how appropriate the brand is for you)
3. Esteem (how you regard the brand)
4. Knowledge (an intimate understanding of the brand)[2]

These pillars represent empirically grounded combinations of the seventy-two dimensions and are the basis of most generally accepted uses of the BAV data. These four pillars, and the subset of the seventy-two brand dimensions that contribute to each of them, are shown in Figure 1-1.

The relationship between differentiation and relevance provides insight into the future of the brand. More relevance than differentiation suggests the brand may be in danger of becoming a commodity. Esteem and knowledge, the other two pillars, make up a brand's stature. A brand with a higher level of esteem than level of knowledge is a brand that enjoys a good reputation, although people may not know a lot about it. This puts the brand in a great position to convince consumers to want to know more about it. Too much knowledge and not enough esteem and consumers might say, "Hey, I know a lot about you and you're nothing special." In the case of leading brands, like Apple, Disney, GE, BMW, Amazon, and Google, all four pillars are strong.

BAV represents the world's largest brand database, and it continues to evolve. In 2005, an additional dimension of Energy was recognized, which relates to forward momentum of a brand. BAV measurements have been successful in predicting stock market performance, and a theoretical portfolio has exceeded the performance of the Standard & Poor's (S&P) index for every year in the last decade. Collaborative work with academia is ongoing to develop a worldwide valuation of a brand's contribution to a firm's market capitalization. The U.S. work

BAV Pillar	Underlying Perceptual Metrics	Survey Scale	BAV Data	Meaning and Role of the Pillar
Differentiation	Unique Distinctive	Yes/No Yes/No	% Responding "yes" % Responding "yes"	Perceived distinctiveness of the brand. Defines the brand and reflects its ability to stand out from competition. Is the "engine of the brand train; . . . if the engine stops, so will the train."
Relevance	Relevant to me	1–7 Scale	Average	Personal relevance and appropriateness and perceived importance of the brand. Drives market penetration and is a source of the brand's staying power.
Esteem	Personal regard leader High quality Reliable	1–7 Scale Yes/No Yes/No Yes/No	Average % Responding "yes" % Responding "yes" % Responding "yes"	Level of regard consumers hold for the brand and valence of consumer attitude. Reflects how well the brand fulfills its promises.
Knowledge	Familiarity with the brand	1–7 Scale	Average	Awareness and understanding of the brand identity. Captures consumer intimacy with the brand. Results from brand-related (marketing) communications and personal experiences with the brand.

Figure 1-1. BAV's work is based on the "Pillars of the Brand Asset."

Source: Adapted from Natalie Mizik and Robert Jacobson, "The Financial Value Impact of Perceptual Brand Attributes," *Journal of Marketing Research* 45 (2008), 16

has expanded to include over 200 categories, representing over 3,000 brands measured each quarter.

We had the opportunity to have an in-depth conversation with John Gerzema, CEO of the BrightSight Group, who helped develop BAV during his tenure as global chief insights officer at Y&R's BAV Consulting. Author of several books, including *Brand Bubble: The Looming Crisis in Brand Value and How to Avoid It,* he is a pioneer in the use of data to identify social change and to anticipate and adapt to new trends and demands. Gerzema's firm marries financial management with brand management to help businesses understand and mine the relationship between their customers and their brands. Talking to us about BAV, he said, "We live in an age of 'compressed change.' Brand building is completely different from the way it used to be. Positioning used to be planting a flag and stepping back. Now the terrain is moving at such speed and ferocity that it's difficult to think in a static way about positioning. Erosion is critical to track. You have to be able to figure out *why* consumers are falling out of love with brands. Consumers don't just want brands to be different and relevant, but to *keep* being different and relevant. . . . Successful brands recognize this and know it's not a place, it's a direction. They must constantly evolve, not stand still."

BAV reflects the spirit of this book. First, it is forward looking; it indicates when a brand's differentiation in the market is starting to lag. This is one of the early indicators that there's trouble ahead and that a brand risks becoming irrelevant if it *doesn't* shift ahead. Second, BAV prevents myopic thinking—another dynamic in being able to stay relevant. By studying brands across categories, BAV allows you to see where your brand resides within the entire consumer experience, not just the category in which you compete. As the lines between industries and offerings continue to blur—especially in media and technology—this is a critical factor in being able to determine whether what you are promising still matters to people. It's essential to be able to see in which competitive set your business or brand sits; in which perceptual space it exists in people's minds. One of the things we'll explore in this book is the ways in which you can see your business or brand within a broader context—a factor critical for shifting initiatives.

Basics covered, we now answer what you can expect to take away from this book. We've taken an iterative approach to shifting ahead, parsing the process as a series of practical and concrete steps, beginning with a discussion of "red flags." Like all red flags, these are the early-warning signals. How do you know when, or if, it's time to shift ahead? How do you know if it's already too late, or if it's too soon? While the lagging indicators that a change is required are pretty easy to see—sales are sluggish, Wall Street is getting testy with performance, or people are unfriending you on Facebook and the like—the leading indicators are not nearly as easy to detect. For instance, consumer attitudes for a certain food group, media choice, exercise-tracking device, gaming app, or automobile are gradually turning one way or another. Will this attitude stick, reach a tipping point, and permeate a wider audience, or will it just fade away? Or, say the implications of a new technology are just starting to take hold. What marketplace markers should you look for as you consider whether to shift your business strategy to chase the shiny new object, whatever the cost, or cool your jets and wait and see how it might apply to your industry in the long run? Using multiple examples, in Chapter 2 we examine the most significant red flags to heed and discuss the potential repercussions for acting, or not, along with the potential steps and resolutions that can help mitigate less-than-positive outcomes.

Throughout the book, we generalize teachable moments from our 100-plus interviews with those who experienced, firsthand, the ramifications of shifting ahead to stay relevantly different in a fast-changing world. Some of our interviewees were successful. Others were not. Others still have not seen their fates decided. Relative to red flags, for instance, we heard Maryam Banikarim, global chief marketing officer (CMO) at Hyatt, delivering a speech at Columbia Business School. Before joining Hyatt, she was the first-ever CMO at media giant Gannett, where she was credited with repositioning the company and its brands. She began her career at Young & Rubicam. "Look at Airbnb and Uber," she shared about early-warning signs. "If you had said to somebody ten years ago there's going to be a business where you're riding around in some stranger's car, they would have been like, 'Are you crazy?' There is no question that what will be here in ten years will not look like what it looks like today. That said," she continued, "it is very hard to get a company to transform when it's not on fire. One of the interesting things about having been in the media business early on is that we experienced disruption [before] other businesses. Most businesses are being disrupted today, but media was one of the earlier industries. We actually saw what was coming and experienced it much faster. It forced us to broaden the way we thought about the business, to broaden our lens. It also taught us to follow our North Star when things get more chaotic.

"We've had to do this in the hospitality industry," Maryam said, "where some think the lane is pretty narrow. We have been forced to think about our category differently, to think about ourselves as creating experiences. But people—like habits—are hard to change, especially when it comes to compensation. I remember hearing about a project that Time Warner was looking at in 1993 called Pathfinder. It was basically the Internet before its time. There was another project in 1993 called the Orlando TV Project, which was like Netflix. The people who had these ideas were at the pinnacles of their careers and, as a result, they were afraid to move forward. They didn't want to take a risk. They killed off their own innovations because they were not being compensated for these types of initiatives. It's a scary lesson to think about. There's not a day that goes by that there isn't some crazy crisis that forces you to have to rethink how you're operating. The world is changing at a rapid pace and you have to be good at being adaptive all the time."

"Adaptive all the time," as Maryam said, is a key headline for being able to shift ahead. While red flags are early-warning signs that a shift is in order, there are some common barriers that inhibit firms from being able to execute a successful shift ahead. In Chapter 3 we take a hard look at these barriers, which can be financial, cultural, and psychological. Again, using specific examples related to the financial, cultural, and psychological barriers to change, we examine some of the usual suspects, among them Kodak, BlackBerry, Toys "R" Us, and Playboy. We look at the causes of the varying degrees of breakdown within these organizations and talk about what they could have done, should have done, and what to look out for in your own organization relative to these scenarios. But we also deconstruct some lesser-known examples of organizations that came up against one or all of the specific barriers and discuss what can be learned from what they did—or didn't do—in response.

More than this, talking to people associated with National Geographic, the American Cancer Society, and Teach for America, we discovered that as well meaning or as altruistic as an organization's promise or purpose might be, internal barriers to change can be present, in both the nontraditional organization as well as the large, publicly traded enterprise. In fact, when dealing with an array of constituents that include volunteers and donors who demand their voices be heard in exchange for their time and money, these barriers can be even more onerous. (Please note for the record: There are—and we acknowledge—impressive results from second attempts at shifting ahead. This is not a one strike and you're out situation!)

Moving on past the red flags and barriers to a strategic shift ahead, we get to the fundamentals. Chapter 4 delves into what's required to ready an organization for a change; the fundamental factors that must be addressed to ensure everyone is on board and all necessary systems are operating optimally. In other words, financially, logistically, and culturally, what must be in top working order to prepare for and execute a shift ahead? In many circumstances, a company might have the best of intentions to make a significant change in strategy. However, the effort is shortsighted because there's not enough money in the bank to deal with snafus, not enough due diligence regarding operational factors, or not enough understanding of the initiative for the rank and file to bring the endeavor to life. Clichéd as it might be, a "can-do attitude" is a key factor for success.

Also, as obvious as it might be—but all too often overlooked—another of the key factors in being able to successfully shift ahead with a relevantly differentiated promise is ensuring you know what is important to your customers. That is, as the world and *their* world evolves, you have to stay ahead of what matters to them—what's relevant to them. Bob Pittman, who was responsible for inventing several powerful brands including MTV and Nickelodeon and, most recently, iHeartRadio, told us, "You have to get to the core of what your brand stands for and then determine its relationship to your customer. I've learned that, before you do anything else, you must understand the relationship to the customer. I've worked in television, in real estate, in theme park companies, with the Internet and digital companies. What ties them together is [knowing] who's the customer and what are they doing? *They* will tell you what matters. *They* will find it. *They* will evaluate it. They will decide if it's good or bad, not me."

Without a deep dive into what matters to the customer, all bets for a successful shift ahead are off. While the categories and industries we examine in this book are as varied as they could be, every person we interviewed emphasized this notion, among them John Hayes, formerly CMO at American Express; Edward Bastian, current CEO of Delta Air Lines; David Kirkpatrick, technology expert and authorized chronicler of Facebook's Mark Zuckerberg; and Joey Bergstein, CMO and general manager of Seventh Generation. From their insider's perspective, we learned about—and share in detail—the fundamentals that must be dealt with before you can even contemplate a successful shift ahead.

Which begs the next questions: ahead of what, and who, and for what reason? In Chapter 5 we look at the many tactics and resources companies use to ascertain, to the best of their (or anyone's) ability, what *does* lie ahead and what it means. While there is absolutely no crystal ball, we discovered that there are several legitimate ways and means to gauge what the future marketplace holds and the inherent implications for one business or another. Some of these things are anecdotal or apparent to even the most casual observer (e.g., sales of artificial intelligence devices are up, people are more often streaming media than watching network television, they're getting rid of telephone landlines, they're cutting gluten from their diets, building smaller homes, buying smart appliances and environmentally safe laundry detergent). More significant to being able to suitably shift ahead, however, are the more sophisticated or high-tech ways and means that companies use to determine what's waiting around corners, to decipher the nebulous writing on the wall, or even (slap to forehead) to expose what has long been hiding in plain sight. We all know that data have never been more copious. That everything from our online searches, texts, and tweets to the IP addresses of our smart appliances offer up a rich source of valuable information to companies waiting to take advantage of it. Organizations that know how to read the signals, to spot trends, to evaluate these data and properly use them to their customers' benefit are those that will, themselves, benefit. Quoting from our conversations with management experts in forecasting and in research and analysis, including Rita McGrath, Paco Underhill, Faith Popcorn, and Amy Webb, we provide myriad recommendations and resources pertaining to how companies can gain insight into what's out there as it relates to their categories and their customers.

Friedman's book, alluded to earlier in this chapter, completely supports the premise of our book—i.e., that we have entered an age of dizzying acceleration, and that has consequences. As for businesses needing to be able to quickly and assuredly connect the dots, to link current activity to future behavior, he told us, "The problem is that our capacity to adapt is being outpaced by a 'supernova' built from three ever-faster things: technology, the market, and climate change. In terms of technology, for example, in 2007, with the arrival of the iPhone, Android, and Kindle, software began to dominate the world. A customer downloads an app from Apple every millisecond. The firm sells 1,000 iPhones, iPads, or Macs every couple of minutes. It whips through its inventories in four days and launches a new product every four weeks. Manic trading by computers and speculators means the average Apple share changes hands every five months.

"For those who may not remember," Friedman pointed out, "AT&T was originally the exclusive service provider for the iPhone. For years, Steve Jobs wouldn't *allow* outside apps on the phone. We forget that there were no outside apps. Then, after 2008, the year they opened the App Store, the demand on AT&T's network increased 1,000 percent over the next seven years. That scale of response set the stage for what was required in networking. It was exponential and, for those who weren't ready for it, overwhelming. A simple act, like opening the App Store, had an exponential impact on the marketplace. It necessitated software-enabled networks, which support the dynamic, scalable computing and storage needs of our current modern computing environment. Without software-enabled networks we couldn't change or expand as quickly or effectively as is necessary to support the modern smartphone and all that it brings. For those who were able to see this coming and prepare for it, it was a game changer."

As Friedman writes, to further support the reality that the speed of change is exponentially altering all manner of business models[3]:

> Such hyperactivity in the world's biggest company by market
> value makes it easy to believe that 21st-century business is push-
> ing its pedals ever harder to the metal. On Apple's home turf in

Silicon Valley the idea that things are continually speeding up is commonplace. The pace of change is accelerating, Eric Schmidt and Jonathan Rosenberg of Google assert in their book *How Google Works*. For evidence look no further than the 'unicorns'—highflying startups—which can win billion-dollar valuations within a year or two of coming into being. In a few years they can erode the profits of industries that took many decades to build.

Like dorks in awe of the cool kids, the rest of America's business establishment chastises itself for being too slow. If you ask the boss of any big American company what is changing his business, odds are he'll say speed. Firms are born and die faster, it is widely claimed. Ideas move around the world more quickly. Supply chains bristle to the instant commands of big-data feeds. Customers' grumbles on Facebook are met with real-time tweaks to products. Some firms are so fast that they can travel into the future: Amazon plans to do 'anticipatory' shipping before orders are placed. The shareholders' reports of the firms in the S&P 500 index of America's biggest are littered with 'speed,' 'fast,' and their synonyms, not to mention a goodly dollop of disruption.

Leaders of all organizations can't help but know today that they face the threat of "disruption," as they've watched companies such as Amazon, Google, Airbnb, and Netflix transform retail, advertising, travel, and media. It's using this threat of disruption as a positive prompt for sustainable, innovative solutions that separates winners from losers in making the shift. It's also having the wherewithal to determine whether this shift necessitates a changing of "gears" or "direction."

We cover this subject matter in Chapter 6 of *Shift Ahead*. Apart from the potential need to change infrastructure, it's obviously much easier to strengthen a current offering. Verizon moving from landline to cable, or Apple shifting from computers to tablets to phones and watches, or HBO moving from paying for the rights to offer Hollywood movies to creating original content, or Starbucks going beyond coffee to offer an ever-expanded café menu—all these examples are in clear alignment with the company's original and core brand purpose, the idea with which consumers understand the company lives behind. More challenging is being able to convince consumers to accept a promise that is not as obviously in keeping with the organization's most recognizable reason for being. This difficulty was faced by Amazon in moving from media sales to media creation and distribution, GE moving from making light bulbs and refrigerators to becoming an interpreter of the "Internet of everything," and BP (formerly British Petroleum) trying to convince people that it does things "beyond petroleum."

If you determine you must shift *direction* to shift ahead of the competition—that is, identify and develop a new way to create customer value altogether—it's critical to ensure that you have significant support for some authentic and credible link to the role you play in your customers' lives. If you don't come by a trait or attribute naturally, and it's a matter of acquiring it or building it out, there are steps that must be taken to guarantee it's believable and sustainable. We talk to senior management from a wide range of businesses about their efforts to shift, the results, and most important, the lessons learned. Among them are Brian Goldner, CEO of Hasbro; the architect of IBM's Smarter Planet and Watson initiatives, Jon Iwata; Peter Seligmann, the founder of Conservation International; CNN's Jeffrey Zucker and former CNN executive Scot Safon, now an independent marketing consultant; and Mark Addicks, who shifted the fortunes of a host of brands while CMO at General Mills.

So critical is leadership in the equation that we give it undivided attention in Chapter 7, getting insight from people who had firsthand experience in steering their organizations through a shift ahead. We share words of both advice and caution from Shelly Lazarus and Ed Vick, titans in the advertising industry; Douglas Blonsky, who led a successful rejuvenation of New York City's Central Park; John Sexton and Richard Soghoian, who spearheaded positive shifts in strategy in the area of academia; and Bruce Rogers, who helped transform the Forbes brand, in a category that, second possibly only to technology, has felt the greatest impact from the rapid changes in the marketplace and the resulting challenges to stay relevant.

Among the people we called on for additional input on what it takes to lead a media organization through a shift ahead in this era of accelerated change is Merrill Brown, a veteran media executive and currently the director of the School of Communication and Media at Montclair State University. In addition to writing for the *Washington Post*, Brown helped launch MSNBC.com in 1996 and was the website's founding editor-in-chief. He was, as he put it, "responsible for connecting Microsoft's 'technology wizards' and NBC's 'news hounds.'" Speaking to him about leading analog-to-digital transformations in the world of news reporting, he talked about the critical importance of vision, or the lack thereof—the ability to see that change is coming, and to be ready and willing to accept it and roll with it. As Brown said, "The greatest obstacle was that the newspaper industry was so insular, like 'We'll be back,' even as recently as the last five or six years. I've spoken at newspaper conferences and have been trying to persuade them, since about 1998, that you're in permanent decline and you guys need to wake up to that. They believed in their monopoly profits," Brown said, "and because they made so much money, it was inconceivable they wouldn't find new ways to continue to do so. For one thing, their ad revenue from classifieds was diminishing, along with revenue from traditional advertising, and it was all brought about by an innovative guy in a townhouse in San Francisco because he had a good idea."

San Francisco–based Craigslist and a host of other innovative advertising sites did their part to rattle the revenue stream for the print media business. But that was just one aspect of what was happening to the industry. More evolutionary, technology was quickly transforming the very way people got and consumed news and information. Vision—forward, peripheral, and hindsight—if not out-and-out prescience was a critical factor in Brown's leadership in a successful succession of industry shifts. The chance to engage with readers, or viewers, via the Internet, on mobile phones, on tablets, whether directly or through social aggregators, was allowing for exciting new formats and targeted content in real time. Brown saw this.

"There were three sets of challenges involved in the founding of MSNBC.com. There were technology challenges, journalistic challenges, and cultural challenges," Brown said. "Doing anything in real-time news on the Internet at that time was challenging. In my work as a journalist I had been writing about technology, like the breakup of the phone company and changes in regulations, that enabled TV to grow. I saw in cable television an enormous creative opportunity to invent new things. In terms of being a leader, I learned by doing. It was sort of a natural progression.

"I started as a consultant at NBC in 1995, and I was able to help them think through their Internet and distribution strategies. MSNBC. com was successful early on because we knew to integrate Microsoft technology from the start. It gave us a huge competitive advantage," Brown said, adding, "Today we see a level of connectivity in people's lives that wasn't possible in the old days of journalism, when things were delivered in a one-way fashion. Today, everything is on demand. The very notions of space and time have changed. That said, this has led to big hiccups in journalism that come from trying to race content to the public. On the one hand, we can't be too smart or too savvy about where technology is taking us. On the other, we need to reinforce the same high standards of integrity in our roles as journalists."

No leader or organization can be too smart or savvy relative to where the changes in the world might take them. And in Chapter 8 we explore what success looks like when leaders and organizations put together all the information found in the first seven chapters of *Shift Ahead*. These are stories that deconstruct the challenges of each organization cited and then reconstruct how the organizations addressed these challenges to stay relevantly differentiated. We show how the Greenwich Public Library successfully shifted ahead in the age of digital information. Marriott and FedEx provide additional examples of companies that put together the insights provided in this book to adapt to their changing environments.

We delve even deeper into this topic in Chapter 9 in *Shift Ahead*, with a look at what we believe are the most important skillsets required to stay relevantly differentiated as the world continues to turn ever faster: the abilities to "see and seize" opportunities. Among the many organizations we profile in our book, two of them in particular, HBO and GE, exemplify these skillsets. Yes, having a founder who exhibits these traits and instills them in the organization from day one is certainly an advantage. But it's been in never losing these traits, and in fact building on them, that has enabled these organizations to unceasingly shift ahead. We'll share critical takeaways from our conversations with top people associated with these organizations and provide a host of applicable lessons learned.

We explore why HBO never has been, and never will be, "TV," and how it stays ahead of the ever-proliferating pack of screen-related media creators and providers. And we talk to and impart lessons learned from senior people at GE, an iconic company with reinvention a trait that has always been part of its corporate DNA, defining what it does and what drives it forward. In essence, we demonstrate why it is that some businesses, organizations, and people can successfully keep up with the continual need to change and meet the marketplace demands, while others can't.

The ability to shift ahead has become table stakes in an organization's ability to *stay ahead* of its competition. Some organizations see it as exciting. Others see it as scary. Whatever the response, it's not just you, it's everyone. We are all feeling the effects of a world that is rapidly changing and where the pace of change is only getting faster. The realities continue to work their way into every aspect of our lives, from economic and technological to social and cultural, with profound implications. Among the most challenging of these implications is keeping up with, if not ahead of, these changes. It is a challenge faced not only by businesses and business leaders, but governmental agencies and nonprofit organizations, politicians and celebrities, academic institutions and job seekers, producers of goods and services and every imaginable brand, including the brands we call ourselves. The challenge is driven by something that is, essentially, Darwinian. It's the need to remain both relevant and competitive.

So, back to the beginning: Why this book? In a world that is changing faster and more furiously than ever, the ability to shift ahead, while not losing focus on who you are, is critical. For many companies, this urgency to stay relevant pushes against the need to protect the brand. *Shift Ahead* offers a smart, calculated approach to knowing when to change course and how to pull it off. Packed with insightful interviews, this book brings every internal and external factor into view: competitors, risks, culture, finances, and more. It teaches readers how to spot the warning signs that it's time for reinvention; how to overcome barriers in the way of future goals; how to maintain authenticity when shifting gears—or direction; and how to execute a bold change . . . brilliantly.

To stay competitive, you must stay relevantly differentiated. To do this, you must shift. To do it credibly, you must focus. *Shift Ahead* turns this difficult maneuver into a straightforward strategy.

2

HEED THE RED FLAGS

In a way, hearing an old advertising tagline is like looking at a forgotten picture in the family photo album. It captures a specific place or moment in time and evokes all sorts of associations and memories. Taglines also capture, in a few simple words, what the brand being advertised stood for—or wanted to stand for—*at* that moment in time. All good taglines express a brand's point of differentiation, how it promises its offering is (relevantly) different from the competition. Avis always tried harder; United's skies were friendly; and Coke was the real thing. A good tagline expresses what's important to consumers, again, at a moment in time.

Over the years, hundreds of taglines have come and gone. Some are remembered and repeated generation after generation, others have become part of the social vernacular (Wendy's "Where's the beef?," Verizon's "Can you hear me now?," Nike's "Just do it!," and the United States Army's "Be All You Can Be").

We're sure you have your own favorites, as we do, or those you find most memorable. In any event, as we began to research companies and organizations that had successfully shifted ahead—along with those that didn't—we talked about some of the most notable taglines and how each summed up, in a dramatic and compelling or aspirational way, the idea driving the organization at that certain point in time. This led us to ask the first and, to us, most obvious questions relative to organizations that had missed the mark: Isn't it obvious to organizations when a promise is becoming less meaningful to consumers? Isn't it obvious that the world is changing, and that the products or services being offered are in danger of becoming obsolete? Couldn't those organizations that did *not* successfully shift ahead see that consumers were losing interest? To paraphrase another tagline, couldn't companies that did not move fast enough to catch the market recognize that they were in danger of becoming their father's Oldsmobile?

For example, the Yellow Pages were identified with an implicit promise to consumers: If you let your fingers do the walking through the Yellow Pages, you can find the phone number of any local business you need. *Advertising Age* named "Let your fingers do the walking" as one of the top ten slogans of the twentieth century. However, with the emergence of Internet and online search directories, fewer and fewer people are letting their fingers do the walking. Seventy percent of Americans did not use a printed phone book at all in 2011.[1] Indeed, their fingers may still be doing the typing, but even that is likely to change with the increased penetration of voice recognition software like Apple's Siri or Amazon's Alexa. The slogan could morph into "Let your voice do the asking." Because of declined usage of print and environmental concerns, phone book delivery is now opt-in in many locations.

Sure, on Monday morning, everyone's a professional quarterback and can tell you which of Sunday's football plays were foolish or made for the turning point in the game. Hindsight is always twenty-twenty. It's foresight, seeing the red flags in advance of the risks, that makes the difference on the road to success. And so, before we get to anything else associated with the process of being able to shift ahead, we get to the red flags. What, exactly, are the signals that companies should be attentive to, indicating that there is a need to course-correct? This was the first thing we looked for as we reviewed our more than 100 interviews, examined our collateral research, and analyzed all the input on organizations that did successfully shift ahead, those that didn't, or those still in the process of doing so. In our compilation and parsing of facts, figures, and anecdotes, we established that there are two key categories of red flags. First, there are the hard business metrics that point to the fact that relevant differentiation is waning. And, then, there are those of a "softer" variety, the cultural dynamics that are inherent in a company and do not bode well for being able to pull off a successful shift in strategy. We'll start with three types of hard metrics in the more straightforward of the two categories.

RED FLAG ONE:
Basic Math

The most apparent red flags are performance-related numbers, the financial data that appears on any CFO's spreadsheet. This basic math would *seem* to be pretty straightforward and would *hopefully* get the message across: Your sales are starting to drop; your revenue, quarter-over quarter, is decreasing; your margins are eroding; your expenses and overhead are spiraling upward. If you're in the nonprofit sector, your donations or charitable gifts are waning year over year, as is your list of new or renewing contributors. Your hard-written grants are being overridden by those of other groups competing for the same pot of money.

Sales and revenue do not have to drop to indicate trouble. Plateaus are bad. If you aren't growing, you are dying. As Shantanu Narayen, the CEO of Adobe, said: "If you believe that growth is a fundamental imperative, and your business is not growing, and you are the market leader in a lot of spaces, you need to broaden the lens by which you look at opportunities." [2]

All organizations operate off fundamental mathematical metrics day-to-day. They have at their immediate disposal the facts that overtly reveal financially related early-warning signs of trouble ahead. We don't need to expound on this. What we do need to do is admonish that these warnings not be ignored. When you see the red ink, look into the cause and act on it as soon as possible. Unfortunately, in the case of many of the organizations we studied that did not shift ahead in time, it *was* a matter of either ignoring the warnings that were clearly in sight or, equally troubling, rationalizing them that led to their problems. By the time they finally did see or acknowledge the red (ink or flag), it was usually too late to do anything about it. They'd run out of, well, runway, in terms of time, money, and opportunity. In Chapter 3, we go into detail about specific organizations that bumped up against a financial barrier. When the numbers start to slide and no one is willing to face the facts or take them literally at face value, chances of future success slide as well.

RED FLAG TWO:
Competing on Price, Not Differentiation

In Chapter 1, we talked about one of the most valuable tools and tactics for determining a brand's value and its standing in a category: Brand Asset Valuator, or BAV. Among the key takeaways from BAV studies is that commodity status is not a good thing. It indicates that your product or service, while it may be relevant currently, is undifferentiated and carries no inherent value beyond how much it costs. A key objective for all brands is to create a promise that customers value at a level significantly greater than a price that includes not only cost, but a reasonable margin as well. Products that create such value for their customers have the potential to dominate their category.

However, companies cannot deliver such value in perpetuity. Innovative competitors will derive ways to deliver similar or superior value to some market segments. As powerful as the *New York Times* has been for a long time, the *Wall Street Journal* delivers news more suited to the business community. Brands must react to these dynamics lest they whither in decline as Pan Am, Blockbuster, Woolworth's, and Borders have done. As one of the developers of the BAV model, John Gerzema, told us, "Branding and growth is a series of constant small risks in decision making. You cannot get to the point where you have waited too long without taking any risks. You'll basically have to throw a Hail Mary."

If you don't make significant shifts at some point, you will find that the only way to keep sales going strong is to adjust the price. If price becomes too important a competitive weapon, it's likely that your brand's point of relevant differentiation is diminishing in the minds of consumers. If they can't see what makes your product or service any different or better, why would they pay more than they had to? Unfortunately, by the time the folks in the C-suites catch on to this idea, a Hail Mary pass might be too little, too late. What we found in our research was that if a company began to address the need to shift the minute there was a slight drop in relevant differentiation scores, they had a fair chance of successfully shifting. But the vast majority did not start to address the relevant differentiation issue before the runway ran out. In fact, many companies don't even track their organization from a brand equity point of view. Not smart. Brand value matters a lot. Heed this red flag.

RED FLAG THREE:
Big on Data, Short on Analysis

In the late 1800s, scientist John Haldane studied the rate of asphyxia in coal miners and recommended that they carry small animals, such as canaries, into the coal mines as carbon monoxide detectors. Given their size, these little birds would die from the toxic gases sooner than the miners and thus served as a warning when it was too dangerous to work. While this inhumane treatment of animals would never pass muster today, the phrase "canary in a coal mine" has come to indicate early-warning signs of major problems. Luckily, there are other inanimate detectors of conditions available to organizations, specifically as they relate to consumer sentiment.

As we know from our extensive work in the field of marketing, sometimes consumers can tell you what they're thinking and how they feel about your offering. More often though, they can't. To paraphrase Apple's Steve Jobs, sometimes consumers don't know what they want until you show it to them.[3] Even with all the qualitative and quantitative research available, we know that consumers tend to be polite, or evasive, when formally surveyed. That's where big data can fill in the gaps. Companies today are investing more and more in data collection, building sophisticated "dashboards" to track how consumers behave in real time. These dashboards can follow what people buy, where they buy, how often they buy, how often they share with others news of what they buy, and whether the news they share is good or bad. Dashboards monitor where people vacation, for how long, and how they arrived at their destination. They can keep tabs on whether someone bought the extended warranty for a product and whether they used it, or took a magazine subscription and whether they renewed it. Name a product, a service, a brand-related activity and there are data on who, what, where, when, and why. These technological dashboards provide a play-by-play of what's going on in a given category. More robust than even just five years ago, big data continues to get even bigger as more sales and goings-on are conducted and tracked online.

The big concern, however, is that many organizations have not figured out how to use all these data quickly enough or accurately enough to be of significant benefit. They can't see the proverbial forest for the trees. They don't always have the ability to detect what's salient to the future of their business. They know they have to keep collecting the data, but don't, or can't, optimally analyze it or evaluate the implications. While it's becoming easier to see consumer behavior in real time, the red flag is in not having the tools or resources to leverage the information effectively—to translate it and apply it. It is essential to invest in a dashboard to collect and track data. It is equally critical to invest in the capability to decode and decipher what the data mean relative to being able to shift ahead in a timely and relevant way.

As early as 1967, in a landmark article called "Management Misinformation Systems," Russ Ackoff, one of the founding fathers of the field of operations research, wrote that the biggest problem facing managers was not that they didn't have enough data, but that they didn't know how to use what they had.[4] With the explosion of big data, management misinformation can only have gotten worse.

If your data are collecting dust, that is another red flag. (More disquieting yet is if your research and development budget has been cut, and if your company has stopped trying to anticipate the next best thing, then maybe it's time to look for another job.)

In Chapter 5, we go into greater depth on the tactics organizations use to gather and analyze the hard business metrics to get a better read on the road ahead. For now, let's go on to the "softer" red flags.

RED FLAG FOUR:
Neglecting Table Stakes

At the global pizza chain Domino's, the recipe for renewed success has been seven years in the making. Domino's is ubiquitous around the world, with 12,500 locations in 80 countries, which in most cases is a marker of success. Indeed, Domino's built its business on the slogan/promise "You got thirty minutes?" However, within the last decade, it experienced falling profits and had a product that was often maligned. In 2009, it needed to take an objective look at what was going on and found that it hadn't been paying attention to what consumers were saying about the product and the brand. The product was perceived as inferior. As Russell Weiner, president of Domino's Pizza USA, told a CBS reporter, "It was a question of taste. People just felt there were better pizzas."[5]

While Domino's was working on making its thirty-minute promise efficient (and safe for deliverers), competitors were improving the taste of their products. Just because a firm exceeds expectations on one important customer attribute does not allow it to fall too far behind competitors on other important attributes. Points of difference can be both positive and negative. In Domino's case, there were both points of superiority (delivery time) and points of inferiority (taste), and they were canceling each other out. In poker and other gambling games, *table stakes* refer to an amount that is required to be able to sit down and play. In pizza delivery, table stakes were going up in taste and Domino's bank ran dry. Its neglect of the product's taste was forcing Domino's to eat its own profits for lunch.

Domino's readjusted its company culture to increase focus on the customer. It required that every employee, from the CEO down, master the skill of making the pizza and do it in-store. These rules were put into place by current CEO Patrick Doyle when he took over in 2010, and they remain in place. All of a sudden, customers had a voice. According to Weiner, the company did the unthinkable. It dumped its marketing campaign, which was based on speedy delivery, and shot a series of commercials that focused on taste.

The turnaround efforts were a success, and Domino's business today is very good. So good, in fact, that in the last seven years the company has outperformed Amazon, Apple, Facebook, and Google, with its stock going from $9 a share to over $180 a share in early 2017. That pizza just generally outsells burgers, tacos, and other fast food is a big advantage for Domino's, as is the fact that pizza literally delivers well. But there is no denying that the company's gain in market share is due to its own motivation and determination. And its recognition that there was a red flag waving. Management saw the red flag and addressed the warning signal. Because of that, Domino's is able to make steady investments in product and technology improvements and make sure it has sufficient table stakes.

RED FLAG FIVE:
Pride Often *Does* Go Before a Fall

While misquoted enough to have become the more commonly used expression, "Pride goeth before a fall" can apply to businesses just as much as it can apply to people. (The biblical proverb is actually, "Pride goes before destruction, a haughty spirit before a fall.") Whatever the verbiage, the point is that arrogance is a less than appealing trait and exhibitions of said trait will likely end in a less than positive way. A company arrogant and in love with its own success and way of doing things brandishes a big red flag on its ability to shift ahead.

In our research and conversations with senior people from a variety of industries, arrogance was often cited as a reason for an organization's failure to stay ahead of the market. Such was the case with Nokia, the Finnish technology company and maker of the first cellular phone. Nokia was the world leader in this technology in 1998, selling over 41 million units and surpassing Motorola as the top producer and seller of cell phones. In 2001, Nokia became the first company to launch a phone with a camera and seemed destined to continue its ascent in the industry. That is until 2007, when Apple entered the picture with its iPhone. By 2009, Nokia had laid off over 1,700 employees, and in 2010, Stephen Elop, who had been head of Microsoft's Business Software Division, was brought in as CEO. But it was too late. The company, grounded in a culture of arrogance and complacency, had by then missed by a mile the rapidly evolving smartphone market. The company's unwillingness to embrace drastic change when it was required the most was the biggest reason for its failure to shift ahead.

We had the opportunity to talk about this with Jerry Howard, a partner in Strategy First, a brand consulting firm, who has provided brand and marketing strategies for a number of Fortune 500 companies, including Procter & Gamble, Xbox, MetLife, and Coca-Cola. His firm worked with Nokia in the early 2000s. "It was a matter of their insularity, and their arrogance," he told us in response to our questions on the topic. "The top people didn't respect Apple and refused to believe that Apple was a viable competitor. A company becomes successful, in part, because its leaders know how to read the market. They know how to take advantage of trends, what to buy and what to sell. The problem enters when they assume that because *they* cracked the code on how to read the market, they can sit back and relax and just use the same approach over and over again. To be fair, some markets are slow moving, but that's becoming increasingly rare. Today, more and more markets are being disrupted by new technologies. An organization must be nimble and agile to keep up. And, even if you are in a slow-moving market, you've got to be paranoid and assume it's only a temporary phase. Eventually someone will disrupt it. If it hasn't come yet, it will.

"You know the old saying," Howard continued. "Culture eats strategy for lunch. There were many smart people at Nokia. They saw what was happening and yet somehow the organization was powerless. It couldn't change. Its very culture kept it from changing. By the time a company realizes that its strategy is subpar, it's often too late to shift."

RED FLAG SIX:
Being Too Deep in Your Comfort Zone

As human beings, it's just natural to want to hang onto things in our comfort zone. Things and ways of doing things that are familiar make us feel safe, especially in a world that is spinning too fast. The faster it spins, the more we want to cling onto something recognizable. Old habits die hard. You know where we're going with this. If your organization's culture is stuck in the mud, if you find it hard to let go of the past even knowing it's detrimental to future pursuits, count that as a red flag.

To illustrate this point, let's go back to another one of those old advertising taglines: "Mm! Mm! Good!" We're dating ourselves, but when we were growing up, you couldn't say "tomato soup" without thinking about Campbell's and its red and white cans. It became one of the country's most iconic brands, and with good reason. In 1897, Dr. John Dorrance, the nephew of the company's founder, invented a formula for five ready-to-eat condensed soups. The product immediately took off with consumers who wanted meals that were inexpensive and convenient. For years and years, Campbell's was *the* soup you turned to in the grocery aisle; tomato soup paired with grilled cheese sandwiches on a snowy day, and cream of mushroom became a staple in millions of American pantries for making your aunt's famous string bean casserole.

Notice the emphasis on calling Campbell's *"the soup."* There is no doubt that Campbell's brand has incredible awareness in the canned soup category. And therein is a good part of the challenge the company has bumped up against in its efforts to shift ahead. The company has been afraid of leaving its comfort zone and risking any damage to its "Mm! Mm! Good!" name, despite the fact that for the past thirty years the data have indicated that consumer tastes and habits dictate the company should be making some big changes in strategy.

In tracking the data, the reasons that the sales of canned soup have been on a steady decline for thirty years are clear to see. Health concerns about too much sodium and increasing consumer preferences for fresh ingredients, no preservatives, and artisanal offerings have been at the core of this decline, along with ongoing changes in demographics and lifestyles. Moms are more likely to be at work than waiting at the back door on a snowy day ready to offer up soup and a sandwich. There's also the matter of millennials who do not purchase food packaged in cans. For years, the management at Campbell's *knew* they had to change, they talked about change, but as the basic math indicated, they couldn't get out of their own way. Year-over-year sales continued to decline. Management was too locked onto protecting the Campbell's soup name. They felt that the strongest thing they had was their brand equity and they didn't want to mess with the recipe. You can't teach an old dog new tricks. Campbell's simply didn't want to change.

As a first attempt at taking a step in a new direction, in 2013, Campbell's brought in Darren Serrao as senior vice president, chief marketing and commercial officer, who oversaw everything from soup to the company's V8 unit. (He has since moved on, becoming chief growth officer for ConAgra in 2015.) The hope was that, as an outsider, he'd help mitigate the cultural risk aversion and inject a new attitude.

As an agent of change, the first thing Serrao did was to get management to take a more honest look at the data. What he got them to see in terms of numbers was that, while dollar sales were sometimes decent, unit sales had been declining for years. The company was using price to reach its dollar sales target and not seeing the whole picture. If you're at the top of the company, you see the numbers you want to see. You say, "great," and don't ask too many questions about how and why you hit the dollar target.

Another thing Serrao did was to get the company to consider a new *demographic* target. He convinced management to put a focus on millennials with Campbell's Go soup, a line of pouched soups with updated flavors such as Golden Lentil with Madras Curry and Creamy Style Thai Chicken. He also spearheaded some much-needed marketing innovation, spreading the word among millennials with "Communal Table" events in New York City and Chicago and creating ventures with BuzzFeed, Spotify, and Angry Birds. There was even a Star Wars–centric advertisement that portrayed a gay couple showing off their Darth Vader impressions as they ate Campbell's soup with their son. This alone was a bold move from a brand that had long been associated with middle-America values for over a hundred years. But all these moves, taken together, were seen as incremental tweaks by Wall Street. Incremental tweaks yield incremental returns. Revenues went up for a short period and then began to plateau and fall. Data, accruing exponentially, were telling Campbell's that a big shift was required to change the outcome.

More recently, there have been signs that Campbell's *may* be taking bigger steps in attempting to move out of its comfort zone. This, paradoxically and happily, while aligning with "authentic," comfortable, and long-held brand associations. The company has, in fact, looked back in order to begin looking forward. It's gone back to its roots to find things that are relevant to customers and, yes, different from what other competing food companies can offer. More specifically, in the Campbell Soup Company archives was Dr. John Dorrance's original beefsteak tomato soup recipe from 1915. In 2016, Campbell's decided to re-create a limited edition of this soup following the recipe as closely as possible, making sure to use as many fresh, organic, and locally sourced ingredients as possible. (The tomatoes Dorrance used came from New Jersey, so that's what Campbell's used.) The packaging for this old-new soup carries a label reflecting both Campbell's heritage and its recognition of the consumer demand for healthier, "cleaner" foods with fewer artificial ingredients and colorings. In addition, at the beginning of 2016, Campbell's created three new divisions, including Campbell's Fresh, Garden Fresh Gourmet, and a refrigerated soup business, all in the effort to cater to health-conscious consumers. The big challenge is to do all this while retaining the company's image of authenticity.

The launch of the original beefsteak tomato soup is a nod to Campbell's past, on which the company built its brand name. But it is also a nod to the company's future, the acknowledgment that people are increasingly turning to food that is more "real." Whether Campbell's newest efforts to shift ahead are significant enough to put the company back on top in the food industry remains to be seen. The brand name is well known. The bigger question is whether the company's culture is strong enough and agile enough to take the calculated risks required to be viewed as relevantly differentiated in the minds of consumers. It's been a story thirty years in the making. And even though the shifting dynamics in food and foodie culture were relatively slow in coalescing into a major market force, Campbell's missed many opportunities to act as early as it could have.

Analysis paralysis is another term that reflects a similar phenomenon. It is the state of overanalyzing (or overthinking) a situation so that a decision or action is never taken—in effect paralyzing the outcome. No one likes to be wrong. When it comes to making a business decision that will affect stakeholders inside and outside the organization, we all want to be right. But delaying action while overanalyzing data is not the best option in today's marketplace. If your organization is behaving like "a deer in the headlights" (another overused but appropriate term), it's literally and figuratively not going to allow you to shift ahead of the competition.

RED FLAG SEVEN:
Yertle the Turtle Is Left Behind

Theodor Seuss Geisel, better known as Dr. Seuss, is among the best-known and best-loved authors of children's books, a storyteller in every sense of the word. His whimsical tales, filled with illustrations of fanciful creatures and fantastical faraway places, have entertained generations of young readers with their freestyle drawings and rhythmic verse that rivals Lewis Carroll's. What many of his youngest fans may not know—or care to know, as they giggle at that super-silly Cat in the

Hat—is that many of Dr. Seuss's books were written to teach a lesson. There is a moral to these stories.

Bear with us. A moral lies at the heart of *this* final red flag story, and while it may not be precisely the one the wise Dr. Seuss had in mind when he wrote it, we think it is an interesting way to make our final point.

Yertle the Turtle, published in 1958, is the story of the king of the pond who one day looks around and decides he needs to increase the area over which he rules. To see what's out there, he demands his turtle subjects climb one on top of the other to build his throne higher so Yertle can "see all he can see." Mack, the turtle at the bottom of the pile, complains about standing too long with turtles on his back. Angered, Yertle demands a higher throne and more turtles are added to the teetering tower. Once again, Mack speaks up, but to no avail. That night, when the moon rises, Yertle, seeing that it is higher than he is, demands even more turtles. Suddenly, Mack, having had enough and in a bit of pain, burps and the whole stack of turtles shakes, throwing Yertle into the mud below.

Moral? Red flag? Looking at the future, surveying as far and wide as possible all that's out there, is a critical endeavor for all organizations in their quest to shift ahead. In this aspect Yertle had the right idea. Yet the most successful organizations are those whose leadership is aware of the vital role *all* members of the organization play. This includes communicating with others to understand how current strategies are doing and, when it is determined that a shift is necessary, communicating to execute the strategy successfully. We cannot overestimate the importance of this fact. Stating that, we go on to Chapter 3, in which we discuss in more detail the three most significant barriers that stand in the way of executing a successful shift ahead.

3

THE ROAD BARRIERS

Marty Crane lives in all of us. Marty Crane is the guy who moves his scruffy, overstuffed, duct-taped recliner into the stunningly sleek and urbane living room of his son Frasier upon coming to live with him. (Watch the reruns of *Frasier* on Netflix. No matter your age, it's still a classic.) Marty is a creature of habit. It's just natural to want to hang onto things that are in our comfort zone. We all do it. The familiar makes us feel safe, especially when our world feels out of control. As the world spins ever faster, more out of control, and more into areas that are unfamiliar, there is a tendency to hold tighter to what's comfortable.

Companies, brands, organizations, and people—including Marty Crane—all face the incredibly hard challenge of being able to shift to stay current, or ahead of the currents of market change, while at the same time not losing what makes them what and who they are. In the course of preparing this book, we studied many companies, brands, and organizations, looking into the root causes for their losing relevance and not acting fast enough to shift to the next successful phase. We investigated what stood in the way of being able to shift and focus in order to maintain a leadership position and what kept them the brethren of Marty Crane, who can't give up something that comforts him, although it's literally falling apart at the seams.

Importantly, there is no single cause that causes most brands or organizations to lose relevance. Rather, there are many, often interrelated. The stories that follow bring them to light.

KODAK READ THE WRITING ON THE WALL
(but Wasn't Willing to Pay the Price)

Paul Simon's song "Kodachrome" refers to the seemingly always-sunny "Kodak moments" in life, captured on film and pasted into millions of analog photo albums that clutter attics and basements worldwide. Unlike what many people may think (including us, before we started researching this book), Kodak did see the "writing on the wall" relative to the rise of the digital age and how it could disrupt picture-taking and, more critically, how it might have an impact on the new ways consumers could interact with their photos, the technology, and the market, specifically social media. Viewing and sharing pictures has become a foundation for everyday socialization. To cut to the chase, Kodak filed for bankruptcy protection in 2012, exited its legacy businesses, sold off promising patents, and now exists as a mere shadow of its former self. Once one of the most profitable companies in the world, Kodak has a market capitalization of less than $1 billion today.

No, Kodak's demise did not come about, as many assume, as the result of myopia. It came about, more so, as the result of not making the big, very necessary financial bet required to stay the incredibly iconic brand it had been. The fact of the matter is that Steve Sasson, an engineer working for Kodak, created the first digital camera in 1975. Kodak invented the technology, but failed to invest in it for over a decade. We will unpack the yellow (Kodak) film box and tell you how and why this all came about.

The Eastman Kodak Company, commonly known as Kodak, was founded by George Eastman in 1888. It followed the "razor and blades" strategy, selling inexpensive cameras and generating large margins from consumables—films, chemicals, and paper. As late as 1976, Kodak commanded 90 percent of film sales and 85 percent of camera sales in the United States. Traveling around the world with their cameras after college, recent graduates could always count on seeing that familiar yellow Kodak signage on street corners from one country to the next where they could purchase more film. Kodak was ubiquitous.

Kodak was one of Allen's key accounts early in his career. He spent many hours at its Rochester, New York, headquarters, where despite a posh lobby with all the accoutrements of Fortune 100-dom, the marketing department and other upper floors were indicative of why what happened did happen. The offices were stodgy and the bureaucratic structure—endless meetings and decision-making processes—equally so. The status-quo-oriented culture was evident long before Instagram was a gleam in someone's eye.

So, it wasn't that the Kodak crew didn't see the train coming or the writing on the wall. It became clear to us, after our conversations with many people who went through this era as company insiders, that the company's own projections of the demise of film were incredibly accurate. Its strategic forecasting group was spot on.

Jim Patton, an executive at Kodak for over thirty years, recounted this state of affairs during our conversation. "We had some really good technical forecasters," he told us. "As a matter of fact, one of them nailed the basic—the major shift from film to digital right to the year it happened. I want to make it very clear that we knew digital was coming. There was a fork in the road and they took the wrong fork. We knew we had to replace film, but the problem with film at the time was that the earnings from film were probably 110 percent of the corporate earnings. And that was not a slip of the tongue. The explanation from the company was, 'This is what we do. We have no choice but to be here.' I think you do have a choice."

Kodak's own in-house experts were saying with great accuracy when the tipping point would occur. The problem, as Patton put it so directly, was an issue of management not wanting to walk away from the easy money flowing from film.

The fork in the road was a pivot point ignored. Kodak had a corporate management team that was Rochester-centric. Despite all the data and prescient presentations, they were firmly entrenched in their way of doing business and in the way they generated money from their business. Film was so profitable, at that moment in time anyway, that management had gotten lazy and fat. The film, chemical, and paper manufacturing and distribution models were wonderfully optimized. Faced with starting over, especially as addicted to this profitable business model as they were, was not something anyone wanted or was willing to take on. It required enormous resources. It required a different assortment of skillsets than existed in-house. And it required a different mindset than existed in-house. With the tension of the golden handcuffs, no one wanted or was willing to face Wall Street pressuring the company to deliver increased revenue and profit. No one had the daring to say, "Hang on for a couple of years, fellas. We're gearing up and going digital." It was a Kodak moment in time that would not go down as a happy memory.

Brands, organizations—and the people who run them—have an extremely difficult time freeing themselves from the pull of the past. And the management teams are generally made up of very competent and very smart people. From Kodak to Blockbuster, Radio Shack to Nokia, the landscape is littered with companies that have done a core set of things well for years and years, and they've made money for years and years. Where they struggle, as this Kodak moment—a teaching moment—tells us, is in their ability (or lack thereof) to make the decision to commit the resources required to fund something that represents the wave of the future. Even, and especially, something in their lane, something the brand is known and respected for, and for which the brand has ultimate credibility: Picture-taking and all its emotional and sociological implications was about to take a left turn, and Kodak refused to follow.

Andrew Salzman, another former Kodak executive, added texture to the nature of the golden handcuffs that shackled Kodak. Salzman, currently a principal at Geoffrey Moore's Chasm Group, a team of technology professionals who specialize in helping technology-based companies deal with the challenges of staying ahead in both emerging and established markets, ran global marketing for Kodak's consumer imaging division at a time when digital technology was transforming the category.

"In the case of Kodak specifically, and this would probably be true for other companies as well, if 95 percent of your revenue is coming from your established lines of business—in this case film, paper, chemicals—your stock price is likely to come under siege if you execute a pivot that would draw resources from those established businesses that are essentially making the numbers for the street. It's very difficult for a smart management team to divert resources from its core revenue," said Salzman. For Kodak, it would have taken what Salzman called an "asymmetrical bet," putting the entire team behind new digital initiatives that promise to deliver ten times improvement on the current category offering. He is referring to the well-understood notion that often it may be more beneficial to place greater investment in what is currently a product with lower profitability than in one that is more profitable.

"They would have had to resource this digital transformation with talent and money, resource commitments in products, sales, marketing, business development, and the like in much the same way they were resourcing their current business model," Salzman continued. "You need to spend a lot of money on it, you need to put the best people on it, and you need to expect and plan for a two-to-three-year J-growth curve that anticipates negative cash flow while growing a new category and business at material scale. It would have to have diverted a disproportionate amount of funding. You have to recognize that the revenue you generate will be a gradual build, but time is of the essence, and the volume of resources—the people and the money required to stand up to that business model, operational, and infrastructure shift—are significant. You must be willing to run the major risk on the new business success and you are likely to miss your overall company revenue and margin performance numbers for a period of time."

Kodak should have resourced the next wave of growth rather than resourcing its current model. As Salzman said, "You need to spend a lot of money on it [the future] and you need to put the best people on it."

Salzman's bottom line is that it's much easier to keep on throwing short-term money to try and prop up short-term business to make the next quarter numbers versus diverting funds for a longer-term business plan with a higher risk profile. If you're the CEO, answering to shareholders, and make an asymmetrical bet on a future growth wave, you'd better have what it takes to stand up to a disappointed Wall Street for at least eight to twelve quarters.

For firms like Kodak, it takes more than just money. You build up an organization to deliver on what's required to win in the current business. Often, if not usually, making a shift of the magnitude Kodak was confronting would require a complete retooling. Kodak's roots were firmly entrenched in Rochester, literally as well as figuratively. This new business, one focused on digital technology, hardware, software, partnership ecosystems, and the continuous beta-centric innovation required to stay ahead of the Silicon Valley curve, was not baked into the Rochester way of doing things.

As Salzman put it, "They required assembly of an entrepreneurial team run by risk-taking leaders, not managers—pretty much like all the start-ups that we see in the Valley. How can we quickly build a viable product? How can we enable the supporting value chain to ensure what we call a 'whole product' solution, such as software partnerships? How can we quickly get traction with a growing base of mainstream customers such that the business begins to represent something material and that will get the attention of—and patience from—Wall Street? The culture would have required a seismic shift to commit to funding a substantial start-up [with] everyone across the company signed up and compensated based on the success of this category reinvention effort.

"When your category and core business is being disrupted," he continued, "you've got to act fast, to be willing to make mistakes, and learn and iterate fast. You need to be willing to operate under a different set of performance metrics relative to the traditional business side, focusing on business traction and user growth over revenues, bookings, and margin. Negative cash flow in the beginning stages isn't particularly well received on that core performance side of the house, the traditional business side. The management-oriented people initially attracted to Kodak were attracted to a well-established, leading, stable company with cyclical growth patterns. They want safety and predictability. Those are not the kind of leadership-oriented people you need to reinvent yourself."

Entrepreneurial companies, with entrepreneurial leaders, are willing to take risks, financial and otherwise. It's not a matter of making small, incremental changes to get where you want to go. As Salzman explained, "It's the difference between death by a thousand cuts and slashing off a limb. In other words, if you miss your number by, say, 5 percent every year, you cannot spend too much time trying to prop up a declining category and business to continue to make [your] numbers for Wall Street, while concurrently dabbling in starting up a new business.

"Kodak did not die overnight," Salzman added. "It saw little signs that things were starting to go south, such as losing a significant contract for photo-processing at Walmart to Fuji because Fuji had committed to losing money and [was] beating them on price in their traditional business. The whole idea [of] being able to capture, store, archive, retrieve, and manipulate images—Kodak's R&D investments in this technology dated back to 1987. What they did not do is commit to commercializing these inventions, suffering the same fate as Xerox did with its many Xerox PARC inventions. Kodak also executed its digital strategy as early as 1994, but it did it without [the] required 'all-in' effort in people, dollars, resources, partnership, etcetera, that was required for starting up a whole new approach to consumer imaging and for owning a category of reinvention. An inherently entrepreneurial company like those we see in Silicon Valley—Apple, Amazon, Google, and many operating in start-up cultures—would have made the investments and commitments into business initiatives [with] the kind of magnitude and power that digital imaging offered."

That the company clearly recognized that digital imaging and all that went with it represented the next wave in the industry was not the issue. The mother ship did not want to jettison the current business to go full throttle into the new business. For Kodak, it was an effort to keep propping up what it had, while also gradually trying to stand up its new business. The company didn't have the mindset that would allow it to accept that film, paper, and chemicals would go away, and that if the company didn't jump on digital it would be obsolete in ten years. Like many companies in similar situations, they didn't have what it took to be able to "go big or go home."

Kodak has been misjudged by people thinking the company had blinders on. Kodak had exceptionally bright and talented engineers and sales people, product people, and marketing people. Across the board, they had what it took to run a traditional, risk-averse, "razor and blades" kind of business. What they didn't have was the desire or wherewithal to make the asymmetrical bet required to seize the day and the future market. Kodak had the inability to free itself from the pull of the past and the revenues that made Wall Street happy. Managers saw the writing on the wall, but didn't—or wouldn't—make the magnitude of shift of resources and effort to bring the future to fruition before others did. They couldn't withstand the gravitational force of the metrics, the process, the strategic planning, or equally important, the change in culture that was required. It's a story of potential lost.

THE MICROSOFT 365 BET

Lest you think bets of the type Salzman thinks Kodak should have made are far too risky to seriously consider, and lest you wonder what organizations have taken on these bets and won, here's an interesting example. Here are some excerpts from a posting by Tim Campos, CIO of Facebook, from the company's blog:

At Facebook, our mission is clear. Give people the power to share and make the world more open and connected. Over 13,000 Facebook employees wake up committed to making this mission a reality for the more than 1 billion people who use Facebook every day.

To enable our productivity, IT at Facebook provides our people with the best tools available. Tools that can mean the difference between just having an idea and bringing that idea to life. All of this means our IT has to be flexible and available over the Web, on mobile, and across platforms—wherever our employees need it. We need the right technology to empower employees, while also ensuring our business is safe at all times.

That is why we've implemented Office 365. Not only is it a mature and comprehensive platform, it meets our stringent security standards, it complements how we work with intelligence, flexibility, and it is continually evolving.

As Microsoft continues to innovate with Office 365, we will continue adding and rolling out more services that have value for Facebook. In that way, we're not just buying the capabilities that Office 365 offers today. We are also buying capabilities that Microsoft will offer over time, and expect even greater things to come.

It bodes well that there are some pretty big players getting in on the ante of Microsoft's bet. A bet that makes clear that while organizations are faced with staying relevant in a fast-changing world, the challenges are exponential when it comes to technology companies. While Kodak knew it had to do something to keep its edge in the photographic category and saw what was headed its way in terms of competition, it chose not to divert the funds that might have kept the company on top. The golden handcuffs were too tight. Microsoft, on the other hand, looked at the future and actually into the "cloud" (i.e., the advances and the fierce competition in cloud computing) and made the decision to make the bet . . . and the beta. In October 2010, it loosened the handcuffs and made the investment required to shift users from MS Office to Microsoft 365, the brand name it uses for a group of software and service subscriptions that together provide tools for productivity. It began with a private beta test, leading to a public beta in 2011, and reaching general availability in 2012. Office 365, unlike the Microsoft Office software product it replaced, is a web-based platform that offers the cloud storage the public will need going forward, is available for use on multiple devices versus a single device, and is offered as a subscription service instead of a onetime, single purchase.

Going back to Andrew Salzman's comments on asymmetrical bets, "It's one thing to go on the offense and start a new business. With Microsoft it was the inverse of that," he said. "They were trying to defend against what was a coming onslaught with mobile and cloud. They needed to make some significant investments outside their core. . . . More than this, they had the right leadership, a CEO who recognized that those things were happening and who took decisive action. Satya Nadella recognized that there were some radical actions that needed to be taken in the face of threats to the Office Suite or Windows, any and all mainstream businesses, under siege based on technological change."

As of July 2016, Office 365 had 23.1 million subscribers, and experts agree that the cloud and subscription-based services are providing steady income and were worth the investment.

XEROX:
Sunk Cost Bias and Golden Handcuffs
Deterrents to Both Business and Brand

In 1959, Xerox joined the ranks of Kleenex as iconic brand names that stand for the product categories they participate in. Decades later, Google joined these ranks, too. "Can you make me a Xerox, hand me a Kleenex, Google this bit of information?" Xerox was huge in its day. In 1959 it launched the Xerox 914 photocopier that revolutionized the document-copying industry by enabling one to make 100,000 copies per month. That may not sound all that amazing nowadays, as a gazillion tweets can circle the globe in a nanosecond. But for 1959, it was amazing. Equally amazing, on a negative, not a positive note, was how relatively quickly this company, whose brand name was synonymous with photocopying, if not all-out technological innovation, lost its footing and fell down the financial rabbit hole, dragging its brand equity with it.

A decade ago Xerox was caught up in the first wave of change, doing what it could and should to shift into the business services landscape instead of just selling product. Its objective was to turn itself into a "solutions" company. To Xerox, a solutions company was one that designed and ran document systems for businesses. Everyone was talking the digital talk, and many were successfully walking the digital walk, and Xerox legitimately wanted—and needed—to follow the digital money. The primary problem Xerox faced was that the relevance of its long-established and heavily funded offering was fast fading. Most of the copying that people did was on desktop printers. More than this, the bread and butter of its business, copying and processing documents and statements for major financial services companies, was crumbling. The world was going paperless. Everything was moving on-screen, online, and eventually into the cloud. This meant that not only did Xerox have the challenge of shifting its business, what it did, and how it operated, but it also faced the challenge of shifting its brand perception, which may be the harder of the two challenges. A brand is what you stand for in consumers' minds. Successful brands stand for something absolutely focused and memorable, as in "Xerox is top-quality copiers." Xerox's vision of where it wanted to go as a business and brand was generic and unfocused. The title of "solutions" company was being touted by everyone, from IBM to boutique management consultants.

The sad irony of the situation was that Xerox was among the early innovators in many of the areas of technology, digital and otherwise, that we take for granted today and that other companies are taking to the bank—big-time. For example, in 1984, Apple, Inc. launched the Macintosh computer, the first computer with a graphical user interface (GUI). This enabled those of us with no knowledge of text-based operating commands to navigate the world of personal computing. What many people don't know, or remember, is that Apple did not invent the

GUI technology. It was one of the many accomplishments that came out of Xerox's Palo Alto Research Center (PARC). Other PARC innovations included the computer mouse, Ethernet, intuitive word processing software, and the laser printer. So what happened? Xerox never concentrated or commercialized these technologies, choosing instead to make copiers more efficient.

Moving quickly ahead in the story, when it wanted and had to catch up with where the market was going, Xerox didn't have the financial wherewithal. It had waited far too long. It had fallen victim to the sunk cost fallacy. In economics, sunk costs are those that have already occurred and cannot be recovered, no matter what you do.[1] In contrast, decisions should always be made according to the future value of the investments you make today. Sunk costs are irrelevant in strategic decision making. A gambler at a Las Vegas table shouldn't base decisions on whether he is up or down. He should never stay simply to try to win back his earlier losses. Those are sunk costs. His decisions should be made according to the odds on the next play. These are always against him, so he should always leave unless he is willing to pay his stake for the entertainment value of gambling. Social scientists often term the behavior of those who refuse to abandon an initial strategy a "commitment bias."[2] The sentiment underlying it is reflected in such clichés as "Throwing good money after bad," or "In for a penny, in for a pound."

Xerox was intent on leveraging a manufacturing process and sales force that were optimized for making and selling back-office products, which is a manifestation of the sunk cost fallacy. Feeling the commitment to sunk costs, Xerox was dividing both time and money, splitting its dwindling investments between past and future. This is not a recipe for success. The sunk cost fallacy and commitment bias can inhibit the asymmetrical bets that Andrew Salzman talked about and that we discussed earlier in the chapter.

Christa Carone spent seventeen years at the company, most recently serving as its chief marketing officer, overseeing all marketing and communications globally. She is currently chief operating officer at Group SJR, a content company in the WPP communications organization. She gave us her firsthand account of the situation.

"I joined Xerox in 1996 at a point where the decline had not yet started," Carone said. "I always say that Xerox is like a cat with nine lives because it had survived a number of business transformations or shifts over the course of its seventy-year history. When I joined, it was going through the shift from analog to digital—analog being the straightforward 'I walk to the copier to make copies' [and] digital, wherein everything is connected to the computer and the printer makes the copies. Then laser printers, connected to computers, became more prominent in the workplace and competitors like Hewlett-Packard grabbed market share. While Xerox was a pioneer in laser printing, competitors were faster to market in scaling down the technology into small laser printers that sat on the top of desks in offices small to large."

Carone went on to confirm that "it wasn't so much that everyone was complacent, just comfortable with the quarter-to-quarter profits." That is, until the quarterly profits started to really dry up. "We were huge in the financial services industries, healthcare, mortgages. Anything that required documentation," she said, then "companies began looking for ways to automate their processes. They realized they could start delivering bank statements, billing statements, mortgage applications, and healthcare forms electronically. Think about all the money this saved these enormous organizations in reducing the cost of printing. However, that cost reduction was starting to have a meaningful impact on Xerox's bottom line."

What happened next in the Xerox timeline was the result of color. People were shifting from printing in just black and white to printing in color. With all that ink, it was more profitable for Xerox and became a relatively healthy business for the company. However, it wasn't enough to offset the fact that people were still copying less. At the end of the day, the advancement in technology translated into less copying. The category became commoditized where price, not brand name, drove revenues, and the category was just basically shrinking as the result of technology trends. Much like the preceding tale of Kodak, Carone made clear that Xerox did see the train coming.

"Yes, and that's when we started to make the shift toward being a professional services company," she said. "Hardware was our bread and butter, but we knew we needed to get into a complementary business to offset the decline of the traditional business. What Xerox did was buy a business, Affiliated Computer Services [ACS], as a way to try and catch evolving market needs. It was an aggressive move and it required a massive shift in the legacy perception of Xerox. But selling copiers and selling services are two completely different business models. To balance the secular challenges of the technology business with the up-front investments needed in the services business, plus the marketing costs to shift perception, Xerox was at a turning point as a company that required patience, prioritization, and a great deal of flexibility with its business model."

So, where is Xerox now? Well, after a series of initiatives, major financial stress, and a bit of soul-searching and fund-sourcing, on January 3, 2017, Xerox separated into two independent, publicly traded companies, each with a single focus and more efficient allocation of capital. One is, yes, a document technology company, called Xerox Corporation, whose objective is to be a global leader in document management and document outsourcing. The other is the business process outsourcing (BPO) company named Conduent Incorporated, which works with clients to improve workflow. Revenue for each of these companies is on the uptick. That Xerox could have been on par with Apple, IBM, or Google had it leveraged its initial brilliance in technological innovation and dealt with sunk costs properly is another, even better thing that might have been. At the very least Xerox could have saved itself some very challenging years, including a close call with bankruptcy. Given its strong brand name and its competitive position, it could have unlocked the future. Instead it was a victim of short-term thinking.

Time and money is the two-pronged moral of the Xerox story. Xerox could not afford the investment required to adequately fund its new business because its traditional business was getting weaker every day. As dedicated as it was to the initiative, by the time it decided to shift, its core business wasn't generating enough cash flow. Another moral? If your brand is so tightly associated with a particular category, it takes a lot of positive, in-market customer experience with the new category, not to mention a lot of marketing muscle, to get consumers to see your brand in a new light.

TOYS "R" US:
Playing Catch-up Is Hard When You're Competing on the Wrong Metrics

The difficulty of sustaining success is a central theme of the teachings of Clayton Christensen of the Harvard Business School. He is the author of *The Innovator's Dilemma: When New Technologies Cause Great Firms to Fail*, once deemed by Andy Grove, the former CEO of Intel, among the "best books I've read in the last ten years." In this classic bestseller, Christensen shows how even the most outstanding companies can do everything right and still lose market leadership. No matter what the industry, his theory goes, a successful company will get pushed aside unless managers know how and when to abandon traditional ways of doing business. As the title states, the innovator's "dilemma" comes from the idea that organizations will reject innovations based on the fact that customers cannot currently use them. He goes into great detail about the way successful organizations adhere to customer needs, adopt new technologies, and take rivals into consideration.

While the first two examples in this section on barriers to successful shifting deal with failure to shift to "new technologies," it's not only technology that can be a disruptive factor in sending a category leader off the rails. Barbara Lawrence, cofounder and managing partner of Lubin Lawrence Inc. (LLI), a consultancy that develops innovative corporate growth strategies, referred to Christensen's teachings when discussing Toys "R" Us, which is one of the large companies LLI works with (other clients are the Walt Disney Company, Johnson & Johnson, PepsiCo, and Fidelity Investments). A few years ago, LLI worked with Toys "R" Us to help the company address the competitive impact of new, low-priced toy-buying channels and the emergence of online buying habits.

As further background, Lawrence explained that although the Toys "R" Us (TRU) everyday low price (EDLP) and "long-standing reputation for good value/low prices had pioneered the low-cost/low-service toy shopping experience . . . this model was facing aggressive new competition from Walmart, Target, and Amazon. These competitors' business models allowed each to profitably out-execute TRU on three levels: lower prices, more inventory breadth, and greater convenience. Essentially, TRU was being 'out-executed' on the business model they had pioneered. The challenge was clear," she said. "We had to figure out what to do, which targets to serve, what to focus on, and where the strategy shift needed to go to return to profitable volume growth. As Christensen writes about, TRU faced a game-changing market event: During this time, you realize that you are losing traction as a leader, and management realizes that a new path forward is needed, yet the organization is resistant to change because everything is built on the initial strategy—in this case, being the low-cost/low-service operator. Toys 'R' Us was a first-mover in the EDLP volume game, but it no longer had the advantage."

Toys "R" Us had been playing a volume game for a very long time, and it had been very good at it. What parent (of a certain age, anyway) didn't live it? Tremendous stores piled high with toys and dolls and Legos and board games. And, oh yes, Geoffrey the Giraffe would be there. You'd bring your holiday gift list, pile your shopping cart high, and go home with the gratification of knowing you got everything everyone wanted for the least amount of money possible. Then, as Lawrence pointed out, Toys "R" Us wasn't the only game in town anymore. First, Target and Walmart eclipsed it on pure price, plus those stores had the advantage that you could buy your toilet paper, a toaster oven, and new pajamas while you were out buying toys. And then you didn't even have to go to Target or Walmart. You could click on Amazon and do all of this shopping in your comfortable new pajamas while sitting at your computer at home and now your phone.

Yet, this was not the only dilemma the early toy retail innovator faced. To address these challenges, LLI conducted qualitative research with a variety of toy-buying parents and grandparents as well as school-age children.

"We needed to find out more about the *ideal* playful experience and fun toy experience, as well as the ideal shopping experience for adults," Lawrence said. "We learned a lot. First, the ideal experience had nothing to do with the lowest toy pricing. The most motivating experience toy buyers wish for is one that will give their children a chance to learn and discover while they are having fun, through experiences that are both educational and entertaining. Toy buyers hope that their choices will expand their child's world through experiences that foster growth. Price alone was not a preference driver.

Said Lawrence, "We also learned that parents have plenty of money to spend on educational toys, but the shopping experience and the merchandise must be presented in a way that feels like a journey of discovery for children. The benefit the mother wants for her children is to develop certain skills early in life. They want a store that is staffed accordingly as opposed to lots of stuff, no staff, and good luck." Service and merchandise that delivered both fun and discovery could withstand premium pricing.

This research led TRU to design, build, and open a massive flagship store in New York City's Times Square, complete with a Ferris wheel and unique merchandise boutiques such as the Imaginarium, designed to foster a child's journey of discovery. Following its opening in 2002, the new flagship store initially saw strong business results. However, over time, and in the wake of internal management changes and growing strategy concerns among some of the new leadership team, focus behind the original vision shifted, which eventually led to declining results as store performance gradually eroded. The Times Square store's performance continued to decline and the store closed fourteen years later, in December 2016.

Toys "R" Us needed to dig itself out of years of morass and re-innovate. Its brand name was associated powerfully with toys. A strong brand name gives a brand permission to shift, to change things up to meet consumers' changing requirements and desires. But it's usually not just one thing when an organization fails to make the shift to a more relevant and sustainable position in its category. There was a lot of shuffling in top management and even in ownership structure in the process of asking,

"Which way do we go?" From 1994 through 2015, there were six CEOs. Toys "R" Us signed a partnership deal with Amazon, only to abandon it six years later. In 2005, it was sold to Bain Capital, Kohlberg Kravis Roberts & Company and became a private company.

"The 'crisis of confidence' and endless internal debates at the board level added to the challenge," Lawrence explained during our conversation. "You have one group saying, 'We've got something that's working, it's too expensive to do anything else,' and another saying, 'No, here's where we have to go.' They're seeing a lot of red ink, they're seeing strategies that are potentially more attractive, and they don't know whether to scale up or scale back."

There was a lot of tension and indecision. In his book, Christensen writes about how the processes that drove previous success will often lead to companies denying the reality of disruption. Christensen also argues that it's critical to listen to customers, to track competitors' actions carefully, to invest in activities that will enable higher profits. Toys "R" Us was brilliant at running its existing business, a discount business, and didn't look at its customers' real needs, or at the spectrum of competition.

Change didn't happen nearly fast enough, nor was there enough cash on hand to keep the company from going through some significant financial setbacks. The predicament was similar to what Kodak and Xerox faced; it was a matter of depriving the future to pay for the current business. Valuable time and several years of lost value ensued. Toys "R" Us continues to struggle.

PROCTER & GAMBLE:
Not Too Big to Fail (or Stumble)

Someone not familiar with the backstory might have good reason to ask, "So what's so bad about that? Those numbers sound pretty good to me." The up-front story, which ran in the *Wall Street Journal* in June 2016, stated that "P&G [Procter & Gamble] hasn't created a blockbuster product with $1 billion in annual sales since 2005. Overall sales growth has been stagnant since the recession, hitting a four-year low of $70.7 billion in 2015." Apparently, $1 billion isn't a good number, nor is $70.7 billion, not when you're P&G.

Procter & Gamble tapped David Taylor as its CEO in 2015, and since then the company continues to be challenged not just by its competitors' pricing, but by a growing consumer appetite for constant innovation. When Taylor was hired, it was to halt the aforementioned falling sales and to streamline the whole process of product development and go-to-market strategies. As part of this process, Taylor cut a number of underperforming brands from the company roster and several advertising agencies as well. It has reinvested those fees into other marketing initiatives, as well as research and development activities. But even this hasn't been enough to change its trajectory, let alone maintain a leadership position in a world that's changing faster and more furiously than ever.

Remarking on his company's challenges in an analyst call after his first year as CEO, Taylor admitted that to "restart" revenue growth, the company needed to "get back to making consumers aware of its products and communicating their benefits. We need to be more relevant in-store and online."

There is that word, *relevant*. Get the consumer's attention with something that is new and different and that genuinely meets an unmet need. To be—and stay—relevant, you need to be able to shift with agility while maintaining a focus on your strengths (which as you know by now is the focus of this book).

P&G had always had the reputation of being ahead of the pack in terms of understanding the consumer, identifying unmet needs, and meeting these needs through comprehensive research and product development. Whether it was keeping babies and their parents happy with diapers that didn't leak, or formulating a dish detergent with the fantastic ability to get rid of grease and minimize the time spent washing dishes, or a laundry detergent that both cleaned and softened your clothing, P&G knew what was important to its myriad target markets, and it delivered brilliantly—and profitably. Its strategies worked for years upon successful years. Until they didn't.

What happened? What barrier stood—and stands—in the way of
P&G being able to shift, stay relevant, and keep its edge in the market?
Whereas P&G always had products that satisfied its customers' needs
better than anyone else, it no longer does. The lack of relevant product
differentiation has made P&G vulnerable to many other things. First is
the pricing issue, or the Internet-pricing issue, with consumers being
able to self-source and buy commodity products at a lower price. Next,
new and innovative competitive business models are taking hold, such
as the Dollar Shave Club that has been cutting mightily into P&G's
Gillette razor sales. (P&G absolutely needs to up its e-commerce game.)
Then there are major global issues, some certainly out of P&G's control, as in the difficult economic conditions plaguing many countries.
But others are very much under its control, such as being able to operate fluidly enough across multiple markets to cater to the idiosyncrasies
of local tastes and preferences. All of these issues need to be addressed,
to be sure. However, they would not be the problems they are if P&G's
products stayed ahead of the competition the way they used to.

Something else has influenced, in one way or another, these key issues. It's the very *culture* of the company. And, more specifically, it's a
culture that is stymied by a "massive middle."

This was at the heart of the conversation we had with Deborah Henretta, formerly Allen's client at P&G when she served as the company's
group president and who is now a senior adviser for SSA & Company,
a management consulting firm that helps Fortune 500 clients use big
data and advanced analytics to drive top-line and bottom-line results.
She shared her perspective relative to P&G and as a lesson of caution
for all big companies, old and new alike.

"What they need to do requires a sense of urgency, and an agility to
shift gears really fast to adjust to new trends and marketplace realities.
But that's not the P&G way," she said. "To be fair, in general, the bigger
the company, the harder it is to activate change. But nevertheless, it can
be done. When I was running P&G Asia for seven years, I was lucky to
have a group with a more entrepreneurial forward-looking mindset—not
tied to the past—and we were making fast, transformational changes to
the business. When I returned to the P&G headquarters in the United

States, I realized how far behind the company was. The organization seemed wedded to the strategies, the systems, the processes they grew up with and had been successful with—and that makes it hard to change. This creates what I call 'the massive middle,' content to deliver in the same old, familiar ways, pulling attention and money away from making the kinds of needed transformational changes. P&G is at a tipping point. They know they need to operate differently and at a faster pace, but they're just not set up to move quickly enough. The middle is so massive at P&G and the movement is so slow, they can't see the path forward."

The challenge, as Henretta reinforced, is that P&G had been so successful operating for so many years in a certain way that there is no objectivity. There are no fresh eyes looking at how things are done. There is no one challenging the status quo. Often, she says, these big, massive-middle companies in need of fresh, objective eyes will call in large consulting companies, who have the same massive-middle problem they do.

"What I encourage businesses in this situation to do," she told us, "is to think like a start-up. One of the great ironies about P&G is that they were actually way ahead and sophisticated in the digitization of the product supply community. Yet it's so difficult for them to apply this agile, inventive thinking to any other area of their business. There's great nervousness about changing for fear of tampering with success models. If you're so desperately trying to protect the business you're in today, you're going to miss [how] your category is evolving. They need to think like market disrupters—the Amazons, the Ubers, the Dollar Shave Clubs, who show us that any industry can be disrupted and will be disrupted if the incumbent doesn't get with the program. It reminds me of kids playing soccer. All the kids are grouped around the ball and no one is on defense. You've got to have a culture that is tuned in to where the ball is going."

We've learned from the many big companies we've worked with, across myriad categories, that the bigger the company, the more massive the middle. We've also learned that successful change can only come about when it's led from the top and executed from the bottom up—with no bottlenecks. Reading about what P&G CEO Taylor is doing, and plans on doing, to inject a "sense of urgency" into the organization, we can't say there are any revolutionary ideas—not so far, anyway. For example, some are concerned that he is not taking millennials into consideration as much as he should be, a group as interested in sustainability as they are product performance. Some don't think his workforce-cutting initiatives will prove all that effective in solving the problem. As the old business saying goes, "Nobody ever cut their way to greatness." Needless to say, constant cost-cutting doesn't do much to help morale.

P&G can't get away from how it used to do things. Too many people in the organization, including the CEO, are tentative about moving out of the comfort zone. As Henretta told us, "I went to work in Asia, thinking I'd left this very developed world to give it a try in an underdeveloped, less advanced world. Fast-forward seven years, I'm back at U.S. headquarters, and I felt like I'd gone backwards again, especially in terms of the application of digital and the Internet. I went back to the future and it was at a standstill. It will be interesting to see where David Taylor, P&G's CEO and a thirty-six-year P&G veteran, will take [the company]. Will he look at the company with fresh, objective eyes and do something revolutionary or will he keep plans close to the vest, trying to build on historical success? All I know is that it's hard to challenge the status quo, especially in these big companies."

BLACKBERRY:
Invincibility Is A Myth

In 1984, Mike Lazaridis, an engineering student at the University of Waterloo, and Douglas Fregin, an engineering student at the University of Windsor, founded an electronics and computer science consulting company called Research in Motion, or RIM. For years, the company worked under the radar until it focused on a breakthrough in technology: an easy, secure, and effective device that allowed workers to send and receive emails while away from the office. They called it the BlackBerry. Located in Waterloo, Canada, RIM grew into one of the world's most valuable technology companies. The BlackBerry became the indispensable accessory of heads of corporations, heads of state, and the Hollywood elite.

Former GE CEO Jack Welch carried one on the golf course. He couldn't afford to miss a critical communication. Barack Obama used one on the campaign trail for the same reason. Investment bankers, hedge fund managers, and IT professionals carried BlackBerry devices on their belt buckles. Working mothers who needed to stay in touch with things in the office and the equally important things at home wouldn't leave the house without their BlackBerry. Police departments across the country handed them out to officers on the beat. It was the requisite device for those working at the Department of Defense. The BlackBerry began life as the must-have communication tool for those whose communications were both time and security sensitive.

Many readers of this book will have lived through the rise and the fall of BlackBerry. In New York, the "masters of the universe" types in the financial services industry started using them as the incredibly efficient and effective business tools they were developed to be. Black-Berry's ubiquity was due to three critical factors. First, the BlackBerry was specifically developed to allow users to very efficiently send hundreds of email responses daily. The functionality of the tactile keyboard made typing fast and easy. Second, BlackBerry was all about security. It built its brand reputation on security. If you're a commander on Wall Street or the commander of the free world, security is essential. Indeed, the "black" in its name evoked images of Black Ops secrecy. Third, when the BlackBerry device was launched, Apple and Android smartphones had not yet taken hold. Those of us who did eventually succumb to the cool allure of the iPhone were—initially—able to segregate our mobile phone activities. We used the BlackBerry for the serious business-related stuff and the iPhone (or Android, if that was your product of choice) for listening to music, or taking pictures, or playing games. You lived with both devices and each had its place in your life.

This story is about the fall. The quick answer is that BlackBerry's inability to shift and move forward was caused by its own sense of invincibility. The longer explanation, along with some critical lessons learned, is as follows. It begins with the mighty rise in popularity of those aforementioned iPhones and Androids. Not only were these smartphones also built for ease of communication on multiple platforms, they were beautiful to look at. The perfect marriage of function and design, the smartphone became just too much to resist for even the most security-centric masters of the universe. When Samsung made security one of its selling points, it made matters that much more challenging for the people up in Waterloo.

What did BlackBerry do as a result? Just what it shouldn't have. Instead of focusing on its core customers and what was critically important to its core customers, it began to chase the market with subpar versions of the competitors' brilliant machines, thinking its core customers would follow them. That did not happen. BlackBerry thought it was invincible. No brand, product, or organization is invincible, especially when it dismisses the needs of its most loyal audience.

The developers at BlackBerry should have doubled down on what made the product so vital to this loyal audience. BlackBerry should have kept its focus on its relevant point of difference in the marketplace—security—and capitalized on it.

We spoke to a number of people who experienced, from the inside, BlackBerry's rise and the beginning of its fall. Among them was David Camp, BlackBerry's vice president of integrated marketing in its earlier years. "BlackBerry suffered from what I'll call institutional arrogance," he told us during one of our conversations. "They had a belief in their own invincibility. They believed that customers were more loyal than they actually were. Or that the competition [was] stupider. BlackBerry had this point of view that, 'Hey, we invented the category,' but when Apple and Android smartphones entered the scene, BlackBerry initially dismissed the notion of the touch screen and an application-driven experience as silliness and nonsense. Their institutional arrogance led to an inability to innovate to keep up, and [then] to an inability to execute quickly enough when they came up with a product they thought would catch the competition. The real problem," Camp said, "was that they didn't have enough clarity around a product vision, nor did they have a road map. They just couldn't build a product that could compete."

Equally important, from a brand perspective, people started to position BlackBerry as the old, as in your father's Oldsmobile. As Camp explained, "It's like, 'This is not for me. I'm creative, I wear a hoodie and use Spotify and Instagram.' They had to fight the perception that they were irrelevant. The business started to crater, confidence was lost." That's around the time Camp showed up, joining the company in 2013, "right before the launch of BlackBerry 10, which had a decent enough operating system and was supposed to be the saving-grace product launch—our version of the other guys' smartphones," he said. "The board expected us to go after Apple and Samsung with a value proposition that was good, but not great. The response was tepid. The thing is, we shouldn't have been going after Apple and Samsung, but rather returning to the roots of our enterprise, which was all about business productivity and security. There was very little chance of winning the consumer business no matter how many marketing dollars we had."

Camp and his team were absolutely right. The company should have had the courage and strength of conviction to go after and own a smaller but intensely dedicated share of the market. BlackBerry was all about security and business productivity and, ironically, security in the mobile communications area has only continued to grow. These days it seems that a week does not go by without some front-page story about a major hacking debacle. The lackluster launch of the BlackBerry 10, a wannabe product, turned out to be the pivot point of no return for BlackBerry. It went through a series of upper management changes, entertained merger and acquisition strategies, and eventually cut thousands of jobs and several operating centers. If the company had stuck with security as its prime selling point, in this hack-a-day age it could have remained a huge player in the industry with a powerful, differentiated, long-term proposition.

"BlackBerry burned up a whole lot of goodwill," Camp said. "But they acted as if they were a monopoly, even after it was clear that they weren't. They continued to act like they were the only game in town. It was institutional arrogance. I think any business, no matter how successful, that can maintain a strong level of humility is destined for great things. As Jeff Bezos at Amazon says, 'No matter how successful your business is, remember, it's always day one.'"

As we were researching this chapter, we found a September 2016 *New York Times* article headlined: "BlackBerry Abandons Its Phone."[3] It began, "Stepping away from its signature product, BlackBerry will no longer make its own smartphones, the device it once defined."

NATIONAL GEOGRAPHIC:
A Well-Documented Case of Cultural Myopia

In November 2015, 21st Century Fox took control of National Geographic's major assets—its stake in the television network, its flagship magazine, and its TV studio—in a $725 million deal. Upon hearing this news, a veteran marine photographer for *National Geographic* magazine said to a reporter covering the story, "I told my wife I would rather see National Geographic die an honorable death than be swept into something it's not supposed to be."

If ever there was danger for a culture clash between two brands joining together, this one was it: lowbrow versus highbrow, sensationalized reality-television versus well-documented academic discourse, a focus on titillating headlines of sex, drugs, and criminal activity versus a focus on science, exploration, and discovery. You get the picture. Except it's not the whole picture. The challenge for National Geographic was how this independent nonprofit organization could keep up in an age of shifting distribution channels, migrating ad dollars, and diminishing loyalty for traditional brands.

The fact is that National Geographic may not have had to follow the Fox-merger route to keep its well-respected brand alive had it more carefully attended to its internal cultural situation, a textbook case of cultural myopia. (And, just for the record, the marriage of these strange bedfellows is not turning out to be nearly as sub-optimal as one might have supposed. But that's a story for another chapter in this book.)

In the summer of 2016, Allen stood on the bow of the *Endeavor*, a National Geographic sailing vessel, staring through the slowly lifting fog at the Margerie Glacier, a massive natural structure situated in

Alaska's Glacier Bay National Park and Preserve, a vast area of southwest Alaska's Inside Passage. It is an awe-inspiring and almost unspeakably beautiful part of our country to be able to explore. The Margerie Glacier was like National Geographic in its heyday. It was massive and impressive. It had gravitas. It was quiet and monumental. Like many of our national monuments, man-made and natural, it had a sense of permanence.

Founded in 1888 as the National Geographic Society by an elite group of scientists, explorers, and wealthy patrons interested in travel, it was "a society for the increase and diffusion of geographical knowledge." Among the founders and presidents of this nonprofit group was Alexander Graham Bell. The National Geographic logo is among the most well-known things about it, a yellow portrait frame, rectangular in shape, which appears on the margins surrounding the front covers of the magazine and the television channel logo.

The *National Geographic* magazine, the product most associated with the National Geographic Society (NGS) historically, is at the same time well respected and the genesis for the organization's decline. Published monthly, the magazine contains articles about geography, popular science, world history, culture, current events, and carries photography of people, places, and things all over the world and the universe. In the 1980s the magazine's subscriptions and newsstand sales peaked at about 10.9 million monthly readers, but began to decline after 1990. Today the publication has a U.S. circulation of about 3.3 million, according to the Alliance for Audited Media. The Internet, cable news channels, and 24/7 news cycles usurped the NGS as a scientific authority and the source for stories about geography, popular science, world history, etc. Aficionados of topics such as these could find content faster, more easily, and in greater abundance through other sources.

The NGS believed that its long-standing position as a respected institution would be enough to insulate it from the fast-changing behaviors in media creation and consumption. Not being able (or not wanting) to see what was happening outside its own monumental—literal and figurative—edifice, it was unready for the changes that were occurring and began to rapidly lose money. While NGS did start its own television and digital media base, it wasn't fast enough.

Linda Berkeley was formerly the executive vice president of the National Geographic Society and president of National Geographic Enterprises. She is now president of LEB Enterprises and an adjunct professor at Harvard and Georgetown Universities. We talked to her at great length about what led to the end of the era for NGS, once the unchallenged leader in its field.

"It did own the category," Berkeley began, "for over 100 years. Its roots [were] things that are eternally relevant: exploration, discovery of new things, curiosity. And, ironically, it was founded as a society, a community of like-minded people, which is so related to the world we live in today. In fact, in this respect, National Geographic was way ahead of everyone else. It had also been very financially successful. It had a truly storied history, in all ways, in documentary television—telling the best nonfiction stories anywhere—and had won a record number of Emmys for outstanding television. The brand was universally known and viewed as in a class by itself. It opened doors anywhere in the world.

"However, the main source of revenue and income was the magazine, which was subscription-based, not reliant on advertising," Berkeley explained. "Because of immense loyalty to the brand and unparalleled reputation, *National Geographic* magazine was able to remain profitable and hold onto its subscriber base even when most other magazines had started to struggle. But the centrality and success of the magazine ultimately made it harder for National Geographic to shift and broaden its main focus to other media channels. First, for too long, they defined themselves, in their tone and culture, as a magazine company. That was where the heartbeat of the organization was. It would have been a perfect example for Theodore Levitt, the marketing expert who wrote the textbook case about railroads starting to fail because they wouldn't define themselves as being in the transportation business, only the railroad business.[4] They could easily have expanded their mission view and launched their own cable channel way before the competition—and were even approached to do so. But, while many people at National Geographic immediately saw the threat of the Discovery Channel, many others felt that National Geographic was in the magazine business, not the cable channel business—or, even more aptly, understood that National Geographic was really in the 'curiosity about the world' business, not in the business of any specific media channel. Thus, so much later, they had to play catch-up."

At this time, the National Geographic Society did begin to bring in people who were fluent in the cable and digital media business. But this decision led to an internal culture clash: one side was ready to move forward, the other held strictly to the view that the National Geographic Society was a magazine-centric institution. "This is so typical [when] trying to change legacy organizations," Berkeley explained. "Even when you bring in people from the outside, you can have immense pushback from people on the inside. You have a world-renowned history for doing things a certain way. The business model was print-oriented and you had a fundamentally magazine-focused print culture that resisted strongly to giving up ground. The endemic culture of the National Geographic Society—its behavior, its values, its style, its attitude—were the opposite of everything that was happening everywhere else, certainly in the media world. It was a slow-moving culture. Historically, stories in the magazine took months to research, fact-check—an increasingly valued skill, even today—[and were] absolutely well documented and incredibly well written, superb quality in every way—but they took lots and lots of time. You couldn't turn on a dime."

The National Geographic Society did not think of itself as a "brand," either. That was far too commercial a term, with all the negative implications of consumerism. The editorial staff decided what was going to be written about, who would write it, and what they wanted the consumer to know. The idea of consumer-generated content was anathema to this ideology. While readers loved and respected the magazine, as the subscription base began to decline and research into the cause ensued, even the proverbial writing on the wall didn't set off the alarms it should have. For starters, people were not reading hard-copy magazines anymore, let alone keeping copies of old ones in the basement. Those inclined were finding lots of media outlets in their quest for interesting stories about our extraordinary planet.

Hoping to make up for falling print revenue, the National Geographic Society invested in everything from Hollywood movies to IMAX theaters to mobile games. It got into cable television, where it did pretty well, but it just wasn't enough to stem the revenue losses. Given that the National Geographic Society was running out of time and money in its fight for relevance, it was in the mid-1990s that the National Geographic Society first approached the Murdoch organization, which had the millions of dollars necessary to shift direction.

As Berkeley explained, "This is a lesson for any legacy organization— [the] legacy organization being a double-edged sword. While you have all these rich assets and history, which are incredibly important to people and bring people together, you can get caught up in this history. A culture like this makes shifting hard. You're holding onto and living in the glory of your past."

Lest you be concerned, the National Geographic Society continues to exist as a separate entity, even after the 21st Century Fox deal. And while Fox has said there would be minimal change and that it was dedicated to maintaining the editorial approach and voice of National Geographic, only time will tell. The much smaller National Geographic will become a for-profit company, perhaps the only way the magazine, founded and edited by the family of Alexander Graham Bell, can survive.

PLAYBOY:
A Yesterday Brand,
with a Lesson Relevant for Today

Ah, Playboy. No matter your age, you've most likely heard about Hef, the bunnies, the Mansion, and of course, the magazine's centerfolds. You've likely seen movies wherein mothers of preadolescent boys find copies of *Playboy* magazine stuffed under their mattresses. And if you're closer in age to our generation, you know it's all about reading said magazine "for the articles." But did you know that Hugh Hefner, the suave guy in the Mansion with the bunnies, initially wanted to call his magazine Stag Party, but had to go with Playboy as a second choice? Stag was the trademarked name of an "outdoorsy" magazine and the editors said Hef's magazine title would have been a conflict.

Given what the mothers of preadolescent boys are finding in their sons' rooms these days, with media channels and the content available having moved far beyond paper and ink, it's pretty easy to understand how Playboy—and Hugh Hefner's empire-as-lifestyle—became irrelevant. Well, partly irrelevant. The Playboy brand had always included two components: the obvious—beautiful, mostly naked young women—but also an intellectual manifesto called "the Playboy Philosophy" that espoused ideas that were way ahead of their time: free, open sexuality; equal access to that freedom for women as well as men; inclusiveness and a welcome mat for blacks, gays and lesbians, and others not considered mainstream in 1950s America; and a fervent respect for the First Amendment. This heady, thinking-person's Playboy was made moot because it largely accomplished its goal. Just about everything the magazine preached actually got accomplished. It's the other stuff— which is the bane of a mother's existence—that got left behind on the ash heap. Lest you think we're not aware that this story itself is so yesterday, it's not. It's representative of the barriers that stand in the way of being ready to shift your business, brand, or organization into the future. If your business, brand, or organization is all about the founder's vision—and if there's no way to profitably reimagine this vision for the present—well, that's not good. But we're getting ahead of ourselves.

Quick, really quick history: Hugh Hefner was Playboy. He embodied the lifestyle: silk robe, martinis, fur-covered pillows, very pretty and very well-endowed ladies always by his side, and just the right amount of interesting and intellectual repartee. In 1953, he launched the magazine out of his kitchen, the first issue quickly selling out nationwide. That it featured photos of Marilyn Monroe didn't hurt. The first Playboy Club opened in Chicago in 1960, creating an opportunity for aspiring Hefners to join in the fun. By 1966, *Playboy* magazine proved itself a credible source for literary excellence, featuring works from well-respected writers including John Updike, Joyce Carol Oates, and Kurt Vonnegut. Whether for the articles or not, by 1972, 25 percent of male American college students were reading the magazine every month. The November 1972 issue sold 7.1 million copies.

Then, in 1988, as Hefner's daughter Christie took the helm, she found an overbloated octopus on the edge of financial extinction. Ego-driven expansions into jets, a publishing imprint, a record label, clubs in less-than-optimal locations (Playboy Club *Des Moines*?), an overprogrammed television channel, and other fledgling diversions were hemorrhaging money. The huge circulation included mostly unprofitable subscription, pumped up to dazzle prospective advertisers. Hef and his team had made some mistakes rooted in arrogance, like angering gaming officials in Nevada and London, which resulted in valuable gaming licenses being revoked. Plus, video porn and its viewers, along with lots of competition from magazines like *Maxim* and *Stuff*, emerged to dig into *Playboy*'s readership.

Christie Hefner's solution was smart enough. She decided to get rid of the losing businesses ASAP and find some new tent poles to prop up the company. She also took the occasion to dump some of Hef's cronies and install new, young, well-credentialed executives to look for business opportunities that were international and electronic. Home video and TV went global, and Playboy jumped on the brand-new Internet market.

The strategy paid off for a while—about fifteen years—then the ship started taking on water once again. While not anywhere near the revenues and profits of the glory years, business grew and newly floated nonvoting stock reached an apogee of $30 by the late 1990s, only to crash back to penny-stock status by the early years of the twenty-first century. The anything-goes Internet really began to pose problems for the Playboy franchise. A 2005 reality TV show that followed the lives of Hef and his girlfriends in the Mansion gave the brand a little, but short-lived, uptick. Print media, in general, began its continuing decline. In 2008, Christie Hefner stepped down as an increasingly rancorous board, channeling the demands of the investment community, flexed its muscles. A new CEO was brought in to pretty-up the company for sale, and even Hef faced the prospect of financial ruin if his huge pile of stock became valuable only to line bird cages around the world. The company was broken up and taken over by a venture capitalist, although Hef gets to stay in the Playboy Mansion until he, too, reaches the end of his life cycle.

What was the core problem? The international and electronic incarnations of the brand maintained increasingly tame and out-of-step "standards of taste and quality," and as emerging markets matured, they ran past Playboy's level of "heat" as fast as they could. The company just kicked the can down the road, because they couldn't shake off the dust of Hef's original vision. When the world started to change, and Hugh Hefner's lifestyle had become passé, there was no ability to reinvent—make that *reenvision*—how this brand … might continue to succeed. Instead of shifting ahead and coming up with a strategy that could truly revitalize revenue streams for the long term, the team ran itself ragged trying to figure out how to sell the Playboy of the 1960s and 1970s to men (and women) born after Hef's seventy-fifth birthday.

Jeff Jenest was one of those young, well-resumed executives brought in to take the brand international and electronic. He put it this way: "It was all too easy to be convinced that the brand continued to be relevant and continued to be valued. We kept uncovering these pools of money—big pools of money in previously untapped markets like Europe, Latin America, and Asia—but we were never able to establish a brand persona that would resonate with consumers under age sixty. Our thinking—for too long—was that if you kept opening new doors, the brand and its content would ride itself out long enough to celebrate its centenary in 2053."

No matter how resourceful company executives were in playing out these scenarios and going for the obvious quick monetary opportunities, the fundamental core premise wasn't working anymore—the founder's vision was irrelevant and no one could come up with a way to capitalize on and optimally leverage any of the other original assets of the brand.

As Jenest said, "It's not that we didn't have a lot of smart people trying to bring the brand up-to-date and reclaim some of its former relevance. We didn't move fast enough. When the brand started to fall off the cliff again in the first decade of the new millennium, that fall was fast and steep." Resources were tight. Layoffs and contraction became the norm. Attracting the new capital necessary for a complete overhaul was impossible.

The fact of the matter is that it is very difficult to resurrect a brand that, once perfect in its day, is no longer relevant. When you have a founder with a vision that was tailor-made for its times, you need an organization whose top priority is to identify and execute complete brand overhauls every decade, if not more frequently. This is a timeless lesson. Oh, and as a footnote, in 2015, Playboy's new owners announced that the magazine would no longer feature nudity in the magazine. Nobody cared.

AMERICAN CANCER SOCIETY:
Leadership on Autopilot Is Fatal in Fast-Changing Conditions

If an organization is financially healthy, the employees are happy, the public continues to give you the thumbs-up for your efforts, and there's no contest when it comes to the competition, an organization might be tempted to proceed "steady as she goes." But one of the themes of this book is that this won't last, and you need to constantly be looking for the curve ahead. In any event, "steady as she goes" is definitely not a good leadership strategy when any or all of these conditions are in less than positive territory. And all of these conditions—a veritable perfect storm—were in pretty negative territory until very recently at the American Cancer Society (ACS).

Revenues for its core fundraising engine, Relay for Life, have been down significantly year-over-year. According to the *Chronicle for Philanthropy*, the event brought in $100 million less in 2014 than it did in 2008, when it raised $439 million—a record for ACS—and was overtaken by newer and more innovative initiatives by other nonprofit groups. ACS was operating as a decentralized group of over 300 local chapters, each with its own governing body, its own internal processes, each empowered to do its own thing. However, the organization was not able to instantly and telegraphically communicate what it stood for.

Was it research, fundraising, advocacy? More than this, there was little indication that anyone at the top had a clear understanding of the biggest population of emerging potential donors — millennials.

The ACS is a textbook case of "hero product leadership," the belief that you can set it on autopilot and keep going, with little regard for the fact that conditions have shifted and, ergo, a shift in operating strategy is required. Rather than assigning judgmental terms such as good or bad, weak or strong, let's say it is more a matter of whether the leader in place has the oversight and agility to navigate in an evolving category, if not marketplace. And all categories and marketplaces eventually evolve. We spoke with Andy Goldsmith, a healthcare executive who formerly worked for the ACS as VP of creative and brand strategy and who currently serves at The Pursuant Group as SVP, creative director, about this topic.

"I was there in the midst of its perfect storm of challenges," he told us. "ACS was a pioneer in community-based fundraising events. It built Relay for Life thirty-five years ago, which generated hundreds of millions of dollars. That said, it was roughly two-thirds of the revenue stream, and they were never successful at fundraising. Because ACS had owned the space for so long, the peer-to-peer fundraising initiative, it didn't really look beyond this. All of a sudden there were several other organizations copying their community framework with more innovative offerings, gaining the philanthropy share of the dollar."

And it wasn't just the larger organizations gaining on ACS, including St. Jude's, for example, or the Susan G. Komen Race for the Cure. It was the smaller, more nimble, and social media–savvy groups. There was the runaway success of the Ice Bucket Challenge sponsored by the ALS Association; the 2014 cancer-fighting St. Baldrick's Foundation, which raised millions of dollars from its hundreds of events during which participants shaved their heads as a show of emotional support; and the Cycle for Survival, a seven-year-old series of indoor cycling events benefiting New York's Memorial Sloan Kettering Hospital.

You would think that with the huge number of people impacted by cancer, simply saying you're raising money for cancer would be enough to keep ACS going strong. But it wasn't. "It was no longer good enough to stand for general cancer," Goldsmith explained. "The market has become very fragmented, cluttered with many important but much more focused causes—pancreatic cancer, leukemia, breast cancer. We had such a broad mission. We tried to be 'all things cancer to all people' and ended up confusing potential donors. People didn't know what they were investing in, what they were writing the checks for. Just because you have a good cause, which ACS does, it's not enough to stand out in an increasingly cluttered marketplace."

It didn't help either that ACS as an organization was so fragmented. "We had a National Home Office as well as eleven different divisions, in many cases led by folks who were there for their entire careers," said Goldsmith. "What you see is that local priorities are different than national priorities, and everyone's making their own decisions about fundraising. There was no core innovation engine in place. You had no one focusing on millennials. It gets down to the strength of nationwide leadership, the skillset of the leadership, and their ability to set a vision for the organization and to get the entire organization behind it. It was a classic case of an organization not paying attention until the revenue really started to drop, which is a lagging indicator, not a leading indicator."

Founded in 1913 by ten doctors and five laypeople in New York City—and originally called the American Society for the Control of Cancer—the ACS has undergone a major restructuring over the last year and will hopefully regain its footing. As ACS states on its website: "We know more about how to fight cancer than ever before but the successful application of that knowledge is dependent on our ability to make a sustainable connection with partners and donors who fuel the mission. The landscape has changed, and the cancer fight is inextricably linked to successful consumer engagement in the face of increased competition for dollars and mindshare."

TEACH FOR AMERICA:
The Challenge to Get Back to the Founder's Mentality

In 1989, Wendy Kopp, a senior at Princeton, had a big idea, one that would change the academic outcomes for thousands of lower-income kids. The idea, Teach for America, the topic of her senior thesis, was to recruit high-performing college graduates to teach in high-need urban and rural schools. It was a truly innovative idea and, as its passionate founder, Kopp went all out to ensure the organization would succeed. It did, incredibly so. By the year 2000, it had over 3,500 alumni and launched an ambitious five-year plan to double the size of its corps of teachers and the number of sites it served.

In the mid-2000s, Teach for America started experiencing growing pains. While its mission to give all students access to excellent education never wavered, there were issues with execution and operations. The ambitious goals were not always being met as hoped. While Teach for America was very good at recruiting teachers, it wasn't nearly as good at supporting the talented young teachers they recruited. Consequently, teacher attrition began to rise. In turn, recruitment efforts became more challenging. Those in charge were not quick enough to grasp and deal with the complexities of changing demographics, both in terms of the communities the organization served and the potential teaching population.

Current CEO Elisa Villanueva Beard told us that the problems stemmed from the role of leadership in a growing organization. "When you're the founder, you feel a deep personal responsibility. If there's a survey, you read every last comment. You don't let others synthesize reports for you. You're obsessed about deeply understanding everything that's going on and coming to your own assessment," she said. "When you grow as big as we have, bureaucracy sets in. Conversations take place in individual silos. Those who are in charge get farther away from what's happening on the front lines."

It was, as Villanueva Beard asserted, a perfect example of "founder's mentality." The problems of fast growth and leadership's concurrent "loss of proximity to the issues" were keeping the organization from shifting in order to stay relevant. A book on this very topic became an essential guide to Beard in refocusing the organization and getting it back on a successful track. *The Founder's Mentality: How to Overcome the Predictable Crises of Growth* was written by Chris Zook and James Allen of Bain & Company. In their book, they look at why profitable growth is so hard to achieve and sustain. The authors explain that most executives manage their companies as if the solution to this problem lies externally. Instead, they found that when companies start to falter in terms of their growth objectives, 90 percent of the causes are internal. As Beard made clear, among these causes are increasing distance from the front lines, loss of accountability, and frustratingly complex processes. Even for the best organizations, Teach for America included, these challenges, if not identified and dealt with properly, can impede future growth.

As Zook and Allen explain, overcoming these internal barriers to restore speed, focus, and a genuine connection to the customer requires, yes, a "founder's mentality" — initiatives embodied by a passionate founder, which might also be called an owner's mindset, a relentless obsession with the front line. Paraphrasing the authors' website:

> The founder's mentality is one of business' most undervalued secrets. Companies start as successful insurgents, at war in their industry doing battle on behalf of underserved or deserving customers. They are fighting industry goliaths. They don't have size on their side, but they have speed. But then they eventually stall out, growth slows, the organization seizes up, the talent you really need leaves. This happens because eventually every leadership team encounters what we call the growth paradox: Growth creates complexity, and complexity kills growth.[5]

This is exactly the situation in which Villanueva Beard found herself when she took over the reins at Teach for America. "Size had become a challenge. We knew we couldn't go back to the future and operate as we had when we were a smaller organization, but we had to figure out how to regain our founder's mentality," she said. "Our core purpose has not changed, but we've had to shift strategies to take advantage of our scale and diversity. The relevance and meaning of our work has never been more important. But, as a result of our bureaucracy, we fell behind the curve of understanding what was happening both in our communities and in the behaviors and expectations of this generation of potential teacher recruits."

When Villanueva Beard came on, the organization had not only grown cumbersome and more complex, fomenting internal challenges, but there were market forces creating strong headwinds. First of all, unlike when Teach for America was launched twenty-five years ago, there was now intense competition for young, talented people who wanted to "change the world." Google, Facebook, Amazon, and all manner of millennial-centric organizations were on campuses across the country vying for the best and brightest. At issue for Teach for America was that these organizations would allow these idealistic kids the opportunity to change the world—and make a lot of money. They could do well, and do good. In particular, as Beard told us, "We . . . missed the cue on the importance of internships. Over the past several years they have become so consequential to the people we wanted to recruit. If you don't get to these students in their sophomore or junior years, you've missed the opportunity."

Second, Teach for America wasn't always as focused as it should have been on the front-line experience of its recruits. Tapping into community issues in addition to individual school issues, Teach for America was not able to ensure that every one of its teachers was having an optimal experience, nor were the students they taught. As Beard told us, social media magnified this challenge. As we all know, social media puts a spotlight on the unhappiest people. Despite the organization's best intentions, the social media buzz on Teach for America was pretty unflattering.

The challenge faced by Teach for America, its inability to shift more quickly to stem years of decline, was not a function of the wrong leadership or poor leadership. Paradoxically it was a function of great leadership—leadership that fueled huge growth, but that made it a less agile, more complex organization.

"We've re-geared," Villanueva Beard said. "We have reset our strategic direction and one of our top-line goals is to build on the strength of our community, at our core member level, at our alumni level, and at our staff level. We have brilliant people; we attract the most brilliant people in our country to this work. What you learn over twenty-five years is that you cannot become too confident. You need to know how to adapt, to refocus the organization in order to allow it to operate like it did when it was founder led," she said. "We are working to become more agile, and trying to reject bureaucracy at every level. It's about creating an incredible organization that doesn't just have a transformational impact on children, but ensures the whole community, the whole city improves."

Lessons Learned ▶

Examining the stories in this chapter reveals three categories of causes, or reasons, for a business's inability to change: financial, cultural, and leadership. Let's review the specifics with respect to each and derive corresponding lessons. We start with financial barriers, by far the most prevalent barriers we found in our research.

Lesson #1: Beware "the golden handcuffs." We use the term "golden handcuffs" to refer to the (perceived) need to deliver short-term financial results to Wall Street, or to investors, at the expense of investing in the change necessary to stay relevant for the longer term. To set off in a new direction, to shift from one business strategy to another, requires a major investment of both money and time. The financial investments will, in almost all situations, decrease current earnings. Wall Street does not like decreased earnings, even if for a short period of time. Some of the companies we studied that failed to stay relevant were making plenty of money with their current business model and were unwilling to free up the funds necessary to make the longer-term investments. Kodak and Xerox are prime examples. The short-term revenues and profits were too good to walk away from—they were too comfortable. And the pressure from investors and Wall Street to deliver these short-term results was too great a challenge. Either the subjects in question ended up underfunding the new initiatives that would potentially keep them relevant, or not funding them at all. This kept Wall Street happy in the short term, but disappointed them in the long term. (Bankruptcy is disappointing.)

Lesson #2: "Empty pockets" restrict options for maintaining relevance. The term "empty pockets" is pretty self-explanatory. That is, by the time the company realizes it's lost relevance, the money has run out. There's insufficient cash on hand to fund a turnaround. Such was the case with Toys "R" Us. Things get so bad that you need to lay off people, close stores, or shut plants. Profits are so squeezed, revenue is so far down, credit is so woefully unavailable that by the time a firm is ready to act, the financial situation is so dire the firm no longer has the wherewithal or scale to execute an effective shift.

Sunk costs present one way in which pockets can be emptied. Xerox, for example, fell victim to the sunk cost fallacy. So much money had been invested in the existing business model. Manufacturing plants had been built; a new sales force had been hired; technology investments had been made. Xerox fed the pet it had raised, despite the fact that it had many more attractive options for its investment. More generally, and keeping with the metaphor, the lost cause or bad idea is followed down the road. As the time and resources devoted to the failing business model add up, it is increasingly difficult to change course.

Lesson #3: Culture clashes kill. We now move to the second category of barriers to maintaining relevancy, cultural barriers. Culture is the inherent qualities that make one organization different from another, comprised of everything from values and beliefs to systems and working habits. Culture is baked into an organization and directs how it operates and why. It's a preexisting condition often perpetuated by the onboarding of employees who exhibit the same values and beliefs as those already there. Culture is often codified in some sort of statement. It might be literally instructive: Consulting firm McKinsey & Company clearly articulates how clients should be served, colleagues treated, and professional standards followed. Or it might be simple and whimsical, but just as directive: Google famously uses the phrase, "Don't be evil." In whatever manner it is verbally communicated, culture manifests itself in myriad ways, both tangible and intangible, from physical environment to dress code and everything in between. To shift, companies need an entrepreneurial spirit as part of the culture.

Sumantra Ghoshal, a noted scholar from the London Business School, who tragically passed away from a brain hemorrhage in 2004, but whose influence continues to this day, produced a set of lectures on culture and organizational strategy that still garner thousands upon thousands of viewers on YouTube. In one particular and very popular lecture, during which he explained his "springtime theory," he would tell audiences about his annual visit to Calcutta to see his parents in July.[6] "Imagine the heat, the humidity, the dirt, the noise. It sucks up all your energy, drains your brain, and exhausts your imagination." He would then go on to talk about the forest of Fontainebleau, close to INSEAD, where he taught at the time, referring to "the smell of the trees, the crispness in the air, the flowers, the grass underfoot. How one's heart lifts up, how the creativity and energy bubble away." Go through the door of any business, he would then tell the audience, and you can tell whether it's Calcutta or Fontainebleau, and whether there is an opportunity for innovation and reinvention.

Just as there are several variations on the financial barrier theme, there are several reasons that organizational culture can get in the way of a successful shift and focus. The 30,000-foot view is that it's just plain hard to overcome how things have always been done. In some instances, it's size that gets in the way.

Larger organizations, like Procter & Gamble, often exhibit the syndrome of the "massive middle." Junior management is open to making a change—these are generally younger folks, possibly millennials, who have an appetite for change—but the hordes of middle managers, long-entrenched in the way things are and were, are more reluctant. They muck up the gears of progress as if they were molasses that the more aggressive managers are trying to get through. At P&G, careful deliberative new product development based on reliable marketing research had always been the firm's modus operandi. They wouldn't tolerate the voices of those among them who recognized the faster pace of change in the modern retail world. Deborah Henretta used the metaphor of kids playing soccer; everyone is focused on offense, because that is what they do, in a game where defense wins.

Lesson # 4: Pride goeth before a fall. This biblical proverb stems from the idea that if you are too proud and overconfident, you will make mistakes leading to your defeat. Pride is one of the seven deadly sins. It leads to arrogance and consequently the tendency to live in a bubble.

The most written-about marketing mistake in history was the recipe change and the introduction of New Coke in 1985. Coca-Cola management could not live with the fact that it lost to Pepsi in a series of blind taste tests. The president of the company felt that no one can beat Coke on anything; Coke had to be number one in everything that matters, including taste. Coca-Cola scientists reworked the recipe over and over until it could beat Pepsi in taste tests. Of course, in doing that, the beverage lost the essence of what made it great. Coke was no longer "the real thing." The consumer backlash is a matter of history. What a display of arrogance!

RIM's experience with BlackBerry mirrors the New Coke story. Preoccupied with matching the apps of the Apple and Android devices, RIM took its eye off the security ball. Its arrogance in fighting the competition led the company to take its customers for granted. The rest is history. The experience of New Coke and RIM suggests a corollary to Lesson #5, which turns to the final category of barriers—leadership.

COROLLARY:

Focusing too much on competition can lead to inappropriate shifts. It's the customer that really counts. In the National Geographic story, Linda Berkeley recounted the classic writings of Theodore (Ted) Levitt on "marketing myopia."[7] Levitt counseled that to move ahead in a changing environment, organizations must define what they do for their customers more broadly; they must act on what consumers want and need, how they fit into customers' lives, without laurel-resting on the longevity of any particular product. Much as Levitt used railroads as an example fifty years ago, today he might well have chosen publishing (e.g., National Geographic), radio, or traditional retail as examples of categories that are challenged by defining their business in too narrow a fashion. Toys "R" Us is one example. Managers focused on lowering costs in a way that would allow them to lower prices. Yet they neglected their customers' needs to have their children grow through educational and entertainment experiences, needs that they were well aware of.

Another way to describe what these companies—RIM, Toys "R" Us, and the National Geographic Society—all experienced is what we'll label "the man in the mirror syndrome." Too internally focused, they may give lip service to staying close to their customers or being in touch with their customers' needs, but they don't deliver. Charlie Wrench, former president and chief executive officer of Landor Associates (Allen's former boss) and now executive vice president of the Engine Group, a communications firm, talked to us about the difference between brands that are too internally focused to jump into new but relevant realms, and those that succeed as a result of being "culturally connected brands."

"When you're trying to ensure your message is always relevant," Wrench began, "what you're looking for is the intersection of what is true about yourself, your culture or some purpose or belief system you have, and what is important to your audience. Then you express it through a prism of what is significant to our time. Success is predicated on finding a way to communicate what's special and different about you and meaningful for your target audience in the context of the cultural phenomenon of our time. Looking at all three vectors, not just two, is what forces you as an organization to constantly look outside and ask, 'What's on people's minds? What's the conversation? What's going on in their lives and how can I fit in?' [That's the opposite of] being just internally focused."

Support for the "man in the mirror" concept was also part of the conversation we had with Joel Benenson, CEO of the Benenson Group and a political consultant known for his role in Barack Obama's 2008 and 2012 presidential campaigns and as chief strategist for Hillary Clinton's presidential campaign. "The best organizations keep that outside view," he said. "When looking in the mirror versus through a prism, say, not to get too metaphorical, [the organization] only sees itself rather than different views of the same object. If you look through a prism you see things you might not see otherwise. That's one thing that I think is an early-warning sign. Conventional thinking is our enemy. You have to challenge what you know. You have to challenge what you *think you know.* And I have seen that when organizations stop asking and facing up to the hard questions internally, they end up like Kodak."

Lesson #5: It takes a special leader to execute a shift. The third major category of barriers to being able to shift and focus with any success, leadership, is tied with absolute certainty to the first two (financial and cultural). There are many types of leaders, but as strategist Joel Benenson said during our discussion, "There has to be a decision maker. Authority, responsibility, and tasks are the three tiers of the decision-making process, but you need a strong leader who will listen to opinions, who will want to make it a consensus decision as much as possible, but is ultimately charged with implementing the decision."

Time and again we've seen situations where there were too many cooks in the kitchen, too many masters, along with superfluous committees and task forces, all without a commander-in-chief. There are many people running in many directions, talking about change, leading change efforts, but the company is fragmenting its efforts and again does not have one person helping focus the efforts. David Ogilvy once said that you can search all the parks and all the city squares, but you'll find no statues of committees.

We learned from information gathered during the research of this book that a lack of urgency on the part of leadership tops the list of complicating issues. Yes, change is coming, but I've got to attend to business as usual. Tightly connected to this is the "future is closer than you think" factor. Leadership knows change is coming in the marketplace, but greatly underestimates how fast the public will react to it. How quickly will people replace film cameras with smartphones? How soon will it be that they get their news from sources other than a newspaper, their clothing from online retailers, shift their travel sleeping accommodations from hotels to the homes of strangers? A third barrier in the realm of leadership is the "which way do I go" syndrome—analysis paralysis as some consultants call it, as Procter & Gamble experienced. While there's no easy choice and there may be several alternatives to staying relevant, each with positive and negative aspects, the person in charge can't make a decision. So what happens? Either they don't decide and continue to evaluate options until the train has left the station, or they're too late to the game to seize an opportunity and their competitors have beat them to the punch ("you snooze you lose"). Or they hedge their bets and pursue several options, not putting the necessary resources behind any one of them and fight a multifront war (in Chapter 4, we describe Sony as a classic example).

Lesson # 6: The magic only happens outside the comfort zone. We end this chapter where we started it, with Marty Crane. Psychologists and behavioral economists have a phrase for the Marty Crane–like preference for the comfort zone. They call it the *status quo bias*, and it refers to the tendency of people to prefer things to stay the same by doing nothing or by sticking with a decision made previously.[8] The status quo bias is related to the previously discussed sunk cost fallacy in that both lead decision makers to stick to decisions already made, even in the face of contradictory evidence. If the world changes and you don't, you lose.

Status quo biases exist even in the face of very important decisions. One study on university health plan enrollments, for example, showed a large disparity in health plan choices between new and existing enrollees. In particular, one new plan with significantly more favorable premiums and deductibles had a much higher market share among new employees than it did among existing employees. The pattern could not be explained by differences in preferences for plan components.

The status quo bias inhibits firms from taking risks. Surely it made it easier for Wall Street to place the golden handcuffs on Kodak. It cemented the culture of the "massive middle" at P&G and created the cultural belief that the National Geographic Society was a magazine-centric organization.

On the other hand, the status quo bias has not prevented Roger Federer from becoming the greatest tennis player of all time. Federer first came into the view of ardent tennis fans (like Joel) at Wimbledon in 2001, where he upset Pete Sampras, then the four-time defending champion and seven-time champion overall, in five sets in the fourth round. What seemed like a monumental upset at the time now does not seem like a bad loss for Sampras in retrospect. Roger employed a serve and volley net-rushing strategy—the strategy that had been the key to success for fifty years on grass courts such as those at Wimbledon. Then in 2002, things changed. Following the 2001 tournament, Wimbledon ripped up all of its courts and sowed new ones made of 100 percent perennial ryegrass. The old courts were a 70–30 split of ryegrass and creeping red fescue. The change was ostensibly made to make the courts more durable. But because ryegrass stands taller and its soil is drier and firmer, the side effect was that the ball now bounced higher and slower. The tried-and-true grass court strategy of taking advantage of low-skidding approach shots to win point after point at the net was no longer unbeatable. Baseline play became much more effective. In the 2002 tournament, Federer lost in the first round and Sampras lost in the second to journeymen Mario Ancic and George Bastl, respectively. Two baseliners, Lleyton Hewitt and David Nalbandian, contested the final. At this point, Federer took off his Marty Crane clothes to reveal a big red "S" on his chest and then restyled his game to be played mostly from the baseline. He then proceeded to be Superman and win the next five Wimbledon titles and three more for eight overall. Take that status quo bias. Roger Federer responded to a change in his world and became the most successful player in the history of his sport.

Fortunately, there are many similar stories of organizations in this book that broke through the status quo bias: Adobe, *Forbes* magazine, IBM, and New York University, among them. There is an old Latin proverb "audentes Fortuna iuvat," which literally means "fortune favors the bold." These organizations had all achieved success in previous incarnations. However, the fast-moving world in which we live was placing a wall right in front of them—a wall seen by effective leaders, but not necessarily by everyone else. Had they imitated Marty Crane, their organizations would have been in trouble. Instead, they made huge investments in changing the fundamental ways they conducted business and, as a result, remain at the forefront of their industries. They followed the advice of the rock band American Authors who sang the 2016 hit song "Go Big or Go Home."

4

READY THE ORGANIZATION FOR A SHIFT

Benjamin Franklin once said that by failing to prepare, you are preparing to fail. We agree. The question we ask in this chapter is how do you prepare to be nimble, to shift and change when the circumstances call for it.

A 2010 article in *Psychology Today* stated:

Success comes from the days, weeks, and months of preparation leading up to the culmination of those efforts. Many businesspeople believe that it's what happens on a key day (e.g., strategic-planning meeting, investor presentation) that matters. But . . . success is determined more by what you do in the days, weeks, and months leading up to the crucial day. If you've put in the time and effort to develop yourself and your team . . . , then you will know that you have done everything you can to achieve your goals and you will perform your best on that important day.[1]

Preparing would be straightforward if we knew what we were preparing for. In physics, the Heisenberg Uncertainty Principle describes how it is impossible to simultaneously know the exact position and momentum of a particle, arguing that there is a fundamental limit on what can be known about a particle at any given moment. Companies often try to prepare for the future by looking at time in a very linear way, often ignoring that one little change, a single event, can alter what happens dramatically. It's necessary to become comfortable with a bit of ambiguity—which is a point we'll discuss further in Chapter 5 with one of our interviewees, futurist Amy Webb.

The stories in this chapter highlight some of the aspects of the preparation (or lack thereof) that will either allow the firm to shift when someday its chance comes or fail because it failed to prepare. We begin with a company that has taught us so much about innovative approaches to ensure that they are prepared to maintain relevance over the many years it has been a public icon.

AMERICAN EXPRESS:
Still Shifting After All Those Years

Founded as an express delivery service, American Express didn't launch its first American Express Card until 1958, when it was already 108 years old. Suffice it to say, American Express has had a lot of experience shifting and refocusing its efforts over the years. From transporting valuable freight across the country, to developing the first traveler's checks, to working with the United States Immigration Department to provide the official currency exchange service, to being a resource for soldiers away from home and their families back home starting with the outbreak of World War I, the company has established itself as dedicated to the needs of its customers.

We have each had the pleasure of working with American Express during our careers and called upon its former chief marketing officer, John Hayes, for his thoughts on what it takes to prepare for such a shift and how this understanding manifested itself in terms of company initiatives and return on investment. In his twenty-one years at American Express, Hayes not only created a number of iconic brand advertising and marketing campaigns, but played a key role in major product innovations.

He began our conversation by talking about the fact that although the business has changed across these many years, there are three basic tenets that have not: trust, security, and service. "American Express started in freight forwarding, hence the 'express' name," he began. "You weren't going to give us your valuables to [ship over] many miles if you didn't trust that your valuables would get where you wanted them to be. Then, security and service emerged as offshoots of trust. We were—and continue to be—a service business. These three things have been the focus throughout our 166-year history," he said. "I'm a big believer that the customer experience has been the most important branding tool we have. It is the principles-based approach we instill in our employees. We don't stifle their ability to serve the customer by giving them lots of rules. Our employees understand the brand and they operationalize it every day in their interactions with the customers."

Knowing that its focus is now and always has been the three fundamental tenets of its business, the next question for Hayes was, How do you shift? How do you remain relevant? To make service relevant, he told us, is a matter of operationalizing and executing it and identifying ways to reinforce that American Express is truly service-minded. "We know the value of being purposeful in today's world. And what we recognized was that small businesses are a very important part of our customer base, and we value them immensely. A number of them were asking why they should accept the American Express Card, given that it cost them more money. We realized we needed to double down and demonstrate our commitment to these small businesses. Delving into the situation," Hayes said, "we came to understand that among their biggest challenges was promoting their businesses. And, not just their businesses, but others in the community. The quality of the community was dependent on the quality of the businesses. We understood the interconnections. We started to see we had the opportunity as a national brand to promote small businesses in a way individual small businesses could never match. It was a fairly junior person in our organization who suggested we 'own' Saturday, much like after Thanksgiving you have Black Friday and Cyber Monday. It was the thinking that led to Small Business Saturday. 'Stay in your community and shop on Main Street.' The results have been astounding. We've been able to actually shift the U.S. economy for the day."

The reaction American Express received has been tremendous. As Hayes explained, the company wanted to see small businesses thrive. Its view was to prompt people to shop locally, even if they didn't use the American Express Card. Demonstrating its understanding of the "ecosystem" of a community, the buyers and the sellers, helped solidify its position as being relevant to people's lives. It's a position that goes back to an earlier point we made in this book, of asking "why" people are doing what they're doing. What is motivating people to behave as they do? You have to understand the "whys," because if you don't, then you can't understand what they're thinking. To be able to shift with authority and credibility, you've got to be externally focused, customer focused, and determine how it will impact your business in the future.

As Hayes said about the continual and necessary changes in business initiatives at American Express, people want to trust. They want to be secure. They want to be well served. Those things don't change. But the way people see the value of these things does change. It changes generationally (think millennials), and it changes when events happen that change everyone's perspective. This means it is essential to be in touch with not just what happens with your business, but what happens in the world. Getting out from behind your desk and talking to consumers is certainly one way to do this, but American Express has been wildly inventive in deriving ways to tap into the general zeitgeist. An example is the company's research enterprise: Artists-in-Residence.

"I gave myself a challenge," Hayes explained. "I have to get the greatest minds in the world thinking about American Express. I want really intelligent people who are part of the popular culture, who understand popular culture, who understand what 'today' means and how it will affect what people want tomorrow. I want people like Bono, like Ellen DeGeneres, Tina Fey, Jane Rosenthal, Robert De Niro, and Martin Scorsese, to help me understand the world from multiple perspectives and definitely from a different perspective than, perhaps, a formal research person. I hired them as my eyes and ears. I got them truly engaged in thinking about our business. These were not consultants being paid to tell me how to make money in the next few quarters. Rather, they were giving me advanced radar. Helping the company see around corners. My objective was, 'How do I engage the most interesting minds in popular culture to help me understand the world as it applies to American Express and keep us ahead of everyone else in the business by giving our customers things of value to them?'"

Being able to extrapolate what you see today into what consumers will want and need tomorrow is the challenge every organization wrestles with. By looking outside the traditional research parameters, American Express has been able to tap into the early-warning signals of consumer sentiment that many companies miss. Early-warning signals that may eventually become pain points, as many marketers call them. Situations that cause consumers to, if not run the other way, wince in frustration. The thing is, if you build your newest offer based on what's happening today, by the time you put it into market, the ball will have moved.

HERTZ:
Research as Waze

Upon arriving in San Francisco to help his son Josh settle into his freshman year at Stanford University, Allen headed to the airport's offsite car rental location. With great impatience, Josh asked, "Why are we wasting all this time? Why can't you just get an Uber?" Allen admittedly was just hardwired to rent a car, even being aware that there may be faster, often more convenient ways to get from point A to point B, this being the age of Uber, Lyft, and Sidecar.

The relevance of rental cars in today's marketplace stimulated our conversation with Stuart Benzal, the former vice president of customer experience at Hertz. How does a company like Hertz, so critically affected by the dynamics of the sharing economy, maintain its relevance when consumer behavior in this arena has been changing in such a seismic manner? Benzal responded, "We don't look at our competitors and say, 'Oh, the customer picked another car rental company.' It's not that we don't care about Avis or National, it's that we do not look at ourselves as a car rental company. We look at how we solve a transportation problem for the consumer. We look at the situation more broadly—mobility on-demand," he said. "We're looking at it beyond A to B. . . . The reason you flew to San Francisco was to close a business deal. How can we be part of the business traveler solution? Or you're going to wine country. What can we do to make your experience more pleasurable? Whether it's a solution having to do with a family visit, or a vacation, or getting a business deal done, we keep the lens broad. What can we do to make the process of mobility on-demand less painful? We look at the pain points and how to mitigate them."

If any "mobility on-demand" company has the depth of familiarity to do this, Hertz does. Almost 100 years old, Hertz was founded by Walter Jacobs in Chicago as Rent-A-Car, Inc. Jacobs expanded the company from a dozen Model Ts to a fleet of 600 cars by 1923, when he sold the company to John D. Hertz, who renamed it Hertz Drive-ur-Self System and made it a subsidiary of his other business, the Yellow Truck and Coach Manufacturing Company.

Like all long-run successful businesses, Hertz solved a problem. In this case, getting around when you don't have a car. As travel grew in scale and scope, both for business and leisure purposes, Hertz expanded to solve the new issues that cropped up. For example, it opened up the nation's first airport rental counter at Chicago Midway Airport to make it easier for travelers to pick up their cars. In 1972, Hertz introduced the # 1 Club, a computerized data system that made inputting customer information more efficient so that customers could get from counter to car more quickly. More recently, Hertz invested in the on-demand valet service, Luxe, which takes the worry out of finding parking in an unfamiliar city.

"For us, it's complexity reduction," Benzal said. "It's looking at the common travel anxieties cited by customers—making it to the airport on time, trying to find the rental counter, getting home as quickly as possible. We look at the pain points to figure out how we can stay a step ahead on relieving them. The only way to do this right is to spend time with customers, not in a focus group asking a bunch of questions, but taking part in the actual journey during which you can get the level of granularity required. Like taking the ride from midtown Manhattan to LaGuardia on a rainy afternoon. If you ask a simple question, you're only going to get a simple answer.

"We're looking for how people are talking and referencing things, the words they use, yes, but also the passion behind the words," Benzal said. "There's an emotion we hear. So, they might say, 'Yeah, Hertz is great. They're at every airport I go to, and they're open twenty-four hours. But it's very different from the tonality you hear when they talk about Uber or Zipcar and, that alone is very indicative of what's going on. They think of Hertz as a good transactional brand, but they don't talk about it with the same passion they use for Uber. It's similar to our social media monitoring. We're actually looking for how people are referencing the category, and whether one company or another has picked up on some pain point and is delivering on it. You can't look at an algorithm. You need the tonality of the conversations, the inflections within the context."

Benzal and his customer experience team at Hertz are on to this, which is why they *don't* just take a laser-beam approach to understanding what's happening with their customers at the airport counter or knowing whether a car is clean. They zoom out to look at the context of a traveler's situation and then they zoom in to alleviate, to the degree possible, the specific pain points so as to improve the customer's overall experience. For those familiar with the app, Hertz takes a "Waze" approach, looking at any barriers in the road ahead and the potential routes out and around them. "It's no longer feasible to say this is the way we've always done business. . . . We have to ask, 'How can we do this differently? How do we do this better?'. . . When Hertz put NeverLost in their cars in the 1980s, no one had ever seen in-car navigation."

Hertz faces huge challenges in its category as technology and consumer habits impact its business model. However, its history of innovation has helped it make impressive inroads in the past. "What can we offer that customers would really value, or make it easier, or make them want to choose you?" said Benzal. "You can't win on table stakes. You need to always be looking for the differentiators. Having that mindset will make it work."

FACEBOOK:
Shifting Gears Comes Naturally

It's pretty amazing to think that Facebook, now virtually baked into many of our daily lives, didn't exist a mere thirteen years ago. For those few of you out there who may not know its history, Facebook is a social networking service founded in 2004 by Mark Zuckerberg and three of his Harvard University classmates, Eduardo Saverin, Dustin Moskovitz, and Chris Hughes, dedicated to the simple proposition of keeping people connected. From connecting a few hundred students on a college campus to connecting one billion users worldwide in 2012, jumping to over 1.8 billion by 2016, Facebook continues to find new ways to keep people connected—and it has paid off. In 2016, Facebook was on pace to reach $27 billion in revenue, defying the slow-down in growth that usually comes with increasing size. Facebook's top-line growth rate is double any other U.S. company with a revenue of $20 billion or more, excluding those growing through acquisitions, according to data from Standard & Poor's Capital IQ.

Facebook's built-in ability to shift and to stay ever-relevant inspired us to have a conversation with Gary Briggs, a seasoned technology marketing executive who was tapped by the company in 2013 to be its first-ever chief marketing officer. While Facebook definitely—and definitively—falls into the category of young, spry companies, there are factors that contribute to its ongoing success that can be adopted by even the most iconic legacy organizations, technology or otherwise.

"We're one percent done," said Briggs at the beginning of our conversation. "It's a saying that we adopted right after we went public in 2012, to make sure people stayed focused. It's an attitude that allows us to stay ahead in an extremely volatile industry. Mark [Zuckerberg] truly believes that his biggest risk is someone else out there in a dorm room or a garage. He keeps an eagle eye on what's happening out there, [which was] part of why he decided to buy Instagram. He's obsessively worried, but in a healthy way. He's totally convinced that if Facebook stops moving for one second, it will die. He *can't* put it on autopilot. He's perfectly aware of the fact that it was among the fastest-growing companies in history and could just as easily become the fastest-disappearing company in history," said Briggs. "An interesting phenomenon, if you take a look, is that over the course of history, the Facebook logo has gotten progressively smaller on the website page. That's because as they build out the platform more and more, [and] embrace their mission to connect consumers, it's a signal that what's important is the user's experience, not the logo.

"That said, there are three basic cultural elements at the core of how we operate," Briggs said. "The first one is that we have a central mission and a clear sense of purpose. Everyone understands Mark's view, and everyone is hardwired to this view. We can operate quickly and autonomously because we each know where we're going, we each know our role in getting us there, and we're all aware of 'why' we're doing what we do. We're pretty singular about this: the concept of having a connected world—giving people the power to share and making the world more open and connected."

Briggs discussed the fact that while "purpose-driven" has become a rallying cry by many companies, it's very often a case of talking the talk without walking the walk. As more and more companies come to the realization that consumers judge brands not just on what they make but on what they are, it's a company whose employees can answer the question, "Why are we here?" that will be most powerful.

That there is no ambiguity in direction is the second core element that enables the company to shift as needed. There is, as Briggs told us, a set of "built-in GPS coordinates. You're not going to make a change that's going to be 'off-brand,' as they say, or something not right for Facebook. Our ability to move fast is because whether we should, or shouldn't, do something is pretty clear." When Zuckerberg envisioned the company, he had a strong sense of the social impact he wanted it to have on the world. "His 'why'—giving people the power to share and making the world more connected and open," as Briggs said, continues to drive the company and everyone in it.

We also spoke to David Kirkpatrick, author of *The Facebook Effect: The Inside Story of a Company That Is Connecting the World*. Kirkpatrick's 2010 book chronicles the history of the company since its inception and documents its global impact. Zuckerberg, he writes, is as much an ideologue as an engineer. He saw, and continues to see, Facebook primarily as a social movement dedicated to keeping people connected. And he practices what he preaches about open communication.

As Briggs told us, this consistency of purpose is validated day in and day out, in the very way the company operates, with openness—which happens to be the third of the company's core cultural elements that give it an edge. "Mark doesn't care about the hierarchy of who's in the room," Briggs said. "It's just the nature of the place. Information flows freely. The ability for anyone in the organization to ask a question with the response being 'thank you for asking a hard question' is stunningly awesome. There's no matrix here. Information is shared so fluidly, it makes it easier for the company to see changes coming and importantly act on these changes without ambiguity. We can seize the opportunity that a changing landscape puts up, and deliver on it."

Asking Kirkpatrick about Facebook's being able to shift so quickly, about seeing what's coming down the road faster than the competition, he commented that it is due to a couple of factors. In addition to consistency of purpose and open communication, he cited the company's ability to leverage its enormous compilation of data so effectively and efficiently. "A majority of companies collect data like they're collecting stamps," he said. "What makes Facebook unique in this regard is its ability to assess the data, to analyze it expeditiously, and critically, to understand it and act on it." It was this sixth sense about what consumers were *going* to want that led it to its 2014 purchase of WhatsApp, bolstering its already-strong position in a crowded messaging market. Similar to text messaging, WhatsApp allows people to connect via their cell phone numbers but without racking up texting fees, because the app sends the actual messages over mobile broadband. This makes it particularly effective for communicating with people overseas.

Facebook's transactions, such as WhatsApp and Instagram, are focused on the goal of assembling an offering that is going to make customers' lives appreciably better than anyone else's offering will. This is a general principle and is especially true in the financial services industry and, more specifically, in the insurance industry. How really different *can* one insurance product be from another? That is why the human element, demonstrating a genuine understanding of the customer, or client, has become the differentiating factor in those that lead in this category.

NEW YORK LIFE:
Mutuality Does Mean a Lot

Not too many people know what a mutual company is. At least, we didn't until we started talking to New York Life. As New York Life's website states, mutuality means that the company operates for the benefit of its policy owners: "Mutuality means we are collectively and entirely owned by our clients, not outside investors. And since we don't have to appease Wall Street, the bulls and the bears, our exclusive focus—every decision we make—is in the best interest of our policy holders. We've stood by our clients since 1845. And we've paid dividends every year since 1854."

To make decisions that are "in the best interest of the policy holders," New York Life needs to understand those interests. That is how the company sets itself apart in a relatively commoditized category. Rather than setting analysts loose on big data (which it has lots of) and the sophisticated analysts to parse those data, New York Life's real secret for success can be found at Little League games, in supermarket aisles, at dog parks, sidewalk sales, and farmers' markets, and wherever else friends and neighbors gather in the 120 communities in which the insurer has offices. Or, as Kelli Parsons, the company's former senior vice president and chief communications and marketing officer, put it, "We do a better job of gaining insights about our clients' needs from our advisers out in the communities because they are boots on the ground every day. They know a lot about what people care about. They have a real sense of what's going on. When people are thinking about their life as a whole, the needs, the challenges, and the opportunities," she said, "having someone who really cares about you, assessing the long term [and] dealing with these complex financial issues, we just believe that human guidance is still very much in style."

While the people at New York Life are certainly experts at numbers and the myriad actuarial details of their industry, this is not their day-to-day focus. Rather, their focus is staying in touch with what's on consumers' minds, gaining an understanding of their clients' lives. They know how to "zoom out" in order to determine where and how a particular product might fit into people's lives. This ability to understand the context, to get to the heart of what makes people tick, has allowed New York Life to be as effective as it has been.

"People say, 'I hate big finance, but I really like my local adviser,'" Parsons told us. "Ours is a relationship-based business from day one. If anything is changing . . . , and where we need to make subtle shifts, is in *how* we nurture these relationships, especially with millennials who are so technology and social media oriented. The more research we've done, both qualitative and quantitative, the more we've come to understand that while we need to communicate with millennials differently, to utilize new tools and technology, at their core millennials want to make good decisions when it comes to their finances. This is partly because they came of age in difficult times, and in many cases saw their parents lose their jobs, their life savings, even their homes. That said, they've also grown up in a world where asking friends for advice is routine behavior. As a company, we equip our agents with all the resources they need to engage in the meaningful conversations that will help clients make good decisions for themselves."

When asked about the notion of being ready to shift to stay relevant and about the "advanced radar" the company uses to ensure it stays relevant, Parsons told us that it was "as simple as taking the time to listen to what their clients really care about and what's going to make a difference in their lives. It's what our agents do best," she said. "It's kind of interesting to think that in a world that is so fast-paced and complex, [being able] to have a conversation with a client that doesn't start with a particular product, but starts with a desire to gain a deeper understanding of needs, aspirations, and dreams, about where you want to be twenty years from now, is the most beneficial tool we have to gauge the future market."

Life insurance is, without question, an emotional sale. You buy it to protect the people you love in the future, while giving yourself present peace of mind. One success factor in the insurance business is being able to connect with people at the right time in their lives with just the right product to give them this peace of mind. As Parsons said, "We believe deeply in the value of conversation, especially when one is making a complex financial decision. The more complex, the more value there is in having an expert talk it through with you to help you make the right decision." As rapidly as the world is changing, the human element, staying in touch one-to-one with what people want and need, cannot be underestimated as a research tool. It's the differentiating factor for New York Life. However, understanding the wants and needs to people is not limited to customers, as the next story shows.

DELTA:
Climbing in Employee Satisfaction, and Otherwise

There is no getting around the fact that the bigger an organization, the harder it will be to shift. If a business is incredibly complex, dependent on multiple moving parts, not to mention variables absolutely out of its control, it only exacerbates the challenge. The airline industry, where the *conceptually* simple task of getting passengers from point A to point B can be disrupted by an unexpected thunderstorm, exemplifies this idea.

Delta is rooted in "southern hospitality," warmth and friendliness being inherent traits. Its roots took hold in Macon, Georgia, in 1924, where the airline began life as a commercial crop-dusting operation, the Huff Deland Dusters. C. E. Woolman bought the airline in 1928 and renamed it Delta Air Service, for the Mississippi Delta region it served. Delta expanded throughout the years, the result of mergers with

Chicago and Southern Airlines in 1953, Northeast Airlines in 1972, and the acquisition of Pan Am in 1991, which officially made Delta a global carrier.

After decades of growth, inclusive of additional mergers and innovative service offerings, there were a series of events that began to severely test Delta's culture of southern charm and hospitality. For example, the September 11, 2001, terrorist attacks rocked the airline industry and sent Delta into financial turmoil. Over the next few years, plagued by rising fuel prices, a global recession, increasing airport security difficulties, a defeated hostile takeover by US Airways, and acknowledged management missteps, the company lost billions of dollars. Ed Bastian, a senior vice president in 2004, had urged his bosses to file for bankruptcy to save the airline from liquidation. When they wouldn't listen, he left the company, returning six months later to help guide Delta through bankruptcy, eventually taking on the role of president. Bastian became the company's CEO in 2015, a year in which the company turned an astounding $5.9 billion profit while the airline moved over 180 million passengers from point A to point B, across 327 cities in 57 countries.

Huge investments in aircraft as well as improvements in basic infrastructure and technology laid the foundation for a strategic shift. Each and every step was undertaken to try to ensure that the customer experience was as stress-free and friendly as possible. For example, the installation of large flat-screen monitors in the gate areas where passengers could see the weather at their destinations, assess their upgrade potential, and watch for delays in departure time made Delta a friendlier airline. While these monitors may have seemed to be simple fixes, they alleviated a lot of anxiety for the gate agents behind the desks, who were then free to deal with triage issues rather than answering questions about weather, upgrades, and delays.

Technology, infrastructure, and airplane upgrades were all necessary, but according to Bastian, the most important factor in shifting the company from negative to positive territory, in every regard, was a heavy investment in employee satisfaction. "We've focused on improving the quality of what we deliver to our customers," he told us, "the product and the service reliability. It's been a long journey and what we are delivering today is head and shoulders above any other airline today. But that's because we concluded ten years back that there was a direct linkage between this and our employees. I'd say that at Delta, the most important thing is to have happy employees. . . .There's a saying that goes back to our founder—'Caring is not something that the airline industry historically has seen a lot of. The better job we do taking care of our employees, the better job they'll be able to do to take care of our customers.' It's a simple premise, but it's in the DNA of Delta's history."

Bastian explained that in its efforts to bolster the company's culture, Delta has launched several new initiatives, including what it calls its Development Series—informal outreach events during which management mixes and mingles with employees to hear about their experiences on the front lines and listens to suggestions for improvement. These events were started immediately after the bankruptcy period, when the company was in its most serious financial predicament. "When you're in a difficult financial condition, it's easy for employees to believe it was their fault—they're making too much money, or they're not productive enough—when, in reality, it's the management's fault. It was important to bring our people together to apologize, to let them know management owned the issue," Bastian said.

This transparent declaration of responsibility, the confession of poor oversight that resulted in pay cuts and lost jobs, went a long way in helping to reignite the passion and the connection between the management team and the employee base, which carries over to this day. The company is committed to a culture of transparency and to the assurance that management will always have its employees' backs. It was this personal engagement immediately following Delta's nadir that Bastian said was a critical catalyst in its transition: "We communicate to our employees that we know they are expected to make decisions that have a direct impact on safety and reliability and service. We want them to know we have confidence in their ability to do a great job, and to do what it takes to serve these customers. Empowerment is a big part of our turnaround success."

So, too, he determined, is sharing in the profits, making it clear—in a tangible way—that there is a direct link between what the employees do every day and the financial rewards due to their efforts. At the same time Delta provided employees arenas in which to voice their opinions, it put together a very impressive profit-sharing arrangement. In 2015, it shared $1.5 billion in profits with its team. It was the largest profit-sharing activity ever. Not in the industry, but in corporate America. As a result of this broad-based universal program, 80,000 employees received a 21 percent bonus for their hard work.

That the employees feel part of the solution is evident in the fact that, as of late August 2016, Delta had fewer cancellations than ever in its mainline operations. Employees getting rewarded for the results of their work (as measured by on-time and completion rates) not only shows up in Delta's internal metrics, but in the company's Net Promoter Scores, an index that measures the willingness of customers to recommend a company's product or service to others.

We also spoke to Roy Bostock, a former member of Delta's Board of Directors and, in the spirit of transparency, Allen's former boss when he was in the ad agency business. "Delta's overall goal was to create a preference for the brand and enable it to be perceived above and beyond a commodity product," Bostock said. "Management set out to achieve operational excellence, which can be measured in a lot of different ways. Just looking at technical operations, it's mind-boggling what happens. You go from dispatchers dealing with delays at LAX, having to ensure planes get positioned faster. You've got the whole mechanical side of it, managing spare parts and inventory, the luggage, the food and drink management. At every touch point along the way you want to deliver a better experience, a more convenient experience, a very enjoyable experience, even accounting for the TSA [security] lines. Instead of saying 'it's not my problem,' every employee sees it as their responsibility to achieve operational excellence, a customer-orientation."

While on the board, Bostock had the opportunity to go down and talk to the employees on the tarmac, the people in technical operations, the pilots and flight attendants, the agents at the ticket counters, and the staff at the airport clubs. They all talked about the "Delta brand," and that they were there to serve the customer, to make the customer experience a great one. As a result, Bostock said that even when there are problems with air traffic control or weather issues, customers are more willing to give Delta the benefit of the doubt because they know that they're putting their best effort into making things right. "People say things like, 'You know, I got stuck for several hours. It was a weather delay. It was unavoidable, they closed the airport. But the Delta people got it right proactively. I'd rather fly Delta because people take care of me.'"

"The people take care of me" is the moral of the story. The culture at Delta is grounded in creating the best possible experience for its customers. The company takes care of its people so the people take care of the company . . . by taking care of its customers. This grounding stems from its roots in southern hospitality, a history of friendliness and welcome, but it's not as simple as that. Building and sustaining a positive culture takes lots of ongoing work. The view of the people at Delta is that this work is never done. Its popular "Keep Climbing" campaign is indicative of this aspirational goal to always find ways to improve.

"Our transformation is largely the story of people," Bastian said at the close of our conversation. "I tell people that while you see airplanes and exotic destinations and fancy airports, that's not the important thing. The important ingredient here is the people. Our success is going to be continued to be defined by the ability of our people to differentiate themselves from the competition. It's the only thing that can't be replicated. It's the people, the culture, and the values we share, and that's why we lean so heavily into that."

SONY:
Going Back to Where It Plays Best

Going back to go forward, reigniting the culture of innovation that sparked its initial success, is the story line for Sony Corporation, the iconic consumer electronics firm that is starting to reclaim some of its former glory after years of steadily declining sales and reputation.

For most readers over the age of forty, Sony transformed the way we listen to music with the invention of the Walkman in 1979. What many don't know is that it was created for one of the company's cofounders, Masaru Ibuka, so he could listen to his beloved operas during the long flights from Japan to the United States. Sony also transformed the way we filmed our kids' birthday parties, weddings, and graduations with its video camcorders. It launched what was among the first and best CD players in 1982. Sony Trinitron color television sets were of such high quality that the company received an Emmy award for their development. Sony was also the first Japanese company to offer shares of its stock in the United States. As a bit more background, Sony made a big move—into Hollywood entertainment—in 1989 with its $3.4 billion purchase of Columbia Pictures, renaming it Sony Pictures Entertainment in 1991. And, of course, there is that PlayStation, one of Sony's biggest success stories, which we'll get back to shortly.

So, the question: After all of these breakthroughs, after being the first-mover with many products and possessing the ingenious thinking and sixth sense to know what consumers would want before it was invented, how did Sony lose its initial traction? Innovation had defined its character and its culture. It was bringing new products to the market while other companies had prototypes still in the lab. Such an innovative culture differentiated it for a long time. Its culture nurtured experimentation. More than this, it was one of the first Asian brands to recognize the importance of branding.

What happened? The simple answer is *too much* happened. Sony was unable to manage consistency across its increasing portfolio of products and services in the face of growing competition from other companies that proved to be more agile and more focused. It could not relevantly differentiate the totality of its offerings. They began putting the Sony name on more and more products that were missing the Sony "magic." The uncontrolled diversification, its toe-dipping into too many areas, caused it to lose its focus on innovation. Where once it had created the playing field and set the rules, its resources were fast draining and, as a culture, it was becoming complacent. With complacency, Sony began to lose relevance with the very audience it had called its own for so many years. The magic was, if not gone, fast eroding.

The good news, and the reason for this story, is that Sony has shifted to embark on a journey to rejuvenation. We spoke with Hideyuki Furumi, the company's executive vice president, Global Sales and Marketing, for Sony Mobile Communications, Inc., to get some commentary on its progress.

"We are going back to our past," he began our conversation. "We needed to step back and say we can't make everything. We can't be a department store. We have to go back and focus on things for which we can truly apply the 'Sony DNA.'" Sony's DNA as captured in the writings of one of its founders, Masaru Ibuka, was to *"deliver moving experiences to consumers through innovation and challenge."*

Furumi went on, saying, "We can't focus on 100 product lines, but a few product lines that are relevantly different. Play where we can play best. The most critical factor for us is that the definition of our business had become unclear, especially for our internal people. They were losing their confidence."

Since its inception, Sony had always been about trying new challenges. Its culture was built on the spirit of innovation. As it became far too diversified, its employees began to lose touch with what the brand stood for. Furumi told us that to re-instill this lost confidence in its employees, the company was paring down its product lines and concentrating on a few "hero products." They are going back to the founding principles of concentrating their energy, not to mention their resources, on selective products that best exemplify who they are and what they stand for and delivering consumer "wow" through innovation. In the United States market, for instance, up until about five years ago, Sony was still in everything from inexpensive clock radios to televisions of every size and price point. They have now winnowed down their offerings and are focusing on the parts of their portfolio where they can truly deliver moving consumer experiences.

"We are focusing on the areas that are most important to drive our business, and our image," said Furumi. "Our character had become too generic, which was reflected not just in financial factors, but in the expectations of our people. We realized we needed to make a painful transformation in order to make ourselves healthier. We needed to streamline, and find ways to communicate openly across functional areas. Our internal silos are diminishing, and that's a good thing. Accountability has become clearer, and our new CEO [Kazuo Hirai] is bringing about a culture of positive thinking. We celebrate even small wins. Our employees' achievements have become much more visible compared to the past."

Furumi went on to say that if you don't have a workforce that is positive and motivated, there is no way you can dig out of a challenge. Becoming more celebratory about successes, even small ones, will help build internal momentum and accelerate change. "By becoming much more selective in the fields in which we play is helping us gain back the confidence of our employees. It goes hand in hand with optimal performance. To excite consumers, our employees need to be emotionally driven. Our people are our greatest asset. They are what will allow us to win in this fiercely competitive market."

That Sony is beginning to win—or win back—in some key areas became evident with the positive marketplace buzz surrounding the newest Sony product, the PlayStation VR (PSVR) game console, which is expected to give other developers in the space a run for their money. The company is among the category leaders in virtual reality. The VR market is expected to rapidly grow, enabling users to do more than just play games. It allows users to enjoy watching sports at home with the sensation that they're right in the stadium, as well as enjoy traveling "virtually" to exotic places around the globe. VR technologies are also used to improve the efficiency of business operations, from construction to healthcare. Another of Sony's star performers isn't a gadget or device like a Walkman or PlayStation. Instead it's a chip found in almost every high-end camera and smartphone, including Apple iPhones. The company that invented the compact disc has, so far, captured almost a third of the $7.6 billion market for low-power sensors that help produce our crisp photographs.

That Sony is beginning to once again distinguish itself by making distinguished products, gauging the market, and beating its competitors to the punch is becoming not a virtual reality, but a real-time reality. Using its founder's principles allowed Sony to reenergize employees and focus the organization on fewer products. This allowed Sony to prepare for a shift as it could better focus resources on products for which it could deliver innovation that made consumers go "wow."

Lessons Learned ▶

The successes and failures of the companies described in the stories in this chapter provide several lessons about how companies, in general, can lay the groundwork for upcoming shifts.

Lesson #1. Have clarity of purpose. Some of our stories shed light on how company purposes should be framed. Facebook's purpose is to connect the world; Hertz's purpose is to make things easier for the business traveler or more pleasurable for the leisure traveler. These are very different from getting more Facebook members or renting more cars. People do not buy products; they buy benefits. When Joel goes to the hardware store to buy a Black & Decker drill, he is not buying a drill; he is buying the holes in the wall. When Allen goes to Ralph Lauren to buy a tie, he is not buying a tie; he is buying a look. Peter Drucker, a late great management guru, once wrote that "business enterprises . . . are organs of society. They do not exist for their own sake, but to fulfill a specific social purpose and to satisfy a specific need of a society, a community, or individuals."[2] When one looks at the objectives of a business as fulfilling a social purpose, it becomes easier to recognize the need and opportunity to shift. It allows Hertz to examine the possibility of parking services and perhaps other concierge activities.

The specific social purpose is often found in the founder's mentality. Authors Zook and Allen found that almost 90 percent of the time, the root causes of trouble in companies that failed to keep pace were internal. The distance between the people at the top and what's happening on the front lines increases and proliferating processes and bureaucratic practices fill that distance. Even in the best of companies, if these processes are not managed properly, the ability to innovate and grow is stifled. Getting around what Zook and Allen call "choke points" requires a founder's mentality; the return to speed, focus, and connection to consumers, and the insurgent's clarity of purpose.

As such, when companies lose sight of their purpose, they lose their focus. Sony had to return to its founder's words to refocus only on products in which the company could innovate and deliver what Sony CEO and President Kazuo Hirai describes as the Japanese concept of *kando* (the ability to stimulate an emotional response in people).

Lesson #2. Understand the ecosystem. When a company embraces its social purpose (i.e., the founder's mentality), the boundaries of the business go way beyond the products and services the company currently offers. At American Express, the Artists-in-Residence program exemplifies how a shift-ready business strives to understand the ecosystem it operates in. This means it's essential to be in touch with not just what happens with your business, but what happens in the world.

Everyone talks about keeping an eye on their business landscapes. But the difference in how one company does it versus another can be likened to the difference between golf and tennis. Astute businesses act more like a golfer than a tennis player. A tennis player is faced with a fixed court with a net, baselines, service lines, sidelines, and a service box. Within that fixed court, the player tries to exploit the weakness of the opponent or the competition. The shift-ready organization focuses much less on the competition. Suzy Deering, chief marketing officer of eBay, told us during our discussion about the company's shift to rebrand itself after its split from PayPal. "I want to keep an eye on my competitor, don't get me wrong," she said. "But too focused on my competitor, then I'm missing the real point. I'd rather spend time with my eyes dead-set at my customer and what their needs are—anticipate their needs and how to best deliver on those needs. We don't talk in terms of a campaign, we talk in terms of the customer experience."

In contrast to the fixed tennis court, a golf course is made up of many variables: It's an ecosystem of wind and trees, sand traps, and water hazards that differ not only from course to course, but from hole to hole within a single course. The golfer must analyze the course, the wind, the topography, and keep his or her eye on the ball, not the competition. The golfer must navigate the entire ecosystem. American Express has been playing golf for over 160 years as illustrated by John Hayes's comments on understanding the interconnections between businesses, consumers, and communities in discussing American Express's approach to small businesses.

What many of those who fall behind their competition don't grasp is that the marketplace is changing so fast that if they don't zoom out, see all the forces that shape the customer experience from as many angles as possible, they're going to miss some critical cues. The smartest organizations, the American Expresses of the world, are always in anticipatory mode, always in touch with not just what customers are doing today or what they did yesterday, but trying to figure out "why" they are behaving in a particular manner. The best companies can extrapolate the implications of what might happen *next* in order to meet a particular customer need before anyone else does.

Going back to what Bob Pittman told us in Chapter 1, you have to get to the core of what your brand stands for and then determine its relationship to your customer. I've learned that before you do anything, you must understand the relationship to the customer. I've worked in television, in real estate, in theme park companies, with the Internet and digital companies. What ties them together is 'who's the consumer and what are they doing?' *They* will tell me what matters. *They* will find it. *They* will evaluate it. *They* will decide if it's good or bad, not me.

"What you realize when you look at consumers is that, more often than not, they value convenience. Something is going to make their life better and easier in some significant way," Pittman said. "It's about looking at what people are looking for and what they want to do. For example, you get a lot of kids not getting their driver's licenses the minute they turn old enough to do it. Why? Because there are too many other ways, more convenient ways to get around than driving your own car. It's critical to get an understanding of what role your product plays in consumers' lives."

Clayton Christensen writes and consults on how new products and services displace established competitors. In his book *Competing Against Luck: The Story of Innovation and Customer Choice*, he writes that consumers hire products to do a certain job. It's the firm's job to figure out what that job is. In one consulting assignment for a fast-food chain, Professor Christensen's colleagues spent a day observing and interviewing customers and found that a number of them came in alone and purchased milkshakes to take along on their daily commutes. "Their surveys suggested that people weren't just looking to buy a beverage; they wanted something to keep them occupied during their drive. Milkshakes are easy to hold and consume and last a long time."[3] What Christensen determined was that milkshakes don't just compete with other beverages, but with everything else people do on a long commute, from eating a bagel to listening to audiobooks. The "job" of the milkshake was to mitigate stress for commuters by keeping them occupied. As a result of its research, the consulting team suggested changes to the fast-food chain that would increase sales of milkshakes and make the purchase process easier for commuters in a rush.

Lesson #3. Bathe with your customers. To completely understand what role or roles your brand or products play in your customers' lives and therefore appreciate the scope of the potential shifts you might have the opportunity to make, you must become intimate with your customer. You must bathe with them to understand how they live. You can actually live with them as New York Life does, or you can bathe yourself in the data you have about them as Facebook does.

Gary Briggs told us, "[Facebook's] move into live video—making video a core component to each of our apps—came out of one of our typical Friday all-hands-on question and answer sessions. In addition to being open and mission-driven, we're also very data-driven. As a result, we're able to read pretty quickly the impact of not just attitudes, but behavior." The company's ability to read and react to behavior is what led Facebook to make some major acquisitions. We have already discussed WhatsApp. Facebook's realization that many of their users were posting photos on the site led to the purchase of Instagram, the popular photo-sharing application, in 2012.

Lesson #4. Be constantly looking out for the next big thing. This book was written under the major premise that one thing we can be sure of is change. With that in mind, it is impossible to imagine how an offering designed for a specific ecosystem, either existing or anticipated, will be optimal for a different evolved one. Under that belief, it becomes imperative that we constantly look for the next big thing. Facebook's saying "we're one percent done" embodies this notion. As Hertz's Stuart Benzal told us, "You can't win on table stakes. You need to always be looking for the differentiators. Having that mindset will make it work." Chapter 6 tells the story of Hasbro's path to a successful shift. There we will learn that the real game changers in enabling Hasbro to make significant gains are the brand blueprints they characterize as "ever-evolving documents."

Joey Bergstein, chief marketing officer of Seventh Generation, Inc., the country's number-one "green brand" and market leader in nontoxic and renewable household cleaning products, told us, "It's a marathon. We do continuous research on our users, but with a focus more on consumers who have not yet made the move to natural, green products. People who are aware of Seventh Generation, but not buying it. We want to understand *why* they're not buying it. 'Does it work? Is there a benefit for my family?' Consumers today want performance and sustainability. While there are a lot of people who say they prefer to buy green things, what they actually do is different. There's a gap and we need to understand the barriers."

Lesson #5. Culture matters. At the outset, we define what we mean by culture: Culture is the sum total of the vision, values, norms, systems, symbols, language, assumptions, beliefs, and habits that shape an individual's choices and behavior within an organization. The company's purpose is among these. According to Francis Frei and Anne Morriss on a *Harvard Business Review* blog, "Culture guides discretionary behavior, and it picks up where the employee handbook leaves off. Culture tells us how to respond to an unprecedented service request. Employees make hundreds of decisions on their own every day, and culture is our guide. Culture tells us what to do when the CEO isn't in the room, which is of course most of the time."[4]

As Professor James L. Heskett wrote in his latest book, *The Culture Cycle,*[5] effective culture can account for 20 to 30 percent of the differential in corporate performance when compared with "culturally unremarkable" competitors. Certainly, the culture at Delta Air Lines, centered around southern hospitality, allowed it to deliver superior value in the form of customer service.

People have to feel that what they do genuinely matters and, more so, they have to be provided with the tools and resources to fulfill their roles in a satisfying way. Far easier said than done, especially when a company is in shift-prep mode. People who share values are people who are excited to be part of the pursuit of a common goal. Last and absolutely not least, a strong company culture is based on trust, both from the top down and the bottom up. Nothing good can come about without trust. (Just for the record, employees don't bring culture with them when they get hired. A company hires employees they feel would be a good fit with the corporate culture.)

In our experience, effective cultures require lines of communication that are open and honest—again, top down and bottom up. Silos have to come down, matrixes disassembled. Literal and even figurative walls stifle innovation, fresh ideas, and collaboration. Transparency is critical. Everyone needs to see what's happening and understand their role in making it happen. Again, the organization's purpose needs to be clear.

One of the first things Steve Jobs did after his return to Apple was to oversee the creation of a still-celebrated advertising campaign for the company titled "Think Different." These ads, featuring an assortment of iconic, idiosyncratic, and incredibly innovative personalities, including Albert Einstein, Bob Dylan, Martin Luther King, Jr., Amelia Earhart, Jim Henson, Martha Graham, and Pablo Picasso, were meant as a signal for the general public, for sure, but also for the people in the organization, that Apple was back in business. At the time the campaign was created in 1997, Apple had about ninety days of operating capital left. It was a campaign that still resonates decades later and that, at least emotionally, put Apple back on the map and sowed the seeds for its future success.

Jobs obviously knew the cost cutting and the brilliant advertising invoking its brilliant culture would only carry the organization so far. It was the result of its truly thinking different that put Apple back on the map in a more tangible way: the launch of the original iMac, the first new product released after Jobs's return as CEO. Although seemingly simple, it was surprising what a difference a little color could make. Adding color to this nifty desktop computer became an instant success and it was an indicator of the things to come from Apple—products that were as beautiful to look at as they were simple to use. With an ad campaign and an iconic product, Jobs ignited a culture of innovation that continues today.

Don't confuse a common purpose with homogeneity of perspective. Cultures that welcome diverse points of view are healthy cultures. Needless to say, organizations that foster diversity in their workplace, in general, are much healthier for it. How can you possibly serve a rapidly changing marketplace if your organization is either of the homogenous or command-and-control variety? In preparing for a shift, organizations must look at things through multiple lenses.

In addition, people need to be heard, not stifled under layers of management. This level of freedom and empowerment not only engenders confidence, but generates creativity. When Steve Jobs designed the headquarters of Pixar studios, for example, he oversaw the creation of areas where people would *have* to bump into each other, share ideas, visualize story lines, light-years ahead of what any other animation studios were doing. Years before this, AT&T Bell Laboratories worked in much the same way. An open campus—an open forum—where people could and would bump into each other and just naturally start chatting about their latest technological breakthroughs. These interactions become part of the culture.

Joel practices this philosophy in his management of the Ph.D. program at NYU Stern as it shifts ever closer to the upper echelon of business school doctoral programs. He emphasizes a culture of "cultivating colleagues" in a common environment. Better doctoral research and dissertation ideas emerge when students and faculty have greater contact. Students and faculty have greater contact when they are seated close together, attend the same events, and eat together. As Joel often says, "Lunch matters."

Howard Stevenson, professor emeritus at Harvard University, has gone so far as to say, "Maintaining an effective culture is so important that it, in fact, trumps even strategy."[6] Others use similar phrases (the idea has also been stated as "Culture eats strategy for breakfast," apocryphally attributed to management guru Peter Drucker). In either case, it means that powerful companies often use culture as competitive advantage. It isn't the enemy of strategy or performance, but an equal player in the game, not to be underestimated or overlooked.

The bottom line on culture, and what those companies gearing up for a shift must keep in mind, is that better moods equal better performance. The workplace should not be something people dread, but something they look forward to. While the work may be challenging and even stressful, the culture, in and of itself, should help mitigate this stress and not add to it. You want your employees as gratified as possible, not just because it makes them more productive, but because how they feel and behave will have a direct impact on the customers (as we saw with Delta Air Lines).

In *The Amazing Spider-Man 2*, Peter Parker, Spider-Man's mild-mannered alter-ego, says, "I like to think Spider-Man gives people hope." This is exactly what CEO Peter Cuneo gave Marvel Entertainment, the company responsible for the Spider-Man movies, when it was coming out of bankruptcy in 1999 and its stock price hovered precipitously at 96 cents per share. As a result of his efforts, the company was later sold to Walt Disney for $4.3 billion with a share price of $54. When asked whether this feat was the result of focusing on the hard numbers or the softer issues, he replied, "You have to do both. You want to understand the business and the language of the business, the numbers, the financials, of course. But, in turnarounds you often find that the culture is completely wrong. The company may or may not be bankrupt financially, but the culture is bankrupt. It's one where the organization is used to losing, failing, and underperforming. You have to change that. You have to give the organization pride."

5

MAKING SENSE OF THE ROAD AHEAD

At this point in the book we have spotted the red flags, overcome the barriers to shifting, and readied the organization for a shift. When an organization actually proactively shifts, it is doing so because it believes that changes in its business environment will require that shift. The organization sees the changes that are happening right in front of it and extrapolates those changes to a longer-time horizon. In other words, organizations shift because they forecast a future for which the shift would be beneficial. Such a forecast requires two skills: the ability to understand what's happening right in front of you and the ability to carry that understanding down the road. The further you can see down the road, the better you can appreciate the need to shift as well as ex- trapolate the implications of a decision to shift in a particular direction. While this has always been the case, it has become harder and harder to do when the world is accelerating at such an incredible pace.

Thomas L. Friedman summarized for us the main argument of his book *Thank You for Being Late* (first discussed in Chapter 1) this way: "How do we align ourselves with these drivers shaping the world to get the most out of them and cushion the worst? That said, you need to focus on your foundation," he told us. "To try and change without that foundation, you'll spin out of control."

That is the subject of this chapter, getting your arms around the drivers shaping *your* world. It's not as easy as checking a GPS device to see where the world is going or looking in the rearview mirror to see if it is safe to change lanes. In fact, looking in the rearview mirror is precisely the wrong thing to do. You have to look forward.

Let's start with the need to better focus on the rapid changes happening daily, right in front of you. Asking people and, more so, watching people in their own environments—obvious, but all too often given short shrift. Paco Underhill, author of *Why We Buy: The Science of Shopping*, is an environmental psychologist who uses anthropological techniques to collect and analyze consumer data. Underhill's approach to consumer behavior differs slightly from the mainstream because he focuses not only on why consumers buy what they do but, perhaps more important for shifting ahead, *why they don't or wouldn't buy* something that is no longer relevant.

He told us, "In order to assess how your business might be losing relevance, it's important to look at it through different lenses." He asks, "How are we doing in terms of addressing . . . female versus male users? Women, for example, are much more conscious of security than men. Ask a man when was the last time he was scared, and he'd have to think about it. Ask a woman, and she'll tell you it was within the last week, when she was in a parking lot, or during an interaction with a stranger. You have to apply different sets of logic."

Underhill believes that "you need to look at different cultures through different lenses to determine if you are relevant or cool on a broad scale." He cited images of a shopping mall in Shanghai where they grow many of the vegetables that are sold in restaurants. It takes the urban agriculture concept of farm-to-table and puts it into a totally different context from which new ideas can be derived. As Underhill said, "The world is global, and having a global perspective is always a lifeline to the future."

Relative to this point, Underhill made an observation that, as simple and as obvious as it sounds, it is a common barrier to companies being able to get a broad, let alone global, perspective on the future. "Find the desk farthest away from the customer and that's where the person in charge sits," he said. "You need to be an observer of people. You need to look at behavior and focus on the piece that's not working. You need to look beyond your own Main Street. You need to learn to think standing up. Many of us are all too comfortable sitting down, looking into a database, or sitting around a conference table. To see what's happening," Underhill said, "go have a meeting where the customer is. Being able to bring senior management [to] where the customer is—that actual point of contact—is critical." To reasonably observe the changes in the world, you need to have a lens that provides a sharp focus on the world you compete in. You don't get that from behind a desk in a corner office.

Underhill's point is valid. Going five miles per hour, the few minor navigational bumps that might be made from sitting behind a desk are unlikely to derail you. It's when you're going 100 miles an hour that those same errors in navigation can have a huge effect and take your car out of control.

When we asked Mark Addicks, former CMO of General Mills, how a company as large and complex as General Mills keeps an eye on the rapidly changing road, he explained that the company actively *leverages* its very scale to take the pulse of its consumers. "You will never get lost if you start with the consumer first," he said. "We are hyper-looking at what the consumer is doing, where they're actually spending their time, and what their behavior is. We see our brand teams not as number crunchers looking at sales, which are lagging indicators, but as journalists and anthropologists. You get people on your team who are used to observing, looking at the culture outside, not just as means to optimize performance, but to look for opportunities. It's critical to see how people are actually engaging with our product, with each other, and what we are missing."

Giving an example, Addicks said, "For instance, relative to Cheerios, a few years back we sent teams out to several cities across the country to do some exploratory work around what Cheerios meant to people's lives. What we found out when we did this—and what continues to give General Mills a sense of how they've needed to shift marketing strategies with Cheerios—is that we heard nothing but emotional stories. Basically, what everyone was telling us was that the true meaning of Cheerios was an emotional connection, a story about nurturing. We came back to the office with all of these stories, laid them out on the floor, and grouped them thematically. This led to a breakthrough in our communications."

Keeping an eye on what's happening right in front of you is challenging enough for most organizations, but to successfully shift ahead you need to be able to look down the road much further, with a longer-term forecast, and try to make sense of what will happen, if not precisely when.

If you go back to the movie *2001: A Space Odyssey*, one of Stanley Kubrick's masterpieces, made in 1968, he got a lot of the "what will happen" right: how a spaceship would dock with a space station, which had never been done before; what the controls on a spaceship would look like, with flat-panel screens; how a space station would look, and how people would communicate on picture phones, a precursor to Facetime calling. The Pan Am plane that launched the spaceship was not too different from Richard Branson's Galactic prototype for a commercial spacecraft. Lots of that was right. The same is true of *Star Trek*, created by Gene Roddenberry, the original television series debuting in 1966. From the flip phones to the tricorders, which resembled today's iPads, to the flat-screen televisions that helped Captain Kirk navigate on the bridge, a lot of the "what will happen" was pretty presciently imagined.

"When it will happen" is a different and perhaps more difficult question. Neither Kubrick nor Roddenberry got this part quite right. As inventive as your thinking might be about the "what," pinning your "what" to a specific "when" can turn the "what" into a "whatever." Apple is an example of a company that famously and fabulously learned from its mistakes. Think about Apple's Newton, the first ever personal digital assistant, or PDA, which hit the market in 1993. People weren't quite ready to have computers in the palms of their hands. That it retailed for between $700 and $1,200, too big to fit in the palm of most people's hands—and that the handwriting recognition software was notoriously inaccurate didn't help.

The bottom line is that success in shifting gears depends on being able to get the best possible sense for what will happen, when it *may* happen, and retaining flexibility to move on a dime when it does happen. The process is both art and science—an art and science practiced by Amy Webb, author, futurist, and founder of the Future Today Institute, a leading future forecasting and strategy firm that researches technology and probes the question "What's the future of X?" for a global client base. Her third book, *The Signals Are Talking: Why Today's Fringe Is Tomorrow's Mainstream*, is about how to predict technological change and what companies can do about it in the present. In her work, Webb uses a systematic way of evaluating new ideas bubbling up on the horizon and, most important, distinguishing what is a real trend, to which attention must be paid, from what is merely trendy. Among the key goals of her work is being able to follow seemingly random ideas at the "fringe" as they begin to converge and move toward the mainstream and have long-term consequence for tomorrow.

During our conversation, Webb made three key points about the work she does with her clients. "First, you need to recognize what I refer to as the 'paradox of the present,'" Webb told us. "Companies and leaders of organizations are focused on what they [believe] to be true, and much of that perspective comes from their past experiences. They perceive what they want to see and hear while ignoring viewpoints that contradict their preferred view. As a result, they will gravitate toward choices that pay off immediately, even if success is minimal—versus larger payoffs that take a longer time. This could explain why in business, companies are reluctant to shift if changing market trends do not fit their worldview."

Behavioral scientists have long known that once we have formed a view, we embrace information that confirms that view while ignoring, or rejecting, information that casts doubt on it. This phenomenon, called *confirmation bias* or, more colloquially, *wishful thinking*, suggests that left to our own devices we do not perceive circumstances objectively. We pick out the information that makes us feel good because it confirms our beliefs or prejudices. We become prisoners of our assumptions. For example, some people will have a very strong inclination to dismiss any claims that marijuana may cause harm. At the same time, some social conservatives will downplay any evidence that marijuana does not cause harm.

The second point Webb made had to do with the perception of time and, specifically, the Heisenberg Uncertainty Principle. As discussed in Chapter 3, the Heisenberg Uncertainty Principle describes how it is impossible to simultaneously know the exact position and momentum of a particle at a specific point in time, arguing that there is a fundamental limit on what can be known about a particle at any given moment. Companies look at time in a very linear way, often ignoring that one little change, a single event, can alter what happens dramatically (again, think of how in *Star Trek*, when they go back in time, inadvertently altering one small event changes everything). In a world of linear rigidity, it's necessary to become comfortable with a bit of ambiguity.

"When forecasting the future, there is no definitive answer to exactly what's coming next. While we perceive time to move in a linear fashion, in reality it is elastic. Therefore, there is no point in making a 'prediction,'" Webb said. "A prediction would imply that the answer is knowable, and the answer is not knowable. There are any number of possible futures; there are probabilities within these possibilities. What's important to consider when future forecasting is that time is arbitrary. It's not based on cycles and quarters. It's really based on internal and external events. Humans understand units of time because that's how we measure things. Companies like to encapsulate strategies in basic units of time—five years, ten years—but that's not how change occurs. A smarter approach is to instead focus on a general direction," said Webb. "Based on what you know right now—and assuming you've done the requisite research [with a] 'fringe sketch' and modeling—this is the best strategy for the next few years. If you understand that time is fluid, then it relieves the pressure of having a ten-year plan."

The third point Webb made was also about how companies have a tendency to look at future forecasting incorrectly. It isn't simply a matter of facilitating a brainstorming group to imagine science-fiction scenarios. She emphasized that future forecasting is data-driven, that it's evidence-driven, based on activities including pattern recognition and regression analysis. She also emphasized that it's not a matter of turning to the "usual suspects," but of putting together a team comprised of creative types and number crunchers. It's essential to look at what might be next from the multiple perspectives of the Kubricks and the Roddenberrys *and* the scientists. You need to look and listen for the "signals" from those on the fringe, and meld them with the insights from the engineers and data thinkers.

"For example," Webb told us, "one of the things that impresses me about IBM is that it often partners with a variety of thinkers, from cartoonists to research scientists, journalists, doctors, and diplomats. That diverse group of thinkers helps the company overcome the paradox of the present and to develop much richer visions of the future. They're not trying to find *the* answer; they are seeking *the path* to an answer, collaborating and sharing information along the way to development of products and services. As futurists, we view trends as guides, not answers. It's a matter of 'these are the places we should be paying attention to over the next year.' A good way to think about it is not trying to figure out what the next light bulb is going to look like, but what's the next phase of light."

Relative to this last point, imagine going to the garage to get your car only to find the battery had died. You call AAA and a millennial-aged service guy shows up. The garage being pretty dark, you go to the car's glove compartment to look for a flashlight. Before you could get to it, Mr. Millennial takes out his iPhone and taps on the flashlight app. If you were advising a manufacturer of flashlights a couple of years ago, would you have been able to see this coming? Would you have been focused only on improving the flashlight, making it more durable or waterproof, or would you have been able to see a point down the road where people would never need flashlights again?

In the film *Creed*, Rocky Balboa shows Apollo Creed's son Donnie a piece of paper that he wants Donnie to study. Donnie takes out his iPhone and snaps a picture and then gives the paper back to Rocky. Rocky then asks him if he wants to take the paper. Donnie replies that it is "in the cloud." Would the manufacturer of a copying machine have been able to see this coming? Would he have been focused only on other copiers, those who made more durable or smaller designs, or would he have been able to see a point down the road where people would snap photos and either view and/or print them when needed, and therefore never need copiers again?

Such a view of the future is what drove Uber's investment in self-driving cars through its purchase of Otto, a developer of self-driving technology. Uber cofounder and former chief executive Travis Kalanick characterized self-driving cars as an "existential" threat to his company.[1] Self-driving cars would be much less expensive to operate than cars with human drivers. Robots work tirelessly, don't demand raises, and don't ask for tips. The first company to deliver a fleet of automated taxis could quickly put the human variety (both conventional taxis and Uber-like companies) out of business very quickly. If Uber is not that company, or at least close in time to that company, it would fall victim to the same technological disruption that it promised to inflict on the auto industry. The Uber philosophy has been that it's a hassle to own a car. Maybe so, but Uber managers don't want someone else to eliminate that hassle in a cheaper way than they can.

Looking outside the obvious parameters, getting a broader view of possible futures, was also something we talked about with Rita Mc-Grath, a professor at Columbia Business School. Her particular emphasis is on developing sound strategy for moving forward in uncertain or volatile environments. One of her bestselling books is *The End of Competitive Advantage: How to Keep Your Strategy Moving as Fast as Your Business*. During our conversation with McGrath on the challenges of staying relevant, she said, "It's as simple and as challenging as keeping your eye on what's going on with consumers today and making a better bet than the competition on where they may be going tomorrow. Among the first steps is to ask if you are framing your category within a wide enough lens. For example, Ford is not looking at cars, but it is looking at 'mobility' as a point of reference. They're very aware that their existing strategy of making a full range of cars globally is going to be changing, based on how people are looking at transportation options. They're switching their language and looking at mobility solutions. When you do this," said McGrath, "it opens up a whole new range of options you might pursue. So, as to your notion of shift, Ford is evaluating which strategies relative to mobility they are going to make a bet on. The next stage is to assess what you're going to *stop* doing, and in some cases, that's even harder than figuring out what you're going to *start* doing."

McGrath went on to explain that what a lot of companies do is make a half-hearted stab toward doing something new, but they're still carrying on things from the old business. "If you want to move ahead, you have to be very clear that 'these are the things we are no longer going to bet on'—and even if you don't get rid of them, shrink them for sure. It's at this juncture that a company also has to be realistic about its skillset. They might have made the right choice in terms of which gear to shift, but they may not be realistic about what it's going to take to execute on a new strategy," she said. In other words, they are susceptible to confirmation biases.

McGrath brings us to another of the factors inherent in successful shifting, which is the ability to get the right balance between "performance" and "opportunity." Performance is a matter of optimizing your current direction and strategy, looking at what you currently do that's working to a great enough extent, and strengthening it. You do what you must to get better at your existing game while balancing other opportunities. Take the *Wall Street Journal*, as an example. For more than 125 years, it has represented the best in business journalism, setting the standard in bringing readers comprehensive business news via the printed page. But the *WSJ* had to confront changes in how people read newspapers and consume media in light of so much information before us and the ever-faster pace of disseminating it. People were reading shorter stories online. So, in late 2016, it launched a reformatted newspaper that is a shorter and more concise read for subscribers. Twenty years earlier, the *WSJ* launched its online site, in response to the same challenges and opportunities presented by people's evolving reading and information-gathering habits. Initially, newspaper websites tried to replicate the actual newspaper. Today, the trend has reversed. The new *Wall Street Journal* print edition was modeled after its online presence. For this to work, the WSJ will have to continue its focus on preserving and building on its heritage as an authority on business news.

Among the most well-known people in the field of predictive research and repositioning for the Fortune 200 is Faith Popcorn, author and founder and CEO of Faith Popcorn's BrainReserve, another of the experts with whom we had the privilege of speaking. Agreeing with others that it takes as much art as science to predict which trends will become sustainable advantages for companies, Popcorn has a very impressive track record. She was one of the first to foresee the demand for fresh foods, the move toward four-wheel-drive vehicles, and the demise of film. She was also among the first to name and frame "cocooning," a term that is now in *Webster's Dictionary*, and to anticipate the boom in home delivery and working from home.

When we spoke with her about the topic of this book, and how she does what she does, among the first things she said to us was, "You can't directly ask a consumer what they want. If you asked someone back before it was invented if they wanted a smartphone, how would they possibly be able to answer that question? You don't ask consumers what they're going to do in 2020; you look for the gaps in their lives. I look for unhappiness. What I try to really get at is, 'Where's the discontent?' If you ask about the discontent," she said, "then you can ask them how they'd fix it. And by getting into a conversation about how you could fix it, you can almost visualize a concept, a company, a new product, a new medium, a new system. You ask people what's bugging them, you'll get fuel for insights about what trends will shape the future. Our predictions have been 95 percent correct, thanks to our two pieces of IP [intellectual property]—TrendBank, a system that includes seventeen trends that we've been tracking since 1975, and TalentBank, a universe of thousands of Futurists in varied fields."

Lessons Learned ▶

No hockey fan, outside of a few diehards in Boston chanting Bobby Orr's name, would deny that the greatest player in the history of the sport was Wayne Gretzky. Gretzky was neither the fastest skater in hockey nor the best, nor did he have the best shot. What made him great was his sixth sense of being in the right place at the right time and getting the puck on a breakaway more than anybody else. He knew where his teammates were going to be when he had the puck and was able to pass it. It was more intuitive than actual physical skill. He had this incredible ability to know where the puck was going and where the other players were going. Those who are most successful at shifting ahead can tell you where the puck is going: where consumers will be, not in weeks, but years from now or even longer. The best companies do whatever they can to get an extended sense of the future.

Sensing the future could be the most important challenge in maintaining the long-term health of an organization, but it is also the most mushy in some sense. Understanding the future for decisions today is not simply the description of what and when. It is more of a "what might be" at some point. The managerial shift needed and preparation activity is not episodic; you don't say, "Okay, here's a forecast and let's make a decision to respond." It's more like, "Okay, here's a likely scenario and let's prepare for the time when it is upon us." We can offer several tips to help get a better sense of the future.

Lesson #1: Get out of the bubble. As Paco Underhill explained, it is hard to see how the world is changing from sitting behind a desk.

Getting out into the world is how Howard Schultz of Starbucks fame transformed a commodity into an upscale cultural phenomenon. In 1971, three coffee aficionados opened a small coffee shop specializing in selling whole arabica beans to a niche market of coffee purists in Seattle's Pike Place Market. Schultz joined the Starbucks marketing team in 1982. Shortly thereafter, he traveled to Italy, where he became fascinated with Milan's coffee culture, in particular, and the role the neighborhood espresso bars played in Italians' everyday social lives.

This inspired Schultz to the point where he convinced the company to set up an espresso bar in the corner of its only downtown Seattle shop. This bar became the prototype for his long-term vision of Starbucks being a "third place"—a place different from home and work where people could go to relax and enjoy others or just be by themselves.

Lesson #2: Find the fringe. So, given that you are going to get out from behind the desk, where do you go? One place to go is what Amy Webb calls "the fringe." Most companies begin their forecasting the future exercises by commissioning some standard marketing research—focus groups, for example. However, such research is more about the past than the future. Participants enter a focus group constrained by their own experiences. Those constraints shackle consumers when they try to imagine the future. Before the advent of personal computers, suppose someone asked you what you would like in a spreadsheet. It would have been almost impossible to answer. Now that we have experience with Excel and Google Sheets, the answer would be much more meaningful, but too late unfortunately.

If not consumers in a focus group, who then? Webb says "the fringe" is the "place where scientists, artists, technologists, philosophers, mathematicians, psychologists, ethicists, and social science thinkers are testing seemingly bizarre hypotheses, undertaking wildly creative research, and trying to discover new kinds of solutions to the problems confronting humanity."[2]

For example, Jane Goodall's foray into Africa to live with the chimps to better understand and learn about them inspired the safari segment of the tourism industry. The massive video game industry is an outgrowth of the training and instructional programs and demonstration programs intended to impress or entertain the public, developed by universities, government organizations, and large corporations a half century ago. In 1971, while he was working with Boeing in Huntsville, Alabama, Theodore Paraskevakos, a Greek-American electronics instructor and inventor, demonstrated a transmitter and receiver that combined data-processing capabilities and visual display screens into a modest-size communications device. By the mid to late 1990s, the technology had advanced to the first generation of what we now call smartphones.

Lesson #3: Look for the pain points. One of the main focuses of Faith Popcorn's work is to locate the discontent in daily life or, as we call them, the pain points. Several stories in this book illustrate companies' searches for the pain points (e.g., Hertz, Marriott). In the spirit of "necessity is the mother of invention," ailments demand cures. Indeed, that is literally the purpose of the medical and pharmaceutical industries in general. Look for ways to heal the sick.

Few commercial developments provide us with as much daily comfort as air-conditioning. Air-conditioning provides a wonderful example that illustrates not only this learning point, but the previous one about the fringe as well. Willis Carrier was a bona fide member of the fringe. While working for the Buffalo Forge Company in 1902, Carrier was tasked with solving a humidity problem that was causing magazine pages to wrinkle at the Sackett-Wilhelms Lithographing and Publishing Company in Brooklyn. Carrier designed a system that controlled humidity using cooling coils. He secured a patent for his "Apparatus for Treating Air" that could either humidify (by heating water) or dehumidify (by cooling water) air. It wasn't long before Carrier realized that humidity control and air-conditioning could benefit many other industries, and he eventually broke off from Buffalo Forge, forming Carrier Engineering Corporation. Today Willis Carrier's company is a world leader in heating, air-conditioning, and refrigeration solutions.

6

WHICH SHIFT TO MAKE?
IT DEPENDS ON WHAT'S AHEAD

Dustin Hoffman spent a good part of the movie *The Graduate* driving a fantastic-looking Alfa Romeo Spider, all the while doing what he could to win the affections of a fantastic-looking Katharine Ross. The Alfa Romeo Spider was Allen's first car. More important, it's a stick-shift. For those who have never driven a car with a stick-shift or manual transmission, it is as if you're sailing down a three-lane highway at sixty-five miles per hour, the traffic moving nicely; there's really not that much difference in how it feels compared to driving a car with automatic transmission. The engine is in fifth gear, not working all that hard, just humming along. There's no real need for "active" driving.

However, the experience of driving a car with a manual versus automatic transmission becomes appreciably different when the road changes or when the conditions change. Maybe the highway narrows down from three lanes to two, or it becomes very hilly, or you must start maneuvering around a series of curves. Or maybe there's an armada of trucks in front of you that requires a strategic passing exercise. It could be that the highway stops being a highway altogether and becomes a local road with traffic lights and lots of oncoming traffic. You could encounter a construction zone, making it necessary to stop and start, slow down and speed up. In these and any number of other situations the experience of driving a car with a manual transmission differs from driving a car with automatic transmission. In situations such as these, you need to be fully attuned to the road *and* to the car.

If there are hills or curves, you listen to the engine and determine if you need more power to take them on, which would necessitate an *active* downshifting to another gear, say, second or third. You shift gears if there is construction or weather to contend with. You need to look at the competition on the road, the trucks in front of you as obstacles that you'll need to pass. You'll need to downshift to get the full throttle and energy required to accelerate and pass. In a car with manual transmission you must *actively* drive. You must be aware of your environment; you must be in touch with the road, and in touch with the nuances of the engine to align your car's power with the terrain and the situation.

The difference between driving a manual transmission versus an automatic is a good analog for what happens in many businesses. To stay successful, to stay relevantly differentiated, a good organization stays attuned to the external conditions—all the things going on in the marketplace and the world that pose potential challenges and a potential need to shift. If you're successful traveling along at sixty-five miles per hour, steady as you go, maybe you make a few minor adjustments to tweak performance or make things more comfortable. Maybe you update the product, redesign a logo to appeal to a younger audience, or speed up production to get out ahead of the competition. In general, the organization's purpose and promise to its customers remain intact and what it stands for in the minds of consumers more or less remains the same. You're on cruise control.

Think Verizon going from landlines to wireless. Think Apple going from computers to tablets and watches. These companies continue to deliver against the same customer promise. In fact, they actually strengthen the promise. They're playing in the same lane, so to speak, and they have the organizational know-how to know *how* to do the same thing, only better, more robustly.

But what if simply changing gears to deliver on the same promise, perhaps in an enhanced way, is no longer the answer? What if it's not a matter of expediting a marketing campaign in light of current events, or changing up your inventory, or tweaking the latest model of whatever it is you manufacture? What if the road you're on is simply the wrong road altogether? It might be that your promise is just totally off-kilter in the new world order and you have to rethink your value proposition. It might be that you have to rethink your employee population—great people, but with skillsets that won't take you where you need to go. Maybe it's that you realize you need to formulate an entirely new customer promise to be relevant. What if you've come to the end of the road with your offering and it's not a matter of shifting gears but shifting direction? There are situations when shifting gears is definitely not enough to give your organization the advantage it needs to stay ahead. We have seen situations (covered throughout the book) where this has been the case: Kodak, IBM, Forbes, Xerox.

This chapter provides a continuum of shift examples from "close-in" gear shifts to more substantial shifts in direction. Using multiple examples, we offer insight from people who have led organizations through a shift in gears, a shift in direction, and those who have changed both gears and direction. In all cases, the stories underscore the importance of understanding organizational DNA, company culture, and effective execution in being able to successfully shift.

The acronym DNA has gained widespread use in the business lexicon. In the biological sciences, DNA is sometimes referred to as the building block of life. It determines who we are and what we can do. If our DNA doesn't dictate large-scale athletic ability, we will not be able to participate in the Olympics no matter how hard we try. Carrying the metaphor over to the business domain, an organization's DNA represents its building blocks of success: the skills, assets, culture, history, and knowledge that guide its ability to succeed—or to have succeeded to this point. The ability to honestly assess inherent organizational strengths and weaknesses impacts the odds of achieving a positive outcome.

For example, take Barnes & Noble, the world's largest brick-and-mortar bookstore chain.

BARNES & NOBLE:
Understand Your DNA

Barnes & Noble is dominated by Amazon, at one end, with its low prices and vast selection, and at the other end by locally owned, carefully curated independent bookstores. Barnes & Noble has been stuck in the middle for almost twenty years, trying a series of gear and directional shifts to find its way. For personal input on this story, we spoke to John Rindlaub, currently vice president of marketing at Health Net, who had previously been vice president of marketing at Barnes & Noble.

"A lot of what happened was due to cultural behavior, norms, DNA, and values," Rindlaub told us. "Everyone in the organization grew up in retail. Leonard Riggio, the former CEO, has been associated with the company for forty-five years. When Amazon launched in 1994, Barnes & Noble didn't see it as a fundamental threat. They didn't even think about launching a website until 1997. When I got there in 1998, the website wasn't what it needed to be because the company basically tried to put the brick-and-mortar process online, without a basic understanding of e-marketing. By that time, Amazon had so much momentum it was impossible to catch up. Amazon had everything on its side. [It was] a founder-led organization; it was a purpose-based e-commerce company. Barnes & Noble looked at online as a hobby. Number-one lesson when trying to make a shift into a new arena? Never underestimate the competition, and never underestimate the effort. You've got to be all in," Rindlaub said, adding, "I'll never forget what Riggio said to me the first year I was there. 'In 1995, why didn't we see this juggernaut coming? Why didn't we set up a website called Book Predator and have rock-bottom prices and just snuff Amazon out? Why didn't we drop our prices and do predatory pricing for six months and have Amazon go out of business?' We all know hindsight is twenty-twenty. But they couldn't get out of their own way and their old way of thinking."

The other thing that was happening during the period Amazon took the book world by storm was that Barnes & Noble was being equally distracted by another challenge. They were being maligned for snuffing out hundreds of little, neighborhood bookstores. (Watch *You've Got Mail*, with Tom Hanks and Meg Ryan, if you want to see the Hollywood version of the story. Spoiler alert. Happy ending.) Because Barnes & Noble's retail sales were still relatively strong at that point, they didn't feel the immediate pain of Amazon's growth. As Rindlaub put it, "Then, all of a sudden, boom, you've got the boiling frog, Clayton Christensen's innovator's dilemma. If you don't feel the pain, you won't change. Dial up the water temperature slowly, and the frog doesn't feel it. If Barnes & Noble had felt the pain, they might have been able to act sooner. But they had a retail mindset. They didn't understand speed to market, or speed once you're *in* market."

Barnes & Noble also underestimated the power of Amazon's Kindle and later the Apple iPad. This was another instance of a shift attempt without having enough of the "right" DNA, being able to execute quickly enough or brilliantly enough to overcome the competition. The essential issue for Barnes & Noble has been its DNA. It is a brick-and-mortar book retailer. In its first attempt to shift gears, to respond to Amazon, it became apparent that the company simply didn't have the people, the tools, or the capabilities to execute an online strategy in a serious way. Then, trying a directional shift—creating an e-reader to compete with Amazon and Apple—again, it was not in the Barnes & Noble genes, not closely enough related to what they were known for and what comes naturally to them to be effective.

As of this writing, Barnes & Noble is trying another shift, one that leverages the company's culture, their "norms and values," and takes the company back to its roots. Leonard Riggio began leading the effort to create smaller community bookstores, with more on-floor sales staff and greater autonomy for store buyers to stock the merchandise that is most relevant to the local customer base. Barnes & Noble has sold more than 3 billion books. That's a hard number to simply dismiss. If Barnes & Noble makes this shift successfully—actually, shifting carefully into reverse—it will be a boon to those of us who want to support neighborhood retailers.

While shifting gears should, in theory, be a bit easier than wholesale shifts in direction, this is not always the case. Each shift has its own set of challenges, risks, and rewards, as the following stories—and lessons learned—will bear out.

KATZ'S DELICATESSEN:
Sometimes Staying in Park Is the Right Gear

Sometimes the best shifts are the ones you don't make. If you ask the customers at Katz's Delicatessen in New York City, they'll tell you, "Please don't change a thing." Personally, as long-standing customers, we agree. Their pastrami, sliced by the cantankerous guys behind the counter, is about as perfect as it can be. That said, the iconic restaurant that's been serving customers for more than a century is shifting gears, just ever so slightly, so as to expand its business without diluting its authentic flavor.

How, exactly, does a veritable New York dining institution expand without losing what makes it special? Very carefully and very conscientiously, explained the restaurant's "Top Dog," Jake Dell, a proud alumnus of the NYU Stern School of Business. After 128 years on Manhattan's Lower East Side, the restaurant, which is known for its mile-high pastrami sandwiches as well as its cameo appearance in the movie *When Harry Met Sally*, is in the process of opening a second location for the first time ever. It is also in the midst of figuring out how best to leverage technology to better share this quintessential New York deli experience.

Before we share the details about its shifting, we want to savor a taste of its history. The restaurant opened in 1888 as a small delicatessen called "Iceland Brothers" at a time when Jewish establishments dotted the neighborhood. Its name changed to "Iceland and Katz," and then to Katz's Delicatessen, after the Katz family bought out the Iceland family. Katz's would later move across the street to its present-day location that today seats 300 people. Opening up a second location is a big deal for a business that is known as the restaurant equivalent of a time capsule. Everything's the same as it's ever been. The counter behind which those cantankerous guys—"cutters," as they're called—yell at each other as they slice the delicious pastrami and corned beef, the aromas of pickles and salami, hot dogs and onions, the neon signs and the mysterious "ticket system," the clamoring throngs of hungry people, New York sanitation workers and Wall Street types freely mingling with each other and with the guide-toting tourists from around the world. It's visual chaos that hits your every sense at once—sight, smell, and hearing.

So, again, think carefully about whether to shift, and how much to shift, and if you can execute before you start down the road. "While we've had several opportunities to branch out over the years," Dell told us, "the family held off until we could figure out how to do it the right way. The history and tradition of this place—it's the classics, what people come here for—the same food every time you come here. All that needs to be the same and not changed. That's what makes this place so special in my mind. When we talk about the core of who we are, it's the food and tradition, the nostalgia, and the atmosphere. We're lucky compared to other businesses [because] not changing is actually what makes us popular, especially in the restaurant industry in New York City. That is rare, but that's who we are."

Dell and his family are attempting to replicate the quality of Katz's food elsewhere, although not at a sit-down restaurant but at a stand at the DeKalb Market Hall in City Point, Brooklyn. "It's in the old Albie Square Mall, near Fulton and Flatbush," Dell explained. "Yes, it's only a small takeout place, but we felt being a part of a vibrant community that's loud and bustling, which this area [the Lower East Side] is, would be true to who we are. It's the kind of environment we love. The Fulton neighborhood is very similar to our Delancey Street area. We know we're never going to re-create the original place, but we want to make it easier for our regulars, who are finding it harder to get to Manhattan, as well as to be able to cater to the millennials in Brooklyn, a group that is keen on authentic experiences. It's a way to bring the tradition and food just a little closer to people who already know who we are."

That millennials are an Instagram-crazy bunch is also not lost on Dell, and a reason for another of the restaurant's minor shifts in gear. After decades without any public relations, Dell actively embraces this social media, audience-activation app as a boon to his business. "I push for Instagram because it reinforces the original aspects of who we are. Any changes we undertake are specifically to reinforce who we are. Social media is good for our business. Instagram really conveys our authenticity to people, especially the sensory part of experience," he told us. "We're the third most Instagrammed restaurant in the country. Our place, our food, our employees, our customers provide great photo opportunities. It's an easy way to grow the business while staying true to who we are. We're balancing change by appropriately leveraging social media and technology to get the experience out to more people."

The shift in tactics to leverage technology is also making it possible to get more of the actual product out to homesick New Yorkers across the country. Without disturbing the "front of the house," Dell's back of the house operation is undertaking a strong push to ship nationally with packages delivered overnight directly to peoples' doorsteps—some pastrami, a rye bread, some pickles, knishes, some mustard. While it can't re-create the real restaurant experience at home, it's still a delicious taste of home.

"The net takeaway for our success," said Dell, "is that you need to stay true to who you are. I think a lot of businesses go under because they lose sight of that, and when they transfer from generation to generation, the next generation wants to change everything. For me, it's a matter of respect the traditions—and respect the things that work. And, yes, you have to change, to adapt and grow, but if you do this while sticking to your core values and traditions, that's what counts. If you're going to make a change, do something different, you'd better be confident that it's your best product and you're putting your best foot forward." Katz's Delicatessen is a restaurant very much in touch with its DNA.

CHEERIOS:
"Small Shifts" to Meet Shifting Attitudes

It's pretty easy to see how rapid and dramatic changes in technology and media necessitate a shift for companies in these categories. It is not quite as easy to see the portents of change that would necessitate a shift for companies in more homespun categories, like packaged goods. But those portents are indeed there. And, as a result of the seismic transformations in media and technology—read, social media—they are not nearly as subtle as they once were. Even the most traditional of packaged goods companies have had to shift, at the very least, *marketing* gears to keep up with changes in consumer attitudes toward everything from what constitutes healthy eating to what constitutes a family unit. When an ultra-traditional megabrand like Cheerios, for example, addresses mixed marriages and makes the daughter of an interracial couple the star of one of its advertising campaigns, it's an indication that no brand is immune from the need to shift to stay relevantly differentiated.

The shift for Cheerios was not in the makeup of its product, but in the makeup of its marketing. Let's start with a bit of background. In 1941, General Mills was looking for a product that would compete with Wheaties and Corn Flakes in the growing ready-to-eat cereal category. Wheaties and Corn Flakes were both made from corn. To differentiate its product, General Mills decided to develop a cereal made from oats. Needing to further differentiate its offering from oatmeal, it perfected a machine that produced puffed oats in the shape of tiny inner tubes—a shape that was to take on iconic status through the years.

Cheerios remains a leading breakfast cereal with Americans who bought $994 million of the brand in 2014.[1] Cheerios was launched in 1941 with two purposes in mind. First, General Mills aimed to bring the health benefits of oats into the mainstream. Second, General Mills positioned the brand to bring families together at the breakfast table.[2] Over the last couple of decades, as concerns about cholesterol and heart disease have taken hold, Cheerios doubled down on the health benefits in its marketing by shifting its message to address the health issue. At the same time, Cheerios executed significant marketing shifts in recognition of how the composition of families has changed.

"Your job as a marketer is to explore an underlying truth," said Mark Addicks, the former chief marketing officer at General Mills, during our conversation. "Consumer attitudes have shifted, and we've had to shift our messaging. A brand's culture should *expect* to be continually changing, especially in this world we live in, which is very fast, very connected, very news-oriented, and in which consumers quickly learn new patterns. We absolutely need to make shifts in recognition of this. It used to be that you had an annual meeting and everyone would just keep following the same GPS. Now, you wake up and life has changed. The place to start shifting your focus for a brand is when the brand is in a healthy place."

Among the societal breakthrough campaigns that General Mills produced in response was an ad titled "Adoption," based on a true event, about a couple that adopts two children from Eastern Europe.[3] The spot starts with a woman and man riding in a van on their way to the orphanage to pick up their children. The children are a little shy, but beyond the uncertainty, the scenes portray a great deal of hope for the new family. On the plane ride home, the woman gives Cheerios to the two children, making a little smiley face out of the Os. The boy and girl smile in response.

Another of the General Mills consumer stories brought to life was a series featuring a little girl named Gracie. In the first spot, "Just Checking," Gracie asks her mother if it's true that Cheerios are good for your heart. A beat later, her father wakes up from a nap in the other room with Cheerios all over his chest. In another spot in the series, during which the family is sharing breakfast together, Gracie's parents share the news that she will soon have a new baby brother; her response is a request for a new puppy. That the mother is white and the father is black won General Mills kudos for showing what real families look like. According to the *Wall Street Journal*, Cheerios has generated 80 percent of all digital engagement in the cereal category.[4] While there was some derogatory feedback, most of the online conversation has been very positive. As for the most recent health-related messaging, General Mills produced a YouTube video starring Manitoba farmer Edgar Scheurer, who supplies oats for Cheerios. From the farm to the table, the company wanted to reinforce that oat seeds, from which Cheerios are produced, are transformed into a healthy breakfast—so it is going back to the, well, roots of its product.

"You need to be culturally in tune with what's important to your customers and potential customers," said Addicks. "We're not looking to make massive shifts. We just need to be constantly ready to make the little shifts—changes that address the conversations people are having—to keep our relevance high. It's a huge challenge to identify and seize an opportunity before performance metrics kick in. But whether it's pure food, or being able to pronounce the ingredients, or family dynamics, the objective is to lock onto a key insight and build on it."

HASBRO:
Game on . . . Shifting by "Zooming Out"

Hasbro's stock is up, literally and figuratively. Over the past few years, the maker of Transformers and My Little Pony, Play-Doh and Nerf, has had a series of outstanding quarters, more than fulfilling the expectations of its shareholders. Its stock is up, too, with kids and parents (and grandparents), whose expectations for entertaining experiences are also being pleasantly fulfilled. We say "entertaining experiences" rather than toys or games because that was the focus of the shift—and the brand blueprint—that emerged after Brian Goldner and his team took to their realignment measures.

But before we get to the here and now and our discussion with Goldner, we quickly serve up the backstory. It was in 1923 that the three Hassenfeld brothers (hence, Hasbro) founded a textile company, selling textile remnants in Providence, Rhode Island.[5] Over the next two decades they expanded to produce, first, pencil boxes and school supplies and later toys and modeling clay. Its first hit toy was Mr. Potato Head, which the company purchased from toy inventor George Learner in 1952.[6] The toy was an incredible success and, in 1954, the company became a Disney major licensee.[7] Another incredible success came with the introduction of the G.I. Joe "action figure," so-labeled to avoid the word "doll" and appeal to boys. In 1964 and 1965, G.I. Joe accounted for two-thirds of the Hassenfeld brothers' sales.[8] (The Vietnam War and, later, the price of plastic and the cost of production, contributed to its decline in sales.[9])

In 1968, the company shortened its name to Hasbro Industries and began a decades-long period of expansion, starting with the purchase of Burt Claster Enterprises, which produced "Romper Room" and an affiliated line of toys, followed in the 1980s and into the 1990s[10] with the acquisition of Playskool, Kenner, Coleco Industries (the maker of Cabbage Patch Kids), as well as the Tonka Corporation and its Parker Brothers unit, creator of Monopoly. Hasbro also purchased Wizards of the Coast and Dungeons and Dragons.

Hasbro's growth activity during these years includes a much longer list of licensing deals with major entertainment franchises and channels, CDs, television and movies, interactive games, and even a venture into virtual reality. It was also over this period of time that the company became a global entity, working with manufacturers and distributors from Mexico to Europe to Asia. Its management, too, went through multiple changes during this period, transferring from fathers to sons and then to a grandson before moving on to leaders from outside the family. The bottom-line results from one year to the next were at times good and at times not so good; the *not* so good due, in part, to too many efforts and not enough vetting of the individual efforts and their implications.

Things were in the *not* so good category when Brian Goldner took the helm and became president and CEO in 2008. The company had not only lost billions of dollars, they were, as Goldner told us, "in need of serious alignment."

"We owned 1,500 brands, had zero economy of scale, zero salience or relevance. It was the world's most complex plate-spinning competition," he said. "We're spinning all these plates to try to eke out sales from lots of things. Letting go of any one of these plates would mean a reduction in revenue and not a lot of ways to replace it."

What they recognized they *needed* to do, Goldner explained, was to start reinvesting in consumer insights as a way to determine which few brands had the potential to be big again. What the company *wanted* to do was go back to a winning strategy that had catapulted the brands at a specific time in its history: connect the brands to consumers through storytelling.

"In the 1980s," Goldner began our conversation, "Hasbro was one of the fastest-growing companies on Wall Street. Our revenues went from $100 million to $1 billion. It did this through a variety of very contemporary means for the time. In fact, in the mid-1980s, the company used kids' syndicated television as a new branding tool to launch brands that are perennials in the toy and the entertainment business, specifically My Little Pony and Transformers. Hasbro was able to unlock the potential of media as a storytelling device before any other toy company did," Goldner said. "They created more relevance and salience around these brands for an audience that was being introduced to a host of storytelling sources. Stephen Hassenfeld, a son of one of the founders, was the visionary leader who took on visionary methodologies to invent and reinvent brands using the storytelling power inherent in media."

Goldner took this strategic cue as he and his team began the process of building a core group of seven brands that they believed could grow to their historical heights, billions of dollars in revenue, by surrounding them with stories. "We used very simple terminology. We said 'we need to build a seven-layer cake.' If we could get these seven layers going, take on the challenge, and succeed in bite-size pieces, it will become a lightning rod for our shareholders, both internally and externally. The seven brands we identified that we were going to focus on represented 17 percent of $2.7 billion. Today those brands represent 50 percent of $4.5 billion. And we still have forty to fifty other brands with the same potential."

Referring to the 2008 time frame, Goldner explained that Hasbro "had to become more 'choiceful.' We had to make the hard decision to let certain brands fall away and go fallow in order to focus the appropriate resources, personnel and otherwise, on the company's rebuilding efforts. We had to have the moral fortitude to say we understand what is happening and we need to communicate it to Wall Street, and to our organization. You have to be able to say 'no.'"

As an example of "saying no," Goldner cited Tonka, producers of iconic toy trucks and a brand that Hasbro had focused on for years. Although Tonka produced quality products, Hasbro assessed the potential growth of the brand and ultimately agreed the brand would never achieve the enterprise value they were looking for. As a result, Hasbro licensed it out to another party.[11] Being selective in the short term meant giving up immediate revenues for the sake of the longer-term picture.

But, let's get back to the focus of Hasbro's shift, the difficult decisions to be made, and the brand blueprints—the real game changers in enabling Goldner and his team to make the significant gains they have. These blueprints are "ever-evolving documents," as Goldner told us, which put individual brands at the center of everything related to its brand experience, brought to life in a variety of forms and formats, from toys and board games, to video games and movies, to television programming and online entertainment.

"Understanding your audience better than anybody else, investing considerably in the time and effort to get under the skin of that consumer, not only in their behavior today, but in the trends from which we then extrapolate, enables us to be ready for where the consumer will be in five or ten years relative to media behavior, family dynamic, and play behavior. We surround our brands with not only proprietary, quantitative consumer insights, but with compelling storytelling. It's our strong suit from a historical perspective," Goldner told us. "The company's successes have drawn largely from its transformational focus on content and storytelling, everything from episodic programming to social media to user-generated content, every screen and every touchpoint that is relevant to our audiences. Our strategy is to build on what we already do well, reinvention and reimagining. Provide children and their families with immersive experiences so they can enjoy Hasbro brands anytime, anywhere. Surrounding our audiences with stories and characters around our brands has always allowed us to engage with consumers in relevant ways."

As he predicted, Hasbro's top-line results following its "seven-layer cake" decision, together with its blueprint strategy to create immersive brand experiences, while choppy at first, would eventually become significantly positive, to which the wizards of Wall Street can happily attest.

Goldner's comments, on both Hasbro's challenges and its ensuing strategy, were reinforced by Kevin Lane Keller, the E.B. Osborn Professor of Marketing at the Tuck School of Business at Dartmouth College and the author of bestselling textbooks on brands and marketing management. "Hasbro had a double challenge," he told us in our conversation. "One was they had too many brands, so they had to really focus on their power brands. But the real shift for them was prompted by the realization that kids' definition of entertainment was changing. Kids were just getting more sophisticated. Hasbro fully understood that entertainment and technology were going to be driving the toy business," Keller said. "The challenge was how to align your forces to make sure you can execute well in these new arenas. How do you get into the digital game in a meaningful way, and how do you integrate well with entertainment?"

As Keller explained, the real "eureka" moment for Hasbro and Goldner came about when they expanded their view of who they really were, what business they were in, not falling prey to marketing myopia: "We're not in the toy business. We're in the entertainment business." That the toy business was an integral part of this was not disputed, but the larger picture was how to employ and optimize movies and music, digital apps and games to expand the entertainment experience. It was because they *were* in the toy business, the business of entertaining kids, that consumers gave them permission to make this shift.

"I always talk about positioning and its three components: desirable, deliverable, differentiate," said Keller. "To succeed, you're always trying to find the new desirable spot from the *consumer's* standpoint. Something that you can truly deliver on and that consumers will accept. Hasbro came to the realization that the company was in the entertainment space, yes, but also that they had the authority to go there. They had been integrating toys and entertainment for years. They had the history and the credibility." They just needed to shift into a higher gear.

In our discussion, we also talked about the courage factor. In Hasbro's case it took courage first to reduce the product lines, some of which had been very popular, and then to shift more fully into the entertainment space. Both were pretty big bets. We agreed as well that you have to not only have the conviction to make these bets, you have to have the DNA that will support your efforts. The Hasbro DNA was—and is—based on the spirit of innovation and reimagination. It is a culture based on fun—in fact, there is a "fun lab" at corporate headquarters. To show commitment to those founding principles, its DNA, Hasbro not only tripled the investment in the fun lab under Goldner's leadership, but it has built fun labs in several countries around the world. "You don't buy research," Goldner said about this investment. "You do it yourself. You put it right under your nose and you lean into it. We took cost out of other areas to focus on things that matter to our customers. There is a mantra in our organization. 'Through curiosity you remain passionate and through passion you remain driven.' This is our culture."

CNN:
An Important Message for Media Companies

That the technology and media industries are intrinsically bound is without question. That when one shifts the other feels an immediate impact has been demonstrated for eons, not just in this era of Facebook, Instagram, and Snapchat. From the printing press to the transistor to the cloud, technology and media have worked together to give people their news and entertainment. That this dynamic has gone into overdrive over the last half century is the point of this story about CNN and the fact that to keep its edge as a premier media company, it can never stop shifting gears.

First, as context, whether or not you were alive at the time, you know of that tragic day in November 1963 when President John F. Kennedy was assassinated. Those of us old enough to remember can tell you that we all stopped what we were doing to find a television to watch. The same thing happened just six years later, in happier circumstances, when men first walked on the moon. That's the way things operated for many years. If you wanted to find out the details of the latest breaking news event, you turned on a television. Seeing an untapped opportunity for people to watch the latest news in real time, Ted Turner launched CNN (Cable Network News), the world's first twenty-four-hour news network on June 1, 1980.[12] CNN went on to change the notion that news could only be reported either at fixed times during the day or as a breaking news flash.

At the time of CNN's debut, television news was dominated by three major networks, ABC, CBS, and NBC, and their thirty-minute nightly broadcasts. Like many new ventures, CNN lost money in its first years of operation. However, Turner continued to invest in building up the network's news bureaus around the world and, in 1983, bought Satellite News Channel.[13] CNN eventually became known for covering live events around the world as they happened, often beating the major networks to the story. The network gained significant traction with its live coverage of the Persian Gulf War in 1991,[14] and continued to grow in popularity along with all of cable television during the 1990s. People were literally and figuratively hardwired to get their news on television—and predominantly on CNN.

Turner had not simply built an innovative distribution channel, but a novel business model with his all-news-all-the-time idea. It was a model built on two revenue streams: one the money the network made from advertisers, and the second from the fees paid by cable operators who were locked into contracts. This double source of revenue gave CNN a huge advantage over broadcast television.[15] And the model worked pretty well, even up until the tragic news event on September 11, 2001, when many people *still* turned to television in the days and weeks that followed to stay current with the details of this horrifying moment in history.

It was at about this time that the terrain in the media industry, and specifically the screen-related side of the industry, began to change. CNN had to shift and maneuver through this terrain if it wanted to maintain its leadership as the go-to twenty-four news source. First, there were the bumps in the road created by competition within television cable news, from MSNBC to Fox News. There was an even more fundamental transformation: Which screens were people watching when they said they were watching television programming? While baby boomers are beginning to turn to their iPads or iPhones for news and views updates, younger viewers never got into the habit of sitting down on a couch to watch the news. How many even get their news from a *news* channel versus a Twitter feed or Facebook page? For that matter, how many teens or millennials curl on the couch to binge-watch their favorite series when viewing these screens? It's no longer a matter of all-news-all-the-time on the family television, but all-news-entertainment-gaming-all-the-time on the screen you carry in your pocket or backpack.

CNN continues to be faced with a challenge of the performance versus opportunity variety. First is the gravitational pull toward the performance of its existing television business on which it built its iconic brand name. For any company, it's simply very hard to move resources and attention toward a new opportunity, which in CNN's case is digital platforms and programming. The balance for CNN is to continue to stay on top of its existing game, not treating it like a second-class citizen, while paying heed to the newest generation of news seekers and their information-gathering platforms of choice. This is not just true of television, but of print media such as the *Wall Street Journal*.

Part of the challenge is, indeed, a generational behavior issue. Another part, and a big part specific to cable news networks, is related to those two streams of revenue generation. First, there is convincing advertisers to deliver platform-specific content for online media instead of reusing television spots online, and then getting customers online—and in a television-on-demand mindset—to watch ads instead of installing ad blockers. Equally important, getting people to pay for content that they can find for free is a major challenge. While 85 percent of millennials say that keeping up with the news is important to them, only 40 percent say they will pay for a news service, app, or digital subscription.[16]

We had the opportunity to speak with Jeffrey Zucker, a long-standing player in the media business and currently the president of CNN

Worldwide, about this scenario. He summed it up this way. "I think the mistake people used to make was that that digital was a complement to linear. It's not a complement. It's its own unique product. We expect CNN to be everywhere. We've invested in keeping our linear television channels strong, keeping our core strong. But we've also had to invest in the future, into digital. Shifting resources from linear to digital, we've had to make sure that linear doesn't suffer. That's the challenge. We are hyper-focused on protecting the core," said Zucker. "Instead of treating digital as a second tier or second priority, we've looked at each vehicle equally, balancing the existing performance metrics against the future opportunities."

With the digital and analog worlds colliding, and the fierce buffeting of revenue sources—advertising and cable operating fees—it's a very difficult balancing act. That CNN maintains focus on what it stands for in the market, the original purpose and values that give it credibility and authority in the category, is critical to its future success. Scot Safon, the former chief marketing officer at CNN Worldwide, gave us his perspective on the shifts in gear that CNN has had to make over the last few years in this environment.

"The underlying business model meant CNN *had* to make some shifts," he said. "There's no way the business could stay the same way for even five years from now. CNN successfully saw digital coming and, while it shifted to offer a digital platform, it stayed pretty true to its original focus—gathering real-time video content when it happened and maintaining the gravitas of its journalistic credentials. Reporters not just pointing a camera, but who had expertise in the field, an expert's perspective."

Even though the digital platform wasn't perfect, Safon said, CNN got into it early enough to stem the flow of viewers going to other sources. Eventually, CNN knew that video was going to dominate online, as more people had broadband connections and video expectations. How did CNN plan for evolving digital demand?

"We knew where the tipping point was. We could see it coming," Safon said. "We have excellent consumer insight simply by being in the space we're in . . . just by watching everyone's behavior on the site and on the network. We could watch them watching us in real time. And CNN lives in the world of watching what was happening . . . and projecting what was going to happen next—the organization is deeply tied to this kind of stuff."

Traditional consumer research was thus less insightful than benchmarking actual consumer behaviors. "If you ask consumers how much television they watch, or where they get their news, they don't even know. They constantly under- or over-estimate how much time they watch television. So, the first priority was making sure that we had the free digital Internet component, because that's where customers were going—especially when they were at work. Then, to remain true to the brand, we had to stay on top of technology that would let us both report from—and be watched in—remote places. And we were going to have to be as strong in digital as we were in television," Safon said. "But those decisions had to be made before we were sure exactly how it was going to be monetized. Nobody was really sure what the business model was going to be in those early days . . . I think people just assumed you had to have strong digital to drive people back to the core business, which would be TV."

This is a shift still in progress for CNN. Its goal over the next year or two is to figure out how to make digital content so irresistible that it will be seen as a must-have service. This is a significant shift in its content model: to find a way to create relevant news stories for a generation that has different expectations from content.

"Facebook gives you a newsfeed. Twitter gives you a newsfeed. They're not reporting, but—like it or not—they're giving you news. CNN and its competitors are all figuring out how to participate in this [environment]," Safon told us. "Suddenly they're competing on a playing field that has a lot of content that looks like news . . . but it's from non-journalists. But CNN is built to pivot quickly and easily into new platforms because it is used to turning around storytelling instantly— high-end productions as well as raw footage and live coverage. Throughout the development of digital content—from desktop websites to mobile apps to social media platforms—CNN shifts quickly to adapt. When we launched iReport, our consumer journalism platform, we essentially deputized our consumers as stringers. But the differentiator will always be the investigative and enterprise reporting—the stuff with context. CNN continues to double-down on this. The focus they've never lost sight of is journalists bringing you the inside story."

CNN is a very robust brand whose view of the business remains the same: "It's what Ted Turner set out to establish. It's a 24/7 global news source." The current challenge for both its cable and digital platforms is how to pay to send a reporter into the line of fire to get the news, to look at news with an insightful perspective in a way that will be appreciated by the next generation. With an endless stream of news events breaking live on an endless stream of social media sites, CNN certainly has the capability to capture everything in dramatic fashion, from natural hurricanes to political hurricanes. That it must not lose control of the steering wheel as the world turns dramatically faster is the most critical challenge for CNN and every other player in the media category.

CONSERVATION INTERNATIONAL:
A Shift to Link Environmental Conservation to Economic Growth

When one thinks of organizations that have undertaken significant shifts, it's not likely that a nonprofit would be among the first on your list; it may not even be on your list at all. That's what makes Conservation International's story so extraordinary. Most nonprofits select a cause or a mission and build their organization to deliver on that cause or mission. They spend most, if not all, of their time and their money and their passion—their existence—traveling down that road to execute the initial vision.

That was the case for the first twenty years of success for Conservation International, a not-for-profit environmental organization, and its founders, Peter Seligmann and Spencer Beebe. After two decades of concentrating on the preservation of "hot spots," or areas with a high level of biodiversity that were being threatened with development, Seligmann and his group redirected their efforts to link environmental conservation to the economic self-interest of surrounding communities. That it has cost the organization both employees and members en route to its current successful position in the category is something Seligmann acknowledged during our conversation, recalling the day he told his staff of the plan. "I said to my team, 'This can't be one more thing we're doing. This has got to be the driving, aligning characteristic of our institution. And we have to redesign the organization. All of our efforts to save the planet will be nothing if we don't make big changes—and fast.'"

To appreciate what prompted Seligmann to make this dramatic shift in direction, it's necessary to look at the organization's initial mission, and its work, to comprehend what it was he saw in the terrain ahead. Founded in 1987, Conservation International focused on identifying the most threatened natural areas in the world, trying to prevent industries from doing further damage in these areas, and establishing policies that would preserve the flora and fauna for the future. For instance, in 1987, they brokered the first-ever debt-for-nature swap with the Bolivian government, purchasing a portion of the nation's debt in exchange for preserving 3.7 million acres of the Beni Biosphere. In the 1990s, Conservation International narrowed its mission to prioritize biodiversity hot spots and establish corporate partnerships with large companies such as McDonald's, Exxon Mobil, and Starbucks to create more sustainable business practices, as well as to get them to support indigenous businesses, in the hopes of making conservation efforts self-sustaining in the future.

"My thought," Seligmann said, "was if we could actually use conservation of these hot spots as a way to generate economic benefits for these communities, they would embrace the conversation. So, that was the approach in the very beginning. This was different from what traditional conservation efforts were doing, and we found great receptivity. We were focusing on how to protect biodiversity hot spots and how to improve the quality of the lives of the people who lived there. Our drive," he said, "was to see if we could have a scale of success that was truly transformative. For example, we told Starbucks, 'You don't have to cut down a forest to grow coffee. In fact, when you cut down the forest, you destroy the biological diversity. Your customers would love it if you actually worked to *protect* these forests and grow coffee.' [In 2015] Starbucks announced that 99 percent of all the coffee it grew and sold was achieved by a standard we created called CAFÉ, which stands for Conservation and Farmer Equity."

Seligmann explained that while the organization was pleased with its initial results, it became clear that the impact was marginal relative to what it could and, importantly, should be doing. His conclusion after looking at several data points was that it was setting up "islands of conservation within a sea of development. The most powerful force on earth was development because that was the way nations measured progress. And it was completely disconnected from the conservational interest. For me, that was a very important recognition. What is threatened is not biodiversity, but the stability of nations, the well-being of communities, and the health of families."

This realization brought Conservation International to the proverbial "fork in the road," and it was the genesis for the changing of its mission from protecting biodiversity to supporting human well-being by procuring the health of ecological systems, with biological diversity being the underpinning of all stable societies. Conservation International was no longer going to be focusing on how to protect a big place or a little place, but shifting attention to the fact that, in terms of business profit and success in the long term, nature needs to be helped. "How do we let people know that a coral reef is not just a beautiful place for fish diversity, but it's a protein factory, the source of protein that all of these people depend upon? Our mission had to shift. If we did not focus on humanity, we were going to be marginalized. Development was going to wipe out ecosystems at the extraordinary pain and suffering of humanity."

As one might expect, Seligmann got a mixed reaction from his staff. Almost all of those who signed up for the organization's guiding mission did so because they so fervently believed in it. Changing course was a jolt. "There was enormous resistance within the organization," said Seligmann. "We lost about 20 percent of the staff. Many people thought I had abandoned conservation and was just someone who was interested in development. I eventually succeeded in explaining that the protection of nature had to be understood as an essential part of the developmental progress activities of communities and organizations that were focused on well-being. I explained that we had been treating a symptom. You can't solve poverty in sub-Saharan Africa by destroying ecological systems that are essential for the production of food."

To overcome obstacles in the way of achieving future goals, Seligmann and his staff made a list of which organizations and companies were acting as positive "global agents of change," as he called it, and they constructed a business model on best practices. More than this, they analyzed and assessed their institutional assets—what skills they had that they could leverage for optimal outcome, the core areas of expertise, and the relevant partnerships that would enable them to maintain credibility with staff and donor groups. These steps were critical to success when considering a shift in either gears or direction. "I felt that if we were going to be honestly successful, we had to redesign our institution. It was not a matter of adding something on to what we were already doing. I believe that to be transformative, you have to be crystal clear about what you are trying to achieve, and you have to put all of your resources into it," Seligmann said. "Being really impactful, really successful requires intensity, excellence in execution, monitoring, and truthfulness. And that's not something you do as a sidebar. For me, the most significant thing is to understand your brand, your purpose, your DNA, your mission, and to focus on them so they are truly aligned. Then you have to hire people who align with this mission and are ready to participate in this way."

Seligmann's understanding that it is essential to have a clear mission before you can execute on it brilliantly is certainly another of the reasons for this organization's success post-directional change. This said, Seligmann agreed that it was relatively easy to communicate the nonprofit's former mission, the conservation of ecosystems. An emotional, beautifully photographed scene of an endangered baby animal is a powerful and memorable branding signal. It has been much more complex to communicate the link between the conservation of nature and the economic well-being of those in the nearby environments. "If you look, for example, at the eastern coast of Brazil and the transformation of the tropical rain forest into a massive eucalyptus plantation, short term you can say it will increase jobs and productivity. What you can't see is the destruction of the soil, long term, and the depletion of watersheds and sources of freshwater and edible fish. These are the types of things we have to communicate, and the measurements we have to prove. To achieve our objectives," he said, "our efforts need to be able to demonstrate relatively complicated ideas in as simple a way as possible to have the required impact."

In the shift that Seligmann and his team are following, there is no simple, telegraphic way to tap quite as evocatively into people's emotions, but they have nonetheless found other, more profound ways to get their message across, and the results are incredibly rewarding. For instance, Conservation International launched a decades-long partnership with Walmart that includes efforts to bring more sustainable products to consumers and support supply chains that are more resilient to climate change and environmental impacts, such as reducing deforestation associated with the global palm oil footprint and implementing innovative sourcing strategies for jewelry and seafood. Rob Walton, son of the company's founder, Sam Walton, serves on Conservation International's executive committee. The Bill and Melinda Gates Foundation announced a $10 million grant to Conservation International to create a global monitoring network, called Vital Signs, focused on the direct connections between ecosystem health and agricultural productivity. To raise awareness of its new mission on the consumer front, Conservation International produced a series of short films titled "Nature Is Speaking," launched in 2014 and narrated by major Hollywood celebrities including Julia Roberts, Penelope Cruz, Robert Redford, and Harrison Ford. "Through these efforts, and many others," said Seligmann, "we are looking at how to accomplish sustainability. If we can identify what is the natural capital and where it is located, we can come up with a plan to protect it. Our goal is clear—to protect nature as a source of food, fresh water, livelihoods, and a stable climate."

Today Conservation International is thriving and growing in scale. Seligmann made a significant strategic shift in direction in what is now a $250 million organization because he recognized that meeting the needs of people is crucial to meeting the needs of nature. By shifting direction and reframing the challenge—asking "What do ecosystems do for people, and what does biodiversity provide?"—Conservational International has made an investment in the planet and the long-term sustainability of its most fragile communities.

IBM:
A Legacy of Continued Shifting

Some organizations are built for rapid gear shifting from the get-go. Everything is set up to enable the company to shift gears quickly and fluidly, from organizational structure to the open-communications policy to the process for fast-tracking ideas. For example, Facebook is a technology company that was established to outpace the fast pace of change. IBM is different. Founded in 1911 as a maker of scales, cheese and meat slicers, coffee grinders, and the like, IBM eventually got into the business of making computers. Then it got out of the business of computers and into business enterprise solutions. IBM has been very adept at shifting direction.

Our conversation with IBM senior vice president of marketing and communications, Jon Iwata, suggests that they view it otherwise. IBM has never defined business as *what* it sells, but rather, what it *believes* in. At IBM's core are a set of values that have remained constant over the years, even as *what* they've done to meet their customers' needs has changed. It is because of this that IBM has been able to shift by degrees while keeping the positive equity in its brand. It may not shift gears as quickly and with the same agility as a Facebook, of course, because of its age (let's call it advanced middle age) and because of its magnitude relative to other tech companies; nonetheless, IBM makes it happen with authority.

Before we get to Iwata's more detailed insight, it is worthwhile to give a brief overview of two famous examples of IBM's shifts. First, in 1993, the once-dominant computer company was on the verge of a breakup. The stock price had hit a twenty-year low. The company that had always maintained a lifetime employment policy let go more than 100,000 employees after posting an $8.1 billion loss. Worse, IBM's way of computing and of working with customers was viewed as antiquated. The company struggled under the weight of a management structure that created independent business units with redundant processes and disconnected information systems. Because of years of operating with few competitors, it had become insular and slow to react to change.

Enter Lou Gerstner, former president of American Express and CEO of RJR Nabisco. While industry pundits assumed Gerstner was brought in to accelerate a breakup of the company into smaller units, Gerstner did just the opposite. He pushed it together, creating a much more streamlined and integrated company. He understood that IBM's inherent strength was in its ability to solve complex (business) problems for its customers. To create value through total solutions, IBM had to become an adviser, not just a vendor. This initiative resulted in a campaign, and a way of doing business, called "Solutions for a Small Planet." The word *solutions* critically expressed the core of IBM's values and belief system.

From the outside, this shift—from manufacturing to advising— might have seemed incongruous with the company's origins. The fact is, however, that IBM had always had a consulting component to its sales. The big mainframes you'd buy from IBM were not just plug and play. They had to be custom-built. There was a huge consulting dimension to the work the company did. Systems were tailored to a customer's specifications.

The second major shift came in 2005 when IBM sold its vaunted ThinkPad PC business to the Chinese company Lenovo. And, yes, these were things you *could* buy off the shelf. But they did it with good reason, which many in the industry considered a win-win scenario. Lenovo had the desire to be in the hardware business, and the wherewithal to grow the business globally. In 2014, Lenovo further acquired IBM's x86 server division, adding strength in this category. IBM, on the other hand, had the desire to shift even further into the enterprise "solutions" category, with a focus on analytics, mobile, security, and cloud, where it saw greater opportunity for future development and, importantly, could further support its customers' needs. It knew it could not shift fast enough to keep up in the PC category.

And this is where Jon Iwata's insight adds support. "Definition is critical," he said. "Think about technology shifts, economic cycles, changing competition, shifting consumer tastes—with all that change, we can't define ourselves by what we've been doing for x number of years. It's important to define our business more broadly than 'We make scales' or 'We make desktop computers.' We define ourselves by our unique and distinctive character. How have we maintained a constant focus on our character over time? If you look at the entire history of IBM," he told us, "you could say the company has transformed itself over and over again, but all in the name of helping solve meaningful business and societal challenges through the application of technology."

Iwata went on to say that continuous focus on different ways to fulfill its purpose is what has enabled IBM to recalibrate how to best serve its customers. While this can be challenging in a company of IBM's size, there are a number of ways it arrives at what Iwata called "pivot points," especially in a marketplace that doesn't change every ten years but every ten days. First is an annual process called the "global technology outlook," a collaboration between IBM's network of scientists, laboratories, and university researchers around the world who synthesize their findings into a point of view that drives the development of products and the merger and acquisition endeavors the company undertakes. As he explained, "It is a forecast, pointing out potential disruptions. The quasi-independence and objectivity of the research division lessens the chance that we'll spend a whole year testing the functionality of a product only to step back and realize it wasn't what the world wanted."

Then, much as the research division takes a step-back global view of what's coming down the turnpike, IBM regularly holds companywide "jam" sessions, engaging over 375,000 employees in more than 170 countries. "We think of it as our social network inside IBM," Iwata said. "We use the input to gauge client experience metrics and measurements. We use it to gauge our employee engagement measurements, to hear people's opinions on company culture and its values. It's a form of crowdsourcing that helps us maintain the constant character of the business. The power of crowdsourcing also preserves authenticity. You get more buy-in on decisions when there's transparency, when everyone can see the thousands and thousands of comments, the debates, the stories of what has worked and what hasn't. We don't constrain behavior, but learn from it. We actually have a term for it: 'treasure wild ducks.' It means we treasure interesting people, different across every dimension," he said.

Iwata also explained that IBM's philosophy relative to the "treasure of wild ducks" plays a significant role in how it recruits people. "We look for people who have a proven track record of reinvention. It's made our gene pool stronger, our capacity for adapting to necessary changes more powerful and nimble. We look not only for people who have deep domain experience, but also people who are comfortable with moving fast, who can engage with colleagues and encourage them to do the same. We prize that at IBM—and I don't think I could have said that about IBM thirty years ago. We put it at the top of our criteria today."

That IBM hires people who have a capacity for reinvention and the ability to move faster is an indication of its awareness that it needs to get into even better shape, up its game in this brutal category if it doesn't want to be eclipsed by younger, more inherently inventive companies. This is a notion that Thomas L. Friedman put forth as critical to succeeding in the hyper-connected world. That a company like IBM continues to define itself by its values, not its product set, also bodes well for its future. As Iwata said, "We say to our new recruits, yeah, you guys are so excited about Watson today, but ten years from now, twenty-five years from now, we will be in new spaces. We are not what we make. That is not how we define ourselves. Our culture is the best way to ensure the future of IBM for another 105 years."

LINDBLAD:
Shifting to Deliver Deeper Expertise to a Core Focus

For those who think of cruising as sitting by a pool with a cocktail and getting off the ship occasionally to shop the jewelry kiosks, a Lindblad cruise is completely different. Regarded as the father of ecotourism, Lars-Eric Lindblad was the first travel company owner to take travelers where only scientists had gone—the first to have the insight that there are folks who want travel to be purposeful and genuinely transformative.

Lars-Eric Lindblad really wanted to be an explorer, and he channeled his passion into his travel business. A noted environmentalist, he was the first to bring those with an adventurous spirit to the most exotic places in the world, including Antarctica, Arctic Svalbard, Galapagos, Easter Island, the Amazon, Papua New Guinea, and Bhutan, all with the focus of creating experiences that fostered an understanding and appreciation for the planet.

In 1979, Lars-Eric's son, Sven-Olof Lindblad, took over the company and expanded the vision by adding newer and more immersive ecotourism experiences. The fact was, however, that despite the incredible experiences, the brand was relatively unknown outside those intrepid types specifically interested in this type of niche travel. Looking for a way to elevate the brand's awareness and adding differentiation to its experience without losing its core focus on authentic eco-experiences, in 2004 Lindblad Expeditions embarked on one of the travel industry's most important strategic alliances when it joined forces with National Geographic to dramatically strengthen the experience they offered customers. By adding the deep expertise and gravitas of National Geographic's scientists, explorers, naturalists, and photographers to their expedition cruises, Lindblad created a dramatically differentiated traveler experience. While other cruise lines could add a naturalist or a photographer, they could not match the depth of knowledge provided by National Geographic employees sharing their expertise with travelers. Today, Lindblad Expeditions-National Geographic operates its own fleet of ten ships, offering life-changing experiences on all seven continents.

Lindblad identified untapped audiences for the type of travel it offered. Its shift to partner with National Geographic was a matter of "playing golf," keeping an eye on the consumers it wanted to attract. We spoke to Richard Fontaine, chief marketing officer of Lindblad Expeditions, about the genesis for this partnership and why it was a win-win.

"When Sven initiated the conversation with National Geographic thirteen years ago, he was looking for a way to elevate our awareness and simultaneously enhance the guest experience," Fontaine said. "By aligning with National Geographic, it allowed us to bring the organization's content, information, and educational programs—authentic real-life explorers and naturalists—into our guest experience. Among the most obvious examples is that on every one of our expeditions we have certified photo-instructors who have been trained by the photographers who are published in *National Geographic* magazine. They are at the top of their profession and you're working side by side with them to improve your own photography skills. More than this," said Fontaine, "the National Geographic alliance has allowed us to create a much more enhanced focus on environmental conservation and sustainability in the areas in which we travel. We are trying to leave the places we visit in better condition than when we started traveling, so future generations will have the same opportunity to see them. Obviously, there is no better partner for us than National Geographic. They have a field staff on the ground all the time, doing research to try to protect and preserve these places." Connecting the two brands allowed Lindblad to add unique differentiation into its original explorer focus.

There is no better partner for Lindblad than National Geographic for another reason. While we analyzed the challenges of the National Geographic Society (NGS) with respect to its faltering magazine business (see Chapter 3), NGS is still perceived as a leading authority on issues of geographic knowledge and information. Its association with Lindblad has brought enormous benefit to both organizations. By shifting to connect with National Geographic, Lindblad adds to its gravitas as the groundbreaker in ecotourism, bringing the words and pictures within the *National Geographic* magazine's iconic yellow border to life. Sven Lindblad knew what his brand stood for and shifted in a way that added more power and authenticity to the brand's simple idea. Other cruise lines can hire photographers and naturalists; Lindblad lets you travel with authentic photographers and naturalists from National Geographic, experts in wildlife, the oceans, and the rain forests. It was a way for Lindblad to dramatically differentiate itself in the sea of cruise and travel companies.

COMCAST:
Two Shifts, Two Roads, One Purpose

You did not need to miss a thing at the 2016 Summer Olympics in Rio de Janeiro if you didn't want to. NBC broadcast every event live, either on television or online—the equivalent of tuning in 24 hours a day for 250 days. We can safely say that it's unlikely that anyone actually watched every minute of this event, but that was okay with Brian Roberts, the chief executive officer of Comcast Corporation, NBC's corporate parent. His objective was to use the Olympic Games to harness the full power of a tool his company had been developing for cable customers, a tool that he hoped would become so essential to their content viewing habits that they'd never give up their Comcast subscriptions. During the Olympics, Comcast subscribers were able to search by event, athlete, or country, get alerts when an American was close to winning gold, and navigate through all these options by speaking into a remote device. The strategy behind this tool was to make it as easy as possible for Comcast customers to find what they wanted to watch on television or online, as the boundary between them continued to erode in the expanding universe of content.

The tool Roberts was betting on was its technology called X1, a black box with a voice-controlled remote developed to take on rival "digital assistants" from Apple or Amazon. Many liken the X1—and the software therein—to Comcast's own version of Android or iOS, a technological platform upon which an empire of software, hardware, and collateral services can be built. It was initially designed for a specific TV-related purpose, the Olympics. However, it has much broader applicability. The incredible proliferation of cable channels, together with the exponential increase in the number of shows and movies available on demand from premium cable networks like HBO, Showtime, and Starz, was found to be overwhelming to many viewers. Instead of just throwing every channel into a linear grid accessed by clicking up and down with a remote, X1 aggregates programming from both television and online sources and arranges it by genre. The voice-activated remote responds to a user's request by showing what's available. The software lives in the cloud, which means Comcast can update it at any time without anyone having to come to your home.

That the X1 has been a game changer for Comcast is certain, as subscriber numbers and revenues from sales of X1 systems confirm. And it is just one of the tangible outcomes of the shifts in direction that Comcast has made over the last few years—shifts that took years to achieve. It's one thing for a small, agile company to make a change in direction, culture, and employee skillset that's cohesive and aligned with the mission. It's another for a massive enterprise, like Comcast, whose infrastructure and culture and competencies are deeply rooted in yesterday's technology. To set the backdrop for these shifts, let's start with a very, *very* brief history.

In 1963, Comcast was formed after Ralph Roberts (father of Brian) purchased a 1,200- subscriber cable system in Tupelo, Mississippi. The name "Comcast" is a combination of the words *communication* and *broadcast*. Back then, cable television was in its nascent period, being slowly installed across the country to give areas with poor reception more channel options than the old rabbit-ear antennas could pick up. Due to federal regulations, cable companies could only serve markets under franchise agreements with local governments, which led to the creation of hundreds of individualized cable companies, each serving their own small markets. The industry began consolidating in the 1990s, specifically after the passage of the Telecommunications Act of 1996. Comcast, a major consolidator, had over one million subscribers by 1998. Acutely aware of what was in the road ahead with regard to technology and media and the concomitant consumer behaviors, Comcast continued its purchasing spree, acquiring not just cable operations but media and Internet companies along the way. In 2001, it announced it would acquire AT&T Broadband, and in 2013 Comcast finalized a deal to take over NBCUniversal, adding the iconic NBC peacock to its logo.

This brief historical overview is a textbook example of something "easier said than done." The terrain and obstacles that had to be overcome for Comcast to attain its current position as a powerful "media" (not cable) company were significant. Along the way, Comcast struggled to stay ahead of the competition; the cable industry was becoming increasingly fragmented with rival companies providing customers with satellite and fiber optics, more reliable technologies than Comcast's in-ground "pipe," as it was called, that provided faster service and an overall better experience. The negative blasts against Comcast were well known. In 2007, the American Customer Satisfaction Index found that Comcast rated lower than the Internal Revenue Service in terms of customer satisfaction.

Changes had to be made. And it was during our conversation with Peter Intermaggio, Comcast's senior vice president of communications, that we talked about the company's initial directional shift. "You had to start with the point of view as to where the industry was going," he told us. "Where technology was going, and most important, what customers would want and need in the next one, three, five, ten years. You had the maturation of the satellite companies into the Direct TV and DISH brands happening in the 2000s. Suddenly the cable companies had real competition, not to mention old infrastructure, key among the causes of poor customer service. Cable companies like Comcast began losing customers to new entrants like AT&T and Verizon Fios."

It was against this backdrop that Comcast made the big bet to make a big investment in network technology, products, and customer service. It took on the installation of an enhanced fiber optic network with more than 145,000 miles of fiber, a network that now provides high-speed and high-definition (HD) services to twenty-nine regional networks in thirty-nine states. Readily scalable, it is the basis for Comcast's Ethernet, Internet, and phone solutions. It has raised the bar within the industry for high-speed Internet, while also substantially increasing on-demand offerings and the number of HD channels available and essentially enabling all-digital video services. At the culmination of this effort, in 2010, Comcast introduced the Xfinity brand to represent its shift to this vastly improved experience above and beyond cable.

"The decision to call this new experience Xfinity was to signal that this wasn't your grandfather's Comcast," said Intermaggio. "It was a vastly improved product. It wasn't a difference in degree. It was a totally new kind of experience. We had been competing in the market as Comcast Digital Cable and it just didn't convey the new vision. The Xfinity name stood for three things: cross-platform, infinite content, and always improving. We knew that we would continue to make investments in digital and network infrastructure. The most important and recent of these improvements was the introduction of the X1, which has resulted in a completely transformative user experience."

As Intermaggio explained, Comcast was a company that had fallen behind in the industry. It had to make the shift, requiring huge investments, if it wanted not only to stay competitive but to lead in its industry. "It is the very nature of technology that it is always improving. Our brand had to demonstrate that its improvements were real and substantive with absolute customer benefit. We could not have made the experiential shift we did without the new infrastructure," he said. "We could not possibly have competed in today's marketplace against the very strong offerings from our competitors, new entrants that we face every day, from Amazon Prime [Video] and Netflix to Google Fiber. We now operate in this really beautiful ecosystem of programmers, content developers, producers and writers, technology companies, and distributors. The velocity in our industry has increased so greatly. I cannot imagine competing against this broader set of competitors as Comcast Digital Cable. What we did gave us the ability to not just compete, but to reshape the direction of the industry."

While Comcast gets credit for helping to reshape the cable industry, another corresponding shift in direction was happening inside the company. And it was about this that we spoke with D'Arcy Rudnay, executive vice president and chief communications officer at Comcast. "One of the shifts we undertook was going from Comcast Cable to Xfinity and integrating NBCUniversal. The broader shift occurred after this acquisition. We are now in the media and technology business. Technology is reshaping the way all consumers look at the products they use. At Comcast, improving customer service is essential. Every time you go online, every time you turn on the camera in your home's security network to watch a baby in the crib, every time your child is studying online, every time there is a crisis in the world, people are depending on our products. One is TV and the other is the Internet, whether the screen is the television, an iPhone, an iPad, or a computer. Being able to get the content they want and need is essential to [people's] lives. They depend on us for the news and entertainment they love. Our purpose is to create and deliver moments that matter for our customers," she said, "whether that means creating or delivering video content, developing products like high-speed Internet or home security, Wi-Fi, or wireless phone. As a media and technology company, we want to deliver on this better than any other company.

"Here's the journey we took," Rudnay explained. "First, we had to take on the basic cable experience, fix the infrastructure, and improve the customer experience. We did that. We are now focused on the next chapter, a shift that means looking at our company through a broader lens. As Peter [Intermaggio] told you, the X1 experience is something that we'd been working on for at least eight years. It was our effort to create a product that blended television and the Internet but, more importantly, that reflected our understanding of what consumers want in terms of easy-to-use navigation, finding the content you want, that uses all the technology of the cloud to make the experience astounding."

These transformative shifts in direction required more than financial investments. Comcast management also determined that it required a transformation of the company's culture, which meant importing new talent that could fill in the gaps in skillset and mindset. In our conversation Intermaggio described the cable industry as a "a very insular industry" and "somewhat self-contained." Comcast made critical hires from outside the company, including the recruitment of Chris Satchel from Nike to be chief product officer, who introduced new ways of thinking. When a ping-pong table arrived on the fifteenth floor of Comcast's corporate headquarters in downtown Philadelphia, it was another signal that the company was embracing the trappings of a more innovative culture. As of today, software nerds and data geeks are key among the thousands of employees. In 2015, Comcast began stamping its remotes with the words "Designed with love ❤ in Philadelphia," an homage to Apple's slogan imprinted on its iPhones. More than this, Comcast is building a skyscraper next to its headquarters that will be the largest building in Philadelphia when it opens in 2018. The sixty-story "laboratory," designed by the same architect behind Apple's new campus, will serve as an incubator for start-ups and the workspace for Comcast's engineers and designers as well as a new Four Seasons Hotel.

"You've got one shift on top of another shift," said Rudnay, "which is Comcast moving from the vertical notion of cable to the broader definition of media and technology and delivery. So many people identify us as just a cable company, but we're not. Through NBCUniversal, we own Universal Parks and Resorts, DreamWorks Animation, Universal Studios, NBC, and Telemundo Broadcast Network and cable networks. The innovation that Comcast has brought to market at scale has now set the standard for the category."

And this brings us back to the 2016 Olympics in Rio, during which Comcast partnered with BuzzFeed to offer 6,000 hours of programming in seventeen days and to create more interactive experiences with viewers using Snapchat, Twitter, and Facebook. It used the Olympics as a way to showcase its new abilities, to give it dimension and bring to life the power of its transformation from a cable company to an innovative media company. The Olympics was a deliberate and strategic activation point in terms of Comcast's shifts in direction. It was a pivotal "moment that mattered" because it enabled the company to communicate what it now stood for after the shifts of massive scale and complexity that took place over many years. Not the least of its efforts was the rebuilding of an infrastructure that could support these shifts in terms of making good on its new promise. Among Comcast's current challenges is demonstrating that it provides good customer experiences and making the experience *better* than ever before—and in the process repairing its reputation for customer service.

Comcast turned itself around and changed directions in a very wide arc. From all indications, it is betting on its new infrastructure, and its new cultural disposition, to support even more shifts in the years ahead. First of all, as sales of X1 increase, Comcast is betting customers will keep paying for cable programming if they can get more benefit from it, and if it's easy to use. It continues to add video options from other sources, including Periscope and Facebook Live, so users can watch live concerts filmed by friends on their phones. As for the future, as more household appliances, from washing machines to thermostats, garage doors to alarm systems, are connected to the Internet, Comcast wants its customers to be able to manage this "Internet of everything" through all their screens, no matter what size. As CEO Roberts stated in an article on *Bloomberg's* technology site, "This is a new world. You have to reset your definition."[17]

BP:
A Lesson Learned

Let's address the elephant in the room that appears when we talk about the global energy company BP: the tragic Deepwater Horizon incident and the 2016 Hollywood movie of the same name that describes itself as "based on true events." The movie generally sticks to what actually happened on April 20, 2010, when an oil rig owned by BP exploded in the Gulf of Mexico, killing eleven people, injuring many more, and creating an environmental disaster of epic proportions. The filmmakers' focus primarily on the oil rig workers and the spill's impact on their lives and the environment turns the audience against BP, by revealing in the epilogue that not a single employee of BP or Transocean, the private contractor operating the rig, were ever prosecuted for their involvement in the disaster.

While BP never faced any criminal charges, the company did not get off scot-free, either. BP eventually paid a $20 billion settlement for the environmental toll and another $4 billion in a criminal probe. Additionally, BP now had a severely damaged reputation in the eyes of consumers. This event is germane to the theme of this chapter to the extent that it is an example of how extraordinarily challenging it is for a company—especially a company as large in scale and scope as BP—to take on a dramatic shift, and more specifically, to take an intellectual brand concept and try to shift it into a business strategy.

As the last story in this chapter, it is a cautionary tale. BP's intention relative to this shift was extremely laudable and forward thinking. It was the first big oil company to acknowledge the link between man-made carbon emissions and global warming. However, it made a fundamental mistake in delivering on its new promise. BP wanted to expand its purpose into supplying new environmentally friendly energy solutions. BP made the change to give itself an edge over other oil companies, to prepare for a future without oil dependency so that BP stays relevant, and to "gain a seat at the table" when environmental regulations increase.

In the spirit of transparency, we begin the story of BP's shift in direction by saying that the company Allen worked at, Landor Associates, helped BP with this program. At the time, Tina Orlando, currently a partner at Indelable, was one of Landor's clients at BP.

In the late 1990s, BP's CEO, Lord John Browne, came up with the idea to forge a new kind of company around the merger of several well-established brands, chief among them British Petroleum, Amoco, Castrol, and parts of major oil and gas companies such as Mobil and Arco. Browne charted a course for how the new direction should be communicated both internally—to BP's thousands of global employees—and to the external markets through powerful branding and marketing. Browne did not want BP to be seen as merely one of the best petroleum companies in the world; management wanted BP to be known as one of the best companies in the world.[18]

We begin with a condensed passage from Lord John Browne, the former BP CEO, taken from his 2015 book, *Connect: How Companies Succeed by Engaging Radically with Society*:

In 1997, I was the first big oil chief to acknowledge the link between man-made carbon emissions and global warming. I believed that oil companies, or at least BP, could no longer deny the problem. It was the realization that Big Oil must move towards a low carbon world that motivated me to change the firm's tagline to Beyond Petroleum.[19]

His idea was to move from being driven by the traditional physical assets of a petroleum company to using knowledge and innovation to create future value beyond petroleum. Through its work with agencies Ogilvy & Mather and Landor, the "beyond petroleum" concept was meant to be much more than a tagline. It was to be a North Star, a clear direction for all of the company's initiatives. Browne wanted BP to be known as the first mover in the energy category in terms of grasping the implications of climate change, and he wanted to demonstrate that the company was able to do something about it. The now-famous yellow and green Helios logo, the evocative representation of the "beyond petroleum" brand idea, signaled BP's determination to be differentiated from its competitors, at the same time highlighting its overarching mission to be a leading energy solutions provider and a good global citizen. Internal brand experience sessions were organized to help the new BP's tens of thousands of employees understand this new mission and their role in bringing it to life.

The problem for BP was that it was so anxious to get the word out and to be seen as the first mover among energy companies into this non-carbon-based world that management forgot to equip the company to actually make the move. It became a branding activity without the substance to deliver upon the promise being made.

According to Orlando, "The internal and external brand engagement activity continued for years after launch. Internally we were up against the complexity of integrating, culturally and operationally, up to five different companies . . . and multiple internal business units, trying to get them all aligned around something that was new to everyone. It was especially hard for the 50 percent of them who were legacy BP people. Here's one of the biggest industrial companies in the world deciding to make a significant shift in what they stood for. The number of people that we needed to reach was massive. In theory, creating a new idea everyone could rally around was good. It was the right theoretical answer. This indicated the dawn of a new era for the company, which believed that the oil and gas industry had a new level of responsibility. They had to change, the old way of operating being no longer acceptable." The problem was that they spent more time telling people, inside and outside the company, that they were changing than they did actually changing.

To say that a lot of competing energy companies were shocked at BP's new branding strategy, let alone the business and policy challenges it would bring, was an understatement. "They called it 'leaving the church,'" Orlando said. "It was obviously a deeply aspirational idea. But the notion of being 'beyond petroleum' for an oil and gas company was inherently a paradox. It was easy for investors *not* to understand it. Analysts' initial response to Browne was that he couldn't ignore his core hydrocarbon income stream. I think it gave those in the industry and on Wall Street an opportunity to doubt and to question. Looking back, the use of this audacious idea was probably a good thing. But the brand idea was complex—it was greater than the sum of the parts.

"The tangible delivery of the idea, being able to drive 'beyond petroleum,' was even more complex," said Orlando. "It was hard enough to explain, and it was going to prove exponentially harder to do. You told people you were going to move to something new, but it was so difficult to fully define what this new was, and while there were pockets of examples across the business, it wasn't standard practice everywhere. It was subject to huge interpretation. You can have the best brand idea in the world, but people didn't get how to operationalize it, and it was hard to standardize at scale. Even though we communicated our approach as 'It's a start' in advertising campaigns, we had raised expectations to the point where stakeholders were looking for the complete package, fully baked and ready to go. The reality is, it takes years for any company to achieve a change on this scale. That said, the company received multiple awards and accolades for the brand, it gained huge traction in numerous rankings, and was the leading industry brand for several years after launch." Ultimately, the expectations it created were not met.

"If you're setting up expectations for a new company direction, remember—it's got to be balanced with the industry you're in and the public perceptions of the industry," said Orlando. "BP was trying to do something new and be responsible and engage with society in a way no energy company had ever done before, but they almost got punished for it because the perception by some was that it was disingenuous, especially around the notion of trying to be green or greener. They devoted lots of time and resources over many years to provide concrete examples of behavior, initiatives, funding, positions, and policies that backed up 'beyond petroleum.'"

But it was too late. To have to go into the nuances and complexities of turning an oil company into a business promising to go "beyond petroleum" was daunting. New technology, expertise, and culture had to be created. Eventually, reality set in and due to the confusion, BP eventually moved away from the "beyond petroleum" concept. The CEO who inspired and drove the brand left the company in 2007. This change in leadership significantly stalled the momentum that had been built over the previous seven years; the commitment wasn't there any longer at the top to continue supporting and investing in the brand.

The lesson, from which all companies can learn, is that you cannot make a promise unless you are ready to deliver on that promise. BP is still paying the price of a broken promise, both financially and from a brand equity point of view. The positive news is that in looking at available data, even though BP went through this tremendous challenge, in general the brand is still leaps and bounds ahead of other energy companies in green initiatives. In taking on such a bold *shift in ideas*—going from fossil fuel to non-fossil fuel—the company definitely did many things right. Some of it may eventually pay off.

In his book, Browne remarks:

In hindsight, this went further than the public would accept. It was a mistake to push so hard. Beyond Petroleum should have been a subheading, not a main line. The renaming symbolized the shortcomings in our climate strategy. In essence the company had gotten ahead of itself and beyond where the industry and government were willing to go at that time. *Beyond Petroleum* was never meant to be literal—not yet, anyway—but there was still too much of a gap between the aspiration and the reality, which I now regret. The actions we took were bold, but they could have been bolder. Ultimately that was my fault, and the barriers I failed to overcome provide a useful lesson for today's CEOs as they attempt to shift ahead.[20]

Lessons Learned ▶

This chapter described a variety of company shifts. They range from Katz's Delicatessen, an enterprise that shifted gears merely by opening a new store and promoting the business using new media, to Comcast, an organization that made a wholesale shift in direction by both getting into the content creation business and upgrading the infrastructure for delivering content. The other companies discussed in this chapter fall along a continuum between the extremes. IBM presents an interesting example that has elements of both. It has changed its DNA by getting into new industries and acquiring the new skills needed. At the same time, IBM views itself as having adhered to its stated purpose of solving problems for customers. But then, isn't the purpose of every business to solve problems for its customers?

The myriad companies along with the scope of shifts described in this chapter provide us the opportunity to draw some interesting generalizations about shifting gears and/or direction. In every case, the marketplace changed, social or cultural or political dynamics changed, technology changed, and the companies we studied had to power up for one reason or another.

For example, in his mission to immediately jump on the new ways to keep people connected—unambiguously—Mark Zuckerberg knew that it was essential for Facebook to embrace mobile early on. It would expand and optimize the user experience. As Facebook turned its focus to its mobile app in 2012, it tapped into a huge market of businesses eager to reach consumers. "People are moving to mobile. . . . Marketers know people are on mobile. The average American consumer is checking his or her smart phone 150 times a day. If you need to reach people, you need to be where they are," Sheryl Sandberg, Facebook's chief operating officer, said in an interview with CNBC in September 2016.[21] In 2016, Facebook added over 270 million new mobile users who log in at least once a month. Of its 1.79 billion monthly users across all platforms, 93 percent are on mobile.

In other cases, you may recognize that if you keep barreling down the road you're on, things will only get worse. It's not a matter of powering up or down while staying the course. You need to shift direction. But, which way do you go? Sometimes the markers are clear, with a very obvious path. Oftentimes, there are multiple options. You can go left or right or, as the Scarecrow in *The Wizard of Oz* says when he tries to guide Dorothy down the Yellow Brick Road, sometimes people go both ways. The very first thing you must ask in this case is, What are your organization's real assets and skillsets? What's in your DNA that will enable you to deliver with credibility? In other words, where can you go and effectively play and win? This leads to our first lesson from this chapter.

Lesson #1. Respect your DNA. Science refers to DNA as the building blocks of life. Deoxyribonucleic acid, DNA, contains the genetic codes that impact what we look like, how intelligent we may be, the extent of our athletic abilities, and to some extent, even our personalities. DNA determines who we are. Of course, we make decisions about our lives, but those decisions are constrained in part by our genetics. For example, both authors are basketball fans; both of us played as kids. However, our DNA dictated that neither of us would grow to the height of six feet (Allen is five foot eight, Joel is five ten). As such, neither one of us could reasonably choose to pursue a career in professional basketball.

Like people, companies are imbued with DNA that govern their choices. Part of the DNA is tangible (e.g., technology); part is intangible (e.g., company culture). Facebook connects the world; Hasbro has relationships that allow it to provide entertainment; IBM solves problems; Cheerios provides health benefits through oats; and Katz's Delicatessen delivers a blockbuster sensory experience through sight, smell, and, of course, taste. Any shifts they make have been and must continue to be guided by their DNA; i.e., who they are. When you stray, you run the risk of not getting back on track. This led to the problems faced by Barnes & Noble and BP. BP in particular made a promise that it did not yet have the DNA to deliver.

Kodak provides another example of a firm that might have fared better had it respected its DNA. Earlier in the book we discussed Kodak's failures in the light of the golden handcuffs they found themselves shackled with. However, that is only part of the story. We discussed earlier that Kodak did not have the mindset to accept that film was on its way to obsolescence. The irony here lies in what was a mismatch between what they knew and what they acted upon. Jim Patton told us that Kodak had some first-rate technical forecasters, one of whom actually nailed the major shift from film to digital right to the year when it happened. In the aftermath of one board meeting, the chairman, Kay Whitmore, described a major philosophical or strategic discussion on Kodak to Patton. The discussion surrounded the question as to whether Kodak was an imaging or a chemistry company. The board answered the question in the wrong way. They decided that Kodak was an imaging, and not chemistry, company. Patton's view was that all the competencies of the company were chemistry. Kodak just happened to be a chemistry company that made really good imaging products. After making the wrong decision in the boardroom that day, Kodak sold off the chemical business and focused on a business that they lacked the basic DNA to compete in.

Lesson #2. As time passes and markets welcome entrants, segments emerge and products must become more specialized—and firms must shift to adapt. Both authors like to play tennis, basketball, and run. Neither of us is as good as he thinks he is. Yet, in a series of vain attempts to recapture a youth long gone by, the floors of our closets are full of tennis shoes, basketball shoes (one pair for indoor and one for outdoor courts), and multiple pairs of running shoes (road trainers, trail shoes, and racers). The irony is that fifty years ago when we engaged in those same three activities, we each only had one pair of shoes—the iconic Chuck Taylors. That's all anyone had. Joel recently visited the Basketball Hall of Fame and saw the NBA all-time leading scorer Kareem Abdul-Jabbar's Chuck Taylors on display.

Then came the transformational year 1972, and Phil Knight, in partnership with the University of Oregon track coach Bill Bowerman, introduced the Nike Waffle shoe, so named because its sole looked like it came out of a waffle iron. At about the same time, Adidas introduced the now iconic Stan Smith tennis shoe, and the world of athletic footwear was never the same again. Models and designs proliferated. The market was no longer a "one size fits all." Different athletes needed different things from their shoes. Some companies, like Babolat for tennis and And1 for basketball, even tied themselves to one and only one sport.

Lindblad was focused on delivering exploration-type experiences but needed to further "specialize" to effectively differentiate. By teaming up with National Geographic, it can now offer exploration-type experiences guided by an authentic scientist, and aboard a Lindblad expedition ship the photographer who helps the guests take pictures of breaching whales is the same photographer who shot the whale picture for the cover of the magazine.

CNN finds itself in the same circumstance. If CNN is going to remain a premier provider, it has to make sure that it has the free digital Internet component. To maintain its reputation, it also has to keep its core business strong, which is being able to report from the small villages where news happens around the world. CNN's goal must be to figure out how to make digital content so irresistible that it will be seen as a must-have service in each and every medium that consumers use to access the news. This will require a significant shift in its content model: to find a way to create relevant news stories for a generation that has different expectations from content while keeping in mind what CNN really is—journalists bringing the public the inside story.

Lesson #3. Update your marketing to conform to and reflect current social norms. This is hardly new, but it is still worth saying. Cheerios updated the people in its advertising to reflect current family structures (e.g., interracial couples), which is the kind of thing that keeps iconic brands relevant for decades. Betty Crocker has evolved through the years. In 1936, her personification had pursed lips, a hard stare, and graying hair. Today, reflecting a different social norm and the role of women in America, she doesn't look a day over thirty-five. Her image is that of a young professional woman who uses Betty Crocker products to save time without sacrificing quality. Coca-Cola has kept its brand iconic by associating with some of the most wholesome American cultural images of its time, from Norman Rockwell to Santa Claus to Kit Carson to Eddie Fisher to Ozzie and Harriet to Bill Cosby. Bill Cosby? Did we say wholesome? Well (LOL), we thought so anyway!

Lesson #4. Shift involves more than meets the eye. Remember that Alfa Romeo that we alluded to at the chapter's outset? That car that Dustin Hoffman shifted so wonderfully driving on the California highways had a lot going on under the hood. To shift gears there is a complex transmission with an intricate mechanism linking it to the shift in the car. Similarly, when Dustin Hoffman uses the steering wheel to turn and change direction, it is not only the wheel that has to work. There is a steering column, axle, and wheel alignment that have to function as well. It is obvious that IBM's shift from manufacturing to service and Comcast's shift from signal transmission to signal delivery require huge changes under the hood, so to speak,

However, less drastic shifts often involve large-scale retooling. The changes in promoting Cheerios are more the exception than the rule. For example, in 2010 Red Lobster was positioned around high value. The restaurant chain implemented numerous promotions of the "all you can eat" variety. Spurred by some informative marketing research, the company's CEO, Kim Lopdrup, decided to shift its positioning from value to freshness and an upscale quality.[22] Gone were the specials; gone were the fried shrimp; and gone were the freezers that stored frozen items. In their place were new wood plank ovens, new higher-end chefs, new procurement processes, more knowledgeable servers, and renovated restaurants resembling something you would find on the New England coast. Red Lobster did not change industry (it is still a casual, table-service restaurant) and it did not even change the sector that it competes in (seafood). Yet the engine under the hood got a complete overhaul. If you think about the complexity behind what seems to be a minor repositioning, then what is involved behind the IBM and Comcast shifts defies imagination.

Lesson #5. Sometimes the best moves are the ones you do not make. Jake Dell and his family have been very cautious in shifting from the core Lower East Side restaurant. They had numerous opportunities, including Las Vegas hotels. They declined all of them largely because the opportunities did not respect Katz's DNA. Furthermore, as the previous point highlighted, shifts require resources, even those that are simply shifts in positioning. Firms should not undertake anything that will absorb too many resources, either people or money. For instance, Barnes & Noble might be in a better position today had it not chased after the tablet business with its Nook, defraying costs, and instead doubled down on figuring out how to make its core retail business work more effectively.

7

LEADERSHIP

In earlier chapters, we illustrated why shifting is so hard, what to do to get ready to shift, and some principles to ensure that the execution of the shift goes according to plan. It takes an extraordinary individual to be able to overcome the obstacles as well as to prepare and successfully execute a meaningful shift. This chapter highlights some of the individuals that fit the bill.

The lay business practitioner often uses the word *vision* to describe the essential characteristic that a leader must have to execute a successful shift. The management literature defines vision along the lines of a strong belief by the manager about the future and the right course of action for the firm or, more simply, as future images of the collective.[1] Such a definition confines vision to forecasting and decision making. We do not believe this characterization captures what is truly required. What is required is a very deep understanding of customers, their problems, how such problems can be solved, how technological advances enable alternative solutions, how organizations can provide alternative solutions using existing and new technology, and how technological advances might differentially impact different competitors. We feel that *peripheral vision* describes this trait much more than mere vision does. Peripheral vision is seeing the broader landscape, seeing the context, seeing both the big picture and the details. It means developing a sensitivity to the ecosystem in which the organization operates. To have peripheral vision requires getting out of the bubble. As we alluded to in Chapter 5, it's hard to see the broader landscape from behind a desk in a corner office, no matter how high that office might be.

Much of the conventional wisdom on leadership, and strategy in general, comes from what has been written by and about the military. Anyone who has seen Michael Douglas's Oscar-winning performance in the movie *Wall Street* will surely remember Gordon Gekko's reliance on *The Art of War* by Sun Tzu for inspiration.

Ed Vick, the former chairman of Young & Rubicam advertising, whose duty in Vietnam earned him two Bronze Stars and a presidential citation, described his combat experience as the spectrum through which he has looked at everything since. "It changed my life," he says. Vick was a naval officer commanding riverboats on more than 100 missions along the Mekong Delta. Almost all of the men manning the fiberglass crafts were volunteers. Their mission was to prevent the Viet Cong from using the Delta to infiltrate Saigon. Half of the men were either killed or wounded in action.

During our conversation on what makes for good leadership in times of market evolution and corporate turnarounds, Vick rendered his opinion that it all comes down to leadership. He said, "I saw it in the military and it's true in business. There are certain leadership characteristics that are more apt to successfully turn around a company. One of my first talks about leadership started out with, 'What do you learn on a small fiberglass boat when you're attacked by a numerically superior force in the middle of the night and, by the way, your boat just took a rocket and you're sinking?' In that kind of situation, you learn to be decisive under pressure, you learn teamwork. You learn courage under fire. Courage under fire is an overstatement when it comes to business, but staying calm under pressure is a gigantic quality of leadership," Vick said.

"In the military, like in business," he said, "you have a mission you are trying to accomplish; only the stakes are higher. The stakes are literally your life, and you go about it and you do it and it's like nothing else. This translates phenomenally into business, and it gets you thinking about problems differently. For example, I learned that you never ask anyone to do what you wouldn't do. It's so common in business where leaders say, 'Do this or do that,' but people want to see the leader actually do that stuff. You can only lead from the front." Vick described his top ten leadership attributes as follows:

- Have vision.
- Think laterally.
- Embrace change.
- Pick the right team.
- Trust your instincts.
- Be tolerant but human.
- Give the credit. Take the blame.
- Be cool under fire.
- Make tough calls.
- Be decisive.

The ability of a leader to engineer a shift successfully has two components. First, of course, there must be peripheral vision. However, peripheral vision by itself will not get it done. Effective leaders must have the temperament and personality that makes others want to follow. In Ed Vick's list, it is fair to say that the first five characteristics on the list go to enhancing ecological sensitivity; the remaining five characteristics go more to temperament and personality.

Recently, management scholars have built a literature on the personal characteristics that make effective leaders. This literature is inextricably tied to the idea of shifting ahead simply because that's what leaders do. They make changes, or at least they look to make changes. Those in charge of organizations that are reluctant to change are not leaders; they are caretakers. The literature uncovers several personal and professional characteristics that are correlated with leadership success and the ability of organizations to shift. These include the variables in Table 7-1.

FIRM PERFORMANCE

Observable Characteristics

- Intelligent leaders are likely to produce success.
- Leadership tenure increases the likelihood of improved firm performance, up to a point. Overall, the tenure performance relationship resembles an inverted U.
- Being embedded in firm social networks has negative implications for firm performance.

Personality Characteristics

- Charismatic leaders inspire followers.
- The ability to tolerate uncertainty opens the door to greater performance.
- Leaders who embrace diversity in their teams enhance firm performance.
- A leader's willingness to empower followers leads to better results.
- The ability of a leader to engage in paradoxical cognition increases the likelihood of enhanced performance.

ABILITY TO SHIFT

Observable Characteristics

- Leaders with a history of career variety are more likely to produce organizational change.

Personality Characteristics

- The tendency to experience positively activated emotions in general, such as excitement, high energy, joy, enthusiasm, and exhilaration, leads to strategies that differ from those previously seen in the industry.
- Self-confidence is likely to lead to strategic change.
- Collectivist values in leaders lead to innovative culture.
- The ability of a leader to engage in paradoxical cognition increases the likelihood of greater innovation.

Table 7-1. Leader characteristics related to firm performance and ability to shift.

Source: Adapted from Philip Bromiley and Devaki Rau, "Social, Behavioral, and Cognitive Influences on Upper Echelons During Strategy Process: A Literature Review," *Journal of Management* 42, no. 1 (January 2016), 174–202.

For example, high on the list of personal characteristics of what enhances a leader's ability to enlist the loyalty and passion of followers is charisma. Charismatic leadership has been one of the most actively studied areas in management literature for the past twenty-five years. The consensus (until recently) has been that charisma has been effective in mobilizing, motivating, and inspiring followers.[2] Recent scholarship has found a few holes in the theory, but not enough to discredit it.[3]

Some of the characteristics in Table 7-1 clearly feed into the ability to develop ecosystem sensitivity; some feed into the ability of leaders to attract followers; and some do both. For example, career variety likely enhances ecosystem sensitivity; charisma leads to the ability to attract followers; and the tendency to experience positively activated emotions likely feeds into both. In particular, joy and excitement in one's work would both stimulate creative thinking and attract followers.

The list in Table 7-1 greatly overlaps with Ed Vick's. The ability to tolerate uncertainty and embrace diversity go hand in hand with embracing change; willingness to empower and collectivist values go hand in hand with accepting blame and giving credit; and self-confidence leads to making tough calls, being decisive, and being cool under fire.

In any case, the leaders discussed in the following stories exemplify many of these characteristics.

JOHN SEXTON:
New York University (NYU)

John Sexton served as the fifteenth president of New York University from 2002 to 2015. His professional credentials are remarkable. He began as a professor of religion at Saint Francis College in Brooklyn, where he was the department chair from 1970 to 1975. He earned a Ph.D. in Religion from Fordham University in 1978 and a J.D. from the Harvard Law School in 1979. Chief Justice Warren Burger employed President Sexton as a law clerk from 1980 to 1981. Prior to becoming NYU's president, Sexton was the dean of the NYU Law School and held that role from 1988 to 2002. From 2003 to 2006, he was also the Chairman of the Board of the Federal Reserve Bank of New York. In 2009, *Time* magazine ranked him as the nation's number-two university president.

John Sexton is a big bear of a man. Smiles are never far from his face. He even greets you with a hug instead of a handshake. One gets the impression that when he meets you, he likes you . . . and you like him. A person would really have to give him a reason not to like him. As the management literature suggests, Sexton's ability to experience positively activated emotions would be a great help in NYU's "shift."

Indeed, one of Sexton's basic values is that he trusts people instinctively. Stemming from his being raised as a devout Catholic and receiving a strong Jesuit education, Sexton describes this value as a "spirituality of hope," a secular ecumenicism, if you will. In fact, as will become self-evident, religion and Jesuit philosophy played a strong role in John Sexton's leadership of NYU. Sexton describes secular ecumenicism as "the intellectual process of viewing the world not through the view you were born with—be it religious or secular—but the many facets of a diamond or windows of a mansion." As a result of this philosophy, he deals with other people by embracing the many differences between them and him. Embracing diversity is one of the traits listed in Table 7-1. He tries to put himself in their place and, by assuming they are of good will, works to understand their viewpoint. There is no such thing as truth with a capital "T," in the sense that it is beyond examination.

Some people find it hard to listen to critics: not John Sexton, the secular ecumenist. He views it as essential that one reflect on what critics are saying. Indeed, their viewpoints must be embraced as part of the tapestry of what a university is and what it should be.

When one embraces diversity, it becomes easier to embrace change. In a study of the semiconductor industry, Professor Warren Boeker, now of the University of Washington, found that diversity in top management teams led to greater strategic change.[4] Consistent with these results, the ecumenist who makes a point of embracing inclusion and diversity becomes a more likely shift agent. Such was John Sexton.

Sexton's religious beliefs led him to the conclusion that, since he was a talented individual, he had the obligation to live a useful life. NYU became the focus of that useful life. Indeed, many leaders bring a sense of spirituality to their work and try to infuse it into the organization and the colleagues that work in it.[5]

Although he surrounded himself with many talented people (e.g., Jack Lew, Cheryl Mills), John Sexton described *his* personal unique talent as "storytelling." A leader asks people to recognize and embrace his beliefs about the organization and its future. These beliefs represent the organization's "mythos," a deeply felt truth that is difficult (but not impossible) to put into words. Being a good storyteller enables the leader to express his mythos. If others do not recognize the mythos, they cannot embrace it. This will surely inhibit any intended shift. When John Sexton became NYU's fifteenth president, he had to decide what his "mythos" was and how he was going to tell the story that reflected it—and it had to be good.

The first step in this adventure was the development of what the Jesuits call the *ratio studiorum*. Marketers call it the value proposition. What is the purpose or value? The *ratio studiorum* guides everything: what classes the university offers, how they are offered, whether the university has big-time athletics. All of it traces back to the *ratio studiorum*. The story had to reflect the enhancement of the *ratio studiorum*.

When Dean Sexton became President Sexton in 2002, NYU was in a precarious position. The university had made significant progress and had pockets of excellence, such as the Law School, the Institute of Fine Arts, and the Courant Institute of Mathematical Sciences. However, NYU had ambitions to become what academics call a leadership university. At the same time, NYU was not in a favorable financial situation to make it happen. Its debt was four times its endowment; its per capita endowment was about $15,000 (Harvard's, Yale's, and Princeton's were all in excess of $2 million). NYU was more in danger of falling from relevance than it was likely to fulfill its ambitions. Any strategy that would propel the university to leadership status could not depend on monetary assets. NYU had to discover its *ratio studiorum*.

In addition to storytelling, Sexton had the skill to derive the story. He had the ability to see the lay of the land in a unique way. It was not hard to see that technology would be a change agent in education, but

Sexton had a knack of getting insight by, as he said, "getting his hands dirty." When he was the law school dean, he attended conferences that were run by and for the benefit of schools ranked quite a bit below NYU. His thinking was that these schools were having problems that NYU and others would soon encounter.

Indeed, this approach resembles one reflected in our conversation with another one of our interviewees, Amy Webb, one of the nation's leading futurists and our colleague at NYU. Amy's philosophy is that the future arrives piece by piece. It begins in what she calls "the fringes" and then migrates to mainstream. Sexton's ability to get his hands dirty in the fringes would be helpful in deriving the *ratio studiorum* that would form the basis of NYU's story.

NYU may have been poor, but New York City is an asset that few universities can match. Inspired by New York City's eventually unsuccessful bid for the 2012 Olympics, which integrated the Games and new venues into the fabric of New York (and was part of the "fringes" of NYU), Sexton found NYU's *ratio studiorum* as well as its DNA, New York City and what it represents. The bid portrayed New York City as a microcosm of the world. NYU, then, is embedded in a microcosm of the world. It has no campus, no gates, no borders. Part of it used to be in the Bronx. At the time, the center was in Greenwich Village, but the university was putting down a footprint in Brooklyn. If NYU was "in and of New York City," it was in and of the world. As such, NYU was uniquely positioned to offer scholars and students access to a truly global education. It would exemplify ecumenism by embracing all parts of the world, all viewpoints, all cultures. Based on the DNA, New York City and what it represents, this positioning became the story; it was the "mythos"; this was, as Plato would have said, John Sexton's "idea of the good." NYU was to shift from being a very good university rooted in the tristate area to becoming a global ecumenical university with Greenwich Village as its capital.

Sexton reasoned that there would be students who came to NYU from certain parts of the country who had probably never had a Chinese meal. Living in New York afforded them the opportunity to take a subway down to Chinatown and have some of the most authentic Chinese food the country had to offer. That's wonderful, but it would be better to send them to Shanghai to study. That notion led Sexton to look for potential study sites around the globe. Today, NYU students have the opportunity to spend time not only in New York, but in the following locations as well:

- Abu Dhabi, United Arab Emirates
- Accra, Ghana
- Berlin, Germany
- Buenos Aires, Argentina
- Florence, Italy
- London, England
- Madrid, Spain
- Paris, France
- Prague, Czech Republic
- Shanghai, China
- Sydney, Australia
- Tel Aviv, Israel
- Washington, D.C.

Two of these locations, Abu Dhabi and Shanghai, have developed into full-fledged portal campuses. These are the first "idea capitals." Sexton saw this as a way not only to fulfill the *ratio studiorum*, but to elevate quality by attracting superior talent, both in drawing students from other parts of the world and making the school more attractive to star faculty. Making the NYU brand more accessible to students in other parts of the world opened up the university to a group of talented young men and women that would not have considered NYU but for the location. In fact, NYU-Shanghai is the only American university licensed in China. The degree counts in China.

Sexton contends that NYU-Abu Dhabi is the best school in the world. It has produced three graduating classes with 600 students. Out of those 600, six have become Rhodes scholars. Kids come from Queens; kids come from tribal villages. Ninety percent of those offered admission accept. Applicants turn down Harvard and Oxford to attend NYU-Abu Dhabi.

With respect to faculty recruiting, Sexton views the structural endowment of multiple campuses as a lure for star faculty. He told the story of a Yale scientist who contemplated returning to his home in China after thirty years in the United States. Sexton would just call him up and ask, "Why do you have to choose? Come to NYU and you can have both worlds!"

When the critics got harsh, as they inevitably did, the former university president retreats not to Twitter, but to the religiously inspired belief that crucifixion for a good cause was a worthy life. In leading NYU through the last fourteen years, John Sexton received a lot of criticism alleging fiscal irresponsibility, lack of inclusion, and cooperating with a government (the Emirates) that did not have a positive record on human rights. Anyone who paid attention knew that he was anything but noninclusive. Anyway, inspired by his faith, John Sexton was very cool under fire. He simply waited out the firestorm and proceeded with the mission. Ed Vick would have approved.

As a result of his foresight shaped by his personal values, his religious background formed by his Jesuit training, his belief in ecumenism, and his ability to tell stories that reflected that foresight, not to mention the force of his personality in connecting with people, John Sexton has transformed New York University into the world's only global network university. NYU today is very much the product of John Sexton. Because of Sexton, it is well positioned to maintain a status as one of the world's leading universities.

When we met, Joel thanked Sexton for all the work he did to bring about the changes in the university that brought along with it an increase in stature. Sexton offered a correction. "The work *we* did," he said. Indeed, that is the kind of message that strong leaders give, the vision of a future for the collective.[6] He gives credit (and takes blame). Joel did nothing really. He was just a foot soldier. John did everything.

Of course, NYU's journey was and remains a risky venture. Sexton relayed a conversation he had with his late wife, Lisa, where she expressed the belief that NYU was the best university in the world that could attempt the transition to a global network university. Harvard wouldn't; Yale wouldn't. It would be too much of a risk for them. But for a school seeking a category change, seeking to elevate its status, risk was an imperative. Sexton accepted the uncertainty, even acknowledging that he thought there was only a 60 percent chance that it would work. It has so far.

SHELLY LAZARUS:
Ogilvy & Mather—Leading the People Who Build Leading Brands

David Ogilvy was one of the most influential and well-respected people in the advertising industry. In 1948, starting with no clients and a staff of two, Ogilvy founded the agency that would become Ogilvy & Mather. He built his company into one of the eight largest marketing firms in the world. Today, it has more than 450 offices in 169 cities around the world.

From the very beginning, Ogilvy intended to build a different kind of company. An expert in branding, he knew that he would need to build a strong *agency* brand. He captured that brand with the snippet, "Only first-class business, and that in a first-class way." The DNA of Ogilvy & Mather was the quality and the diversity of the people, and the quality and the class of the operation. Over time, Ogilvy & Mather has helped to build some of the most recognizable brands in the world, among them American Express, Ford, Nestlé, Maxwell House, Dove, Ponds, and IBM.

In 2016, *Adweek* selected Ogilvy & Mather as its 2016 Global Agency of the year. *Adweek* cited Ogilvy's range of creative diversity as a key reason for its win. *Adweek* attributed the success of Ogilvy's work to its consistency in talent development and leadership.

You can see where we're going with this. In the almost seventy years since its founding, Ogilvy & Mather's dedication to talent development and leadership continues to keep it at the head of the class in a first-class way. And it was about talent development, among other things, that we spoke to Shelly Lazarus, who spent forty-plus years at the company, most recently as CEO and chairman of Ogilvy & Mather Worldwide, and then chairman emeritus. She saw the agency through two complex shifts, each a consequence of a fast-shifting marketing landscape. First, she helped broaden the organization's scope from an ad agency that did primarily general advertising as a way to support client efforts to one that offered a full range of communication and branding tools, including direct marketing, public relations, and promotions. Then, with the advent of the Internet age, she presided over Ogilvy's shift into the world of digital marketing, helping it to become among the first adopters—and adapters—in this ever-burgeoning field.

In their attempt to make even one of these shifts—the move from general advertising to integrated marketing or from analog to digital—many of Ogilvy's former competitors fell to the wayside. How did Ogilvy not just survive these shifts, but orchestrate them so successfully?

"As David said to me, 'It's always and only about the people,'" Lazarus told us when we spoke. "This was the most meaningful advice I received from him. It's about the people—the people we serve, our clients, and nurturing the relationships that help us drive their business forward. In terms of the clients, doing what's right for them means staying curious. To bring the right solutions to clients, it will not be of sufficient value unless you start with the right questions and really listen to the answer. I'll give you an example," she said. "I met once a month with the head of sales at IBM specifically to hear what the sales force needed, what was valuable to them in their interactions with *their* customers. I didn't just sit down and ask him if he liked a specific piece of advertising but, rather, what things were driving the business. I'd say, 'Tell me what you want to have happen. What do you want your respective customer to think as a result of seeing your marketing? What do you want them to do?' You have to get a real sense, get to the root cause, of the problem they're trying to solve before you can offer up a solution."

It's been our experience that all great ad people are inherently curious. To succeed, as Lazarus did, you *do* have to be motivated to ask the right question and be passionate about getting to the "so what?" Inherent curiosity, and the ability to listen, *really* listen and hear what was being said, were both key leadership skills that enabled Lazarus to build long-term relationships with agency clients. They also enabled her to successfully manage the shifts in agency composition that were required to stay relevant to these clients. Back to David Ogilvy's advice to her, what made these shifts so very challenging was not necessarily getting a handle on the newest resources and tools of the trade, be it technology or otherwise, but getting a handle on the people who could most effectively and efficiently leverage these new resources for the benefit of the clients. The mitigating factor that made Ogilvy & Mather's shifts so complex had to do with people, not the processes. It's easy to build a new manufacturing plant, install the latest robotics, or shift your operations to deal with the new realities of your category. Lazarus had to manage a shift in her workforce.

Ultimately, the trick to making a shift in a business where people are your competitive advantage is that you either have to be able to get your people to evolve, or you have to go out and find the right people. Leading an organization through the types of transformation Lazarus faced posed a very huge risk to the culture. The unique and powerful culture created by David Ogilvy *was*, in fact, the company's core competitive advantage. It was a culture that allowed them to produce better solutions for their clients—better than many competitors. That Lazarus was passionate about protecting this culture was important. That she possessed the deliberate and strategic—and very objective—leadership qualities required to deal with the employee aspect of the shift was equally important.

"The biggest challenge of all is moving people on," she explained. "It is the people who become completely comfortable in an environment that is fast receding and being able to provide the environment where they can move along and develop new skills. Not all of them can, or want to, do this. At a certain point, you have to make a decision and say, 'Okay, these people are brilliant at creating television commercials. Do we keep them because they are great at this, and hope for the best, hope that they can broaden their outlook?' You find there are people who resent being asked to move out of their comfort zones. At some point you've got to say we need people who are going to come up with ideas that are brilliant at their core and can then figure out how to make them work through whatever channel meets the client's objectives.

You've got to move on to people who are excited by new challenges. This was the hardest part of our transitions."

As Lazarus made clear to us, sure, you can *say* you want to shift an organization. But you need people who are able to shift with you. Easy in theory. Hard in execution. Lazarus was able to do so in a way that teed up the organization for future success. She clearly used her acute listening skills, asked difficult questions, gleaned nuances and subtexts in the answers, and made some difficult decisions in order to shift the company without destroying its long-standing and venerated culture. It was a culture she had grown up in, lived in, was comfortable in. Just as she was comfortable "in her own skin," as she put it when we asked about other leadership traits she believed were critical to success. "David's imprint on the company was deep," she said. "He established the culture that still exists today. Among my challenges was to lead this company, through all its iterations, in the spirit of the founder. This meant feeling comfortable in your own skin, being true to yourself, not pretending to be someone you're not. When you're leading people toward something important, losing your authenticity is the last thing you want to do."

As a good leader, what Lazarus also understood was that purposeful change takes time. She was determined in her efforts, but strategic enough to systematically make the reforms and adjustments required. Shifting from a pure-play agency to a marketing communications firm for the digital age was, literally, a marathon effort. She explained to us that, as a leader, she had to be willing, patient enough, and forward-thinking enough to make investments that didn't have short-term results. As she told us, "You want to sit down once a year and think about what you want to accomplish over the next period of time. I would actually have a small piece of paper sitting on my desk on which I wrote the five big things I wanted to accomplish over the next twelve months. To manage my time properly, I would think which of the multiple activities on a given day's to-do list would have an impact on achieving these big things. There's a challenge in not letting yourself get caught up in the day-to-day fires. I'd keep my five key goals front and center on my desk to make sure I stayed focused."

CENTRAL PARK:
Holding People Accountable—
and Getting Your Own Hands Dirty

Douglas Blonsky understood that you *can't* just snap your fingers and make change happen. For almost twenty years, Douglas Blonsky has led the efforts to make—and keep—Central Park the marvelous centerpiece of Manhattan that it is today. Enjoyed by millions of the city's residents along with visitors from around the world, Central Park is, more than 100 years after its founding as America's first major landscaped public park, among the nation's most cherished. That it went through a period of terrible decline is pretty well known. Less well known is how Blonsky led a diverse group of constituents to take Central Park from its lowest point to its highest, both in condition and reputation.

In 1853, the New York State Legislature set aside more than 750 acres of land in central Manhattan and selected two landscape architects, Frederick Law Olmsted and Calvert Vaux, to turn the tract into a great urban park that would "improve public health and contribute greatly to the formation of a civil society." By the early-twentieth century, changes in the social, economic, and political climate combined to send the park into its first serious decline. Robert Moses, park commissioner from 1934 to 1960, received federal funding for many of the eroded landscapes and crumbling structures and took on substantial public programming as a result. When he left office, however, there was no management strategy in place for seeing these improvements through, let alone for educating park visitors about responsible treatment of the natural treasure. For the next two decades, the second and most destructive decline took place.

As stated on the Central Park Conservancy website:

Physically the park was in a chronic state of decay. Meadows had become barren dustbowls; benches, lights, and playground equipment were broken, and the one-hundred-year-old infrastructure was crumbling. Socially, the park bred a careless, even abusive attitude towards the park evidenced by unchecked amounts of garbage, graffiti, and vandalism. Positive use had been displaced by illicit and illegal activity. The perception—and, in many cases, the reality—of Central Park was of a lawless and dangerous ruin. Despite a workforce of over three hundred Parks Department employees assigned to Central Park, there was no accountability. New York City had abdicated their responsibility as Park stewards and, as a result, this national treasure became a national disgrace.

To the rescue came George Soros and Richard Gilder, who underwrote a management study of the situation led by E. S. Savas, a Columbia University professor.[7] The groundbreaking study proposed that two major organizational changes be implemented: one, that a chief executive officer be given authority for park operations, and two, that a Central Park Board of Guardians be created to oversee strategic planning and policy, instituting a way for private citizens to become involved in their public park. In 1979, Betsy Barlow (now Rogers), a Yale-educated urban planner, took on the role of administrator, overseeing all aspects of Central Park's daily operations. It was during her tenure that she created a public/private partnership with the support of then Park Commissioner Gordon Davis, allowing private monies to be donated to the park's restoration. In 1980, the two prominent private advocacy groups the Central Park Task Force and the Central Park Community Fund merged to become the Central Park Conservancy. Under a Conservancy-funded master plan, the gradual restoration of Central Park began to take shape and, as a result of its early and significant successes, more private individuals, foundations, and corporations put their trust—and their money—into the further restoration and maintenance of the park.

In 1998, the Conservancy and the City of New York formalized a management agreement. With this agreement, Blonsky, who began his career in 1985 as a landscape architect, took over from Rogers and assumed the title of park administrator. In 2004, he assumed the additional role of CEO and president of the Conservancy, responsible for not only management of Central Park, but also fundraising. Under his leadership, the Conservancy has made an even greater shift toward becoming the benchmark for innovative practices in green urban spaces. We had the good fortune to be able to talk to Blonsky about his work in this role, and to glean some insight as to what it takes to shift a nonprofit organization with a diverse group of very involved constituents. We also were delighted to be able to gain additional perspective on Blonsky's initiatives from Steve Zammarchi, a former advertising agency executive and founding advisory board member of the Central Park Conservancy Institute for Urban Parks, who took on the role of the Conservancy's chief creative officer.

"I'll never forget when I first met Doug," Zammarchi told us. "He walked into my office wearing a sports jacket and a tie, but he also had on a baseball cap and sneakers, and his sneakers were covered with dirt. And right away, he credentialed himself. He was folksy, but I knew he knew his stuff. He didn't walk in like some banker, but like a guy who spends his days walking through the park talking to the women's committee volunteers about the flowers, the gardeners about what type of grass will stand up to a lot of foot traffic, the maintenance people about the playgrounds. He's the personification of the brand. Yet he can go toe-to-toe with the business folks he deals with, the people who write the checks, because they know that their money will be well used. On top of his landscape expertise," Zammarchi said, "Doug has a record of accountability. He has a proven track record for giving people responsibility to get things done and making them accountable for their actions."

Zammarchi went on to tell us the story about the day a large group from Alcoa, one of the largest aluminum suppliers in the world, came into Central Park as part of the Conservancy's Day-in-the-Dirt program, where companies bring in employees to work "in the dirt" as a way to build corporate camaraderie, yes, but also to give back to the city. According to Zammarchi, the CEO of Alcoa picked up a microphone and, after cheering on his troops and thanking them for their efforts, chided Blonsky for the fact that the garbage cans in Central Park were made of plastic.

"Doug, because he knows the park and all the issues it faces, turns directly to the Alcoa CEO, thanks him for his employees' efforts, and says, 'You know, if someone were to give us trash cans made of recycled aluminum, it would be a lot better for the park.' The next day he received a grant for several hundred thousand dollars to do that. Those trash cans eventually became the platform for a successful recycling program at the park. He's just that kind of engaging guy," said Zammarchi. "He can talk to anyone with great passion and sincerity about anything having to do with his vision for the Conservancy."

Blonsky had—and *has*—a clear vision for Central Park, a key factor in his being able to continue to shift its fortunes forward as its leader. Over the past several years, he has created innovative management practices to ensure that the landscape would continue to be tended in a skilled and professional manner. More than this, to put his words into action relative to the need for accountability, he implemented what is called the Zone Management System, which provides not just clear and measurable results for park preservation, but instills a pride of workmanship—and ownership—in those who are employed by, or volunteer at, the Conservancy.

"I think accountability is one of the biggest things for us," Blonsky told us. "Betsy Rogers was the first accountable person for the park. Before that, the buck didn't stop anywhere. Someone would bring in a tree crew to do tree work. Then they'd leave. There was no one in charge of mechanics, of infrastructure, of long-term planning. Luckily, the need for administrative oversight was one of the first things that came out in the study we did many years ago. Betsy took the first step, and then I took the next step in further bringing accountability to the landscape level. That was the whole Zone Management System, whereby we assigned a specific person to 'own' a specific area of the park, from the garbage cans to graffiti, to the condition of the gardens, to the walkways, to the playgrounds."

As Blonsky explained, he literally sat down with his team and mapped out the total geography of Central Park, determining what made sense, size-wise, in the assignment of areas. They eventually came up with breaking things up into forty-nine zones, each with a designated individual accountable for the conditions in that zone. "Each person was given responsibility for learning about the landscape they oversaw, the traffic flow, [and] how those who lived in the neighborhoods nearby one zone or another made use of the park. The first couple of years it was pretty difficult. But, slowly, every year things improved and improved and improved," he said. "Connecting accountability to a space is a very simple concept, and eventually those in charge felt a real sense of ownership that was terrific. You're in charge of everything in your zone. If you see a branch that needs cutting down, or a garbage can that's overflowing, or graffiti that needs to be removed, you have the power to do something about it, and we provide the resources to see that it gets done."

Splitting the park into zones and giving people accountability for their own "backyards" induced friendly competitions between groundskeepers, gardeners, and volunteers in one zone versus another. Those in the East 84th Street zone would compare what they were doing against those in the West 96th Street zone. As such, empowerment, purpose, and personal pride translated into executional excellence through personal accountability.

As a landscape architect, Blonsky understood both the strategic and the implementation aspects of what had to get accomplished. Blonsky had credibility, on the level necessary, with each of his constituent groups. "You can't run a park from an office," he said. "I think a big thing for me, what's really unique about my job, is the variety of people I have to deal with. From dog walkers, to the Zone techs, to billionaire fundraisers, to the mayor of the city. For many, having to make such a diverse group of people happy could lead to analysis paralysis. The answer is, I just keep meeting with people, talking to them. The fact is, I know what I'm doing. I've got a sensitivity to, and understanding of, what it takes to manage a public park. To me, everyone involved in the process is important. I've learned that you can turn people around by making it clear that my objective is to make the park work for what I call 'the person on the bench.' The senior citizen who wants to sit quietly and read the paper. The guy or girl who comes in to sit and just watch people walk by. The mother with the baby in the stroller. The woman who just lost her husband. This park is critical to their quality of life, to their mental well-being," Blonsky said. "It's the 80 percent, the non-vocal users. I keep in mind that it's not the loudest voice that is the most important."

As Blonsky makes evident, there is nothing more important to positive leadership than understanding the product (and the people who use the product) better than anyone else, and being able to make that clear through both words and actions. Blonsky knows his product. He can't be talked out of doing what's right for Central Park. He has purpose and the drive to continue to build and maintain a sustainable model for the park, knowing that he must take a long and deliberate view. He does not rest on his laurels and comes up with new innovations for the park. For example, he formalized the Central Park Conservancy Institute for Urban Parks, which serves as the educational arm of Central Park Conservancy, and provides environmental education for children and a variety of lectures and tours for adults. The Institute also shares the best practices in urban park management locally, nationally, and internationally so that others may enjoy their parks the way New York City residents and visitors appreciate Central Park. He genuinely walks the walk and talks the talk, building consensus among diverse groups, managing both up and down. He is a skilled listener and communicator to all constituents.

Blonsky and team accomplished all of the above over many years. What they built were best practices. Cities from all over the country and the world would come to the Conservancy to learn how to build and manage their own Central Park. Instead of sitting on his laurels, Blonsky laid the foundation for an institute so that these best practices could be handed down to the next generation. Blonsky is credible and trusted, and he continues to be effective in the ongoing shifting of the Central Park Conservancy because he knows his stuff from, well, the ground up.

FORBES MEDIA:
Adversity Was the Mother of Reinvention

"We were facing a true existential moment," Bruce Rogers, chief insights officer of Forbes Media, told us within the first few minutes of our conversation. "This was not a 'We need to think about a long-term strat-egy' situation. We knew we needed to do something very different, very quickly, or we'd slowly go out of business. The business model for the media industry was broken, and Forbes was at a tipping point. But, ad-versity is the mother of invention. It forces you to examine things."

There was no question to anyone that mobile technology was dra-matically transforming the way people around the globe consumed me-dia. People were fast abandoning news outlets that no longer served their needs. Anyone with a computer, a mobile phone, a tablet and a Twitter, Facebook, Instagram, or any other social media account expe-riences this new paradigm for information gathering every day. Millen-nials, who by 2020 will make up more than 50 percent of the workforce, have likely not spent much time with a print newspaper or news maga-zine. Elementary schoolchildren even less. That a tweet became the "news" dissemination channel of choice by a certain president of the United States is just one example of how this state of affairs is manifest-ing itself. According to studies from the Pew Research Center and Niel-sen Media Research, cable and network news have been in decline since the 1980s, with small boosts during election years.[8] Yesterday's paradigm was fast becoming obsolete, even for baby boomers who con-tinue to turn more and more to their smaller screens for news flashes that hit cyberspace not on the hour but by the minute. Examples of the effect of this shift in consumer behavior on analog news sources abound. To name just a few, in 2009, *BusinessWeek* was sold to Bloomberg. *Time* has laid off hundreds of staffers. The *Wall Street Journal* condensed the number of sections in its weekday print edition. And *Newsweek*, along with myriad newspapers, went to online-only platforms.

The fact of the matter in this case was that adversity was the mother of *reinvention* when it came to Forbes meeting the challenges of the analog-to-digital news media revolution. The company's leadership under CEO Mike Perlis was forced to examine the business model of the iconic publisher and come up with a sustainable business model that would not diminish the "success through visionary entrepreneur-ship" image of the brand, which was once so carefully cultivated by its founder, B. C. Forbes, and perhaps more famously so by his son,

Malcolm Forbes. What they did not only *elevated* the brand's standing in the media category, but demonstrated that those at the helm genuinely knew how to practice what the media company had long preached.

Leadership at this point in the history of Forbes—around 2010—was shared by several people: Mike Perlis, COO Timothy Forbes, Bruce Rogers, and Chief Product Officer Lewis DVorkin, who had rejoined Forbes after leaving to found True/Slant, a digital news network and a start-up that was acquired by Forbes and played an integral part in Forbes.com's transformation from a website to a publishing platform. Those in charge shared more than just a post at the helm. They shared two crucial character traits that enabled them to turn a long-standing and legacy media business model—advertising-supported print journalism—on its head.

First, those on the team had the ability not just to see the changes ahead in the media landscape, but to more astutely grasp the dire implications of what they saw coming at them than did the competition. This allowed them to identify not just what they should do, but what they *shouldn't* do. Second, they were willing to take the bold actions required to do what they had to do to stay relevant, as risky as these actions may have seemed to others in the industry.

Moving to an online-only platform did not, in and of itself, solve the problem. While media organizations may have looked down the road, many of them did not look with a wide enough or far-reaching enough lens. While they knew that digital was fast overtaking analog as a medium of choice, the general and immediate reaction was to simply put their print content online and call it a day. Using the Internet for reposting existing content, making it as a secondary distribution channel, posed a real monetization dilemma. That's because people consume media differently when they're online. They're in a different functional mode. They don't browse and consume advertising in the same way. For a majority of news companies, advertising revenue began to decline precipitously.

As if this weren't enough, a second—and collateral—problem resulted from the shortsightedness of many traditional news organizations: content *creation*. Consumer demand for more and new content, not just repurposed content, was steadily rising. And the competitive set for this content was steadily expanding. Long-standing content creators were now not only competing with an ever-widening array of formal sources for content, be it inherently online purveyors of news and information like the *Huffington Post, Politico, Google News,* and *Al Jazeera* or anyone and everyone with an Internet connection. It continues to be the case, more so than ever, that anyone can publish, edit, and republish information. However, even as many media organizations saw this development, they couldn't move fast enough, or their content creation initiatives were not sufficient enough, to meet the overwhelming challenge.

How, then, did the leadership at Forbes shift the paradigm to take on the interrelated challenges of monetization and content? They evolved Forbes.com into a publishing platform that allowed the bona fide full-time staff journalists along with a curated network of outside contributors—experts in different fields—to publish content on the site to their own home pages. The contributor platform enabled the Forbes brand to continue to provide quality writing while offering a variety of voices and increasing the content. At the same time, they also came up with an innovative way to generate revenue from advertisers.

As Rogers explained, "We shifted from a traditional staff-based, re-sourced content model to a contributor model. There would be a multitude of voices, all who had relevance in the marketplace. This allowed us to take advantage of the power of the *Forbes* name, but at the same time, change our cost structure dramatically, and [as] dramatically increase the amount of content in a world where search identifies the right content. Content equals audience—more and better content, a larger audience. Scale is critical. The business over the course of nearly 100 years had gone through many ebbs and flows, wildly successful under Malcolm. But then the disruption of the digital world was a huge challenge. By doing what we did, it was a pretty dramatic turnaround."

What's important to highlight here is that Timothy Forbes recognized that this bold effort was not something the organization could get up and running fast enough to outrun the evolving market. Time being of the essence, he and his team made the decision to first invest in DVorkin's True/Slant and then to acquire it, using its unique content creation capability as a catalyst to fundamentally change the Forbes business model without having to start from scratch. It was sort of like starting at the thirty-yard line versus the end zone.

Before rejoining Forbes after an initial stint there, DVorkin had pioneered and refined a system with True/Slant, in which contributors were compensated according to the visitors they attracted. Then, in what many saw as controversial but DVorkin saw as necessary, he also allowed marketers and brands, for a fee, to publish their thought leadership marketing content on Forbes.com, transparently labeled "Brand-Voice," the company's name for sponsored content. DVorkin understood that content engines needed to be continuously reconfigured to match the trifecta of audience, device, and context, which was critical to the eventual success of the venture. DVorkin had also previously worked at Forbes and understood the culture, which was also critical to the preservation of the brand's equality.

After years of working as a writer and editor at some of America's best-known publications, DVorkin was in the perfect position to identify a sustainable business model for advertising-supported journalism. Under DVorkin's leadership as chief product officer, Forbes departed radically from the path taken by most magazines and newspapers online, contracting with more than 2,000 contributors (authors, academics, business leaders, and freelance journalists, among others) who write posts, load them into the Forbes.com content management system, and hit "publish." Each contributor writes on a specific topic and is supervised by a channel editor. A team of producers is constantly monitoring the content on the platform for quality control. Onboarding contributors, together with opening its site to marketers, was a strategy that enabled Forbes to monetize its efforts. From 2010 to 2017, unique monthly visitors rose from 15 million to a record 56 million. "We have channels, such as technology, investing, entrepreneurs, and at the head of every channel is a Forbes editor who has worked for the company for ten or twenty years," DVorkin says. "They are responsible, along with a producer or two, for their contributors."[9]

Take the example of Forbes's technology coverage: There's a channel editor who's responsible for the overall content as well as full-time staffers and contributors who publish to the technology channel. This channel editor works with a deputy editor who's responsible for quality control, recruiting new contributors and the general voice of that channel. Then there's a senior producer who works with new contributors on their particular beat—making sure they stay focused on that beat and resolving any content questions or issues with contributor content. Forbes also has a producer who helps contributors understand how to use the publishing tools and to answer questions they have about producing content on Forbes.com. Both producers monitor content closely after it's been published to make sure it lives up to Forbes's quality standards.

In response to those who saw this move as anathema to journalistic ethics, DVorkin replied, "Journalists believe they are the protectors of the audience. There are great skills that journalists bring to the game, whether or not this is on Forbes.com, but there are also the skills of experts," referring to Forbes.com's contributors and marketers who can serve as domain experts. "The result of these efforts—a high-quality, scalable, and efficient model for journalism—enables Forbes to provide its readers with more comprehensive and in-depth coverage on myriad news and business topics."[10] (In the spirit of transparency, one of this book's authors, Allen, is a contributor to Forbes.com, writing about the intersection of branding and cultural trends.)

"We did the unthinkable in content creation," Rogers told us. "We said we are going to carefully vet and select experts to create content for Forbes, as long as it goes through a Forbes filter and quality control. As a result, we have a stronger, more robust content engine. Tim had the foresight and realized the business model needed changing. He saw an interesting contributor platform DVorkin had developed and bought it and integrated it into Forbes.com. This action allowed us to liberate our brand essence, something that has been true about Forbes since its inception—the idea of free market capitalism, the market of ideas, a focus on wealth creation through entrepreneurship. This has always been the cornerstone of what the Forbes brand was all about. It is synonymous with the word *success*, which resonates across the world in any language."

Interviewed on CNBC in the spring of 2016 about the shift in strategy and, specifically, the monetization aspect, Forbes CEO Mike Perlis told his interviewer, "I am a content person. Everything comes down to having great content. If you have great content you will have a fiercely loyal and compelled audience. And if you have this strong relationship between content and the audience, you can monetize it. You can figure out how to charge for subscriptions, and you have a strong story for advertisers. Our audience now exceeds 75 million worldwide across all platforms. [*Author's Note*: As of this writing, Forbes.com's audience has increased to 94 million.] Seventy-five to eighty percent of our total advertising revenue comes from digital, but it's a constant effort to make sure everything is in place—from the platform to the content. My advice to anyone in business," Perlis told CNBC, "is that you have to start with a great product. If you have a great product that people want, and that people love, they'll be willing to pay for it."

When we asked Bruce Rogers about this book's central premise, he said, "In any business, especially the media business, you have to be in a constant state of reinvention. With the digital landscape changing every year, it forces you to constantly reevaluate where you are heading. That said, a business model change is not without its pain, the shifting from old to new, going from the old command-and-control model of journalism to a model that is inherently more flexible, responsive to the vagaries of the marketplace. We want to be on the leading edge of how to be a media company in the digital age. What we did with our effort was to build a sustainable business model for advertising-supported journalism. But, to be credible requires that you have to have a clear focus on your internal GPS. The how and what of your business is less important than *who* you are, and *why* you are. Malcolm lived the brand and was the brand face for many years."

Rogers added that "Mike [Perlis] likes to say, 'Malcolm Forbes turned the business into a brand. We are about entrepreneurial capitalism, a disruptive force with traditional values. From Malcolm Forbes on, this has been the driving spirit of the company's journalistic efforts.' Since its founding in 1917, Forbes has been providing insights, information, and inspiration to further the success of those who are dedicated to the spirit of free enterprise. Our readers expect nothing less from a brand with our entrepreneurial heritage. We will continue to strive to make the business of Forbes as big as the Forbes brand. The brand succeeds him."

The shift in strategy for Forbes Media, conceived and delivered under its forward-looking and bold-minded leadership team, has rattled the media industry, but it has paid dividends many times over, demonstrating how journalism can be reinvented—and monetized—in an increasingly mobile and social media–dominated world. In the era of the social Web, it has demonstrated that journalism can best fulfill its essential mission to inform when the individual who possesses information connects, or transacts, one-on-one with the individual who desires it. Forbes reinvented a century-old, timeworn newsroom process to cover and report news in a totally new way.

COLUMBIA GRAMMAR & PREPARATORY SCHOOL:
Guiding Kids—and Parents—with Honesty and Determination

"That's what I inherited—a bankrupt school [whose] buildings were up for sale, teachers underpaid, facilities were totally inadequate and in disrepair, parents discontent, kids weren't getting into the right colleges. I had all those issues to deal with in order to put it together. I had to focus on what to change, what to change first, what not to change."

Upon taking the role of headmaster at Columbia Grammar & Preparatory School (CGPS) in 1981, Dr. Richard J. Soghoian did not merely face a shift in strategy but, rather, a complete rebuild, literal and figurative. With a rich history dating back to 1764, this well-respected coeducational institution on Manhattan's Upper West Side had most certainly seen better days. Over the past three decades, Soghoian has guided the school's growth without ever losing sight of its high standards. With the largest campus among Manhattan independent schools and 1,300 students from pre-K to grade 12, CGPS celebrated its 250th anniversary in 2014 as one of the oldest independent schools in the United States. But we're getting ahead of ourselves. This is a case study in the attributes of leadership and, specifically, what it was that enabled Soghoian to reestablish—and then some—the once prodigious reputation of CGPS. As one of us (Allen) had a personal connection to the school, we're going to make this a firsthand account.

When Allen's youngest son finished preschool, he and his wife began the long, notoriously difficult search for a New York City school that would provide the best educational environment for their child, both academically and in terms of social responsibility. No matter who they talked to in the initial information-gathering phase, everyone praised the Columbia Grammar & Preparatory School for having a rigorous curriculum while, at the same time, being a caring, family-oriented school.

It was a reputation that Dr. Soghoian had worked to cultivate and maintain, demonstrated in small part by the fact that he would stand at the front door of the school, every day, rain or shine. When Allen would drop off his children (his daughter eventually joined his son as a student there), they would run into the building to begin their day. That Soghoian took the time to greet you with a friendly smile and, most importantly, by name, was among the personality traits that helped him lead the school's remarkable turnaround.

The current warm welcoming environment of CGPS is in sharp contrast to the image the school had in the 1980s when it was on the verge of bankruptcy. Originally founded in 1764 as a boy's preparatory school for King's College, the then name for Columbia University, CGPS eventually ended its partnership with the university to become a private, independent school in 1864. The school enjoyed a long era of comfortable stability until the 1970s when it, along with a great many of New York City's institutions—academic, cultural, and otherwise— entered a state of decline due to the economic difficulties faced by New York and its residents.

As Soghoian told us during our conversation, when he was appointed as the school's thirteenth headmaster in 1981, he found a bankrupt school and inadequate facilities, yes. But, perhaps most pressing of all, he found extremely unhappy parents who were ready to take their children out of the school. To reverse the school's decline, Soghoian told us, he knew he personally needed to roll up his sleeves and get to work. "I had to take it on with a start-up mentality. You can't just send out a letter telling people what your strengths are, or that you have a vision. Those are just words. You've got to somehow convey it through your character and your personality and your actions. I knew I had to do it myself, with my strength of determination, if you will. It just had to be done."

Soghoian has an informal, soft-spoken manner, he is ardently purpose-driven, conveying genuine passion for the tasks for which he has been charged. He is also absolutely honest. This combination of approachability, passion, and transparency allowed people to trust his leadership when he first took on the challenge of a bankrupt school.

In one of the first town hall–style meetings he held in these early days, Soghoian gathered the CGPS parents and asked for a 20 percent deposit on the next year's tuition. He then made clear that the tuition would increase in the year, and the years ahead, to cover the costs of the physical repairs to the school, to hire more educators, and to enrich the curriculum. He did this against the advice of board members who feared that even *talk* of the increased costs at CGPS would drive parents to look at other schools. Instead, it was this transparency, along with the genuine enthusiasm and belief in what was to come, that aided Soghoian in his initial efforts. "So parents would come in and I would warn them tuition is going to go up 17.5 percent," he said. "That's how much money I need to repair buildings, to hire better teachers and to pay them better. I told them you're going to get a better school, and you're going to be part of something exciting over the coming years, starting now. Believe it or not, that worked. Nobody, except for one family, left because of that, and we were off to the races."

The first order of business was to get the school in physical working order, to fix the leaking pipes, the peeling paint, the substandard electrical system, the unusable water fountains, along with myriad other issues. "I had so many problems, just to get the environment workable,"

Soghoian told us. "This was in addition to thinking about the longer-term issues, like teacher salaries, [and] how I could get a reading
and math specialist. How do you hire new people when you can't even
pay your existing staff? Funds were limited. I knew I couldn't afford a
subcontractor, so one of the first hires I made was a jack-of-all-trades,
someone who would be able to do the electrical work, the plumbing,
and other repairs without having to outsource. I knew I had to be resourceful. It saved the school a lot of money."

Soghoian then applied this streamlined, start-up mentality to other
areas of CGPS's administrative costs. In his book *Mind the Gap! An
Insider's Irreverent Look at Private School Finances and Management—
with a Lesson for Government and Industry, Too*, Soghoian details how
he pulled CGPS's finances from the brink, including lessons learned
on how to lead a private school by operating on tuition alone, instead
of relying on endowments. "We never allowed ourselves the luxury of
using a dollar of voluntary giving to supplement our operating budget
or to 'close the gap'—to use the euphemism of private school fundraising," he said. "Our mantra, or operating philosophy, is neatly summarized in the following proposition: 'Tuition is for the present, voluntary
giving for the future.' Learning to live within our means forced us to
streamline our administrative structure and keep it that way."

By focusing on keeping operating expenses low, Soghoian could put
every dollar generated by fundraising straight back into the buildings or
faculty salaries. These were his two top priorities, the objective being to
be more attractive to prospective parents, leading to increased enroll-
ment. That, combined with a streamlined bureaucracy, enhanced the
solvency of CGPS. What enhanced the overall outlook for the school's
future was Soghoian's natural skills as a candid communicator. "I had
to be out there and make a personal commitment to everyone," he said.
"I used to sit in a little cafeteria at 5 West 93rd Street and talk to parents
about how excited I was about what I was doing, and would they like to
join the board, or help develop a fundraising capability. At one of the
parents' evenings, a woman offered to start a street fair fundraiser, which
has now been a continuous part of CGPS's fundraising for the past
thirty-four years. Another [parent], just based on what we were talking

about, wrote the largest check he had ever written for an organization in his life. He became treasurer of the board for ten years. That's the kind of thing I did. You talk person-to-person about your vision and about the exciting opportunity. If you're trying to turn something around, you can put up pie charts filled with data. The more important thing, especially when it comes to a nonprofit organization, is that people need to feel some emotional connection," Soghoian said. "You need to convey that your heart is in it, and do things that prove it."

As the parent of students at CGPS, Allen can attest to the fact that Dr. Soghoian's person-to-person leadership practices were not meant solely as a way to get the school off the ground after its near bankruptcy. They are part and parcel of who he is. "I've always wanted this school to have a hands-on, family-friendly feel," Soghoian explained. "I've written very few memos in my thirty-five years here. Faculty are totally unaccustomed to getting formal dictates from the headmaster. They are so used to talking to me in the cafeteria, in the halls, in the street, in the classrooms. That's the way I've continued, even though the school is so much larger, so much more formal, so to speak. I've maintained my way of communicating, to get out there, become a part of the community, to connect and continue to build connections."

Soghoian has been able to maintain such an informal style of leading this school after all these years as it has grown exponentially in size and status. Because of his openness, his approachability, and his one-on-one communication style, Columbia Grammar & Preparatory School has become what it is. "It's the personal experiences with no strings attached, the non-rigid format, that appealed to people," he said. "I've had so much fun. But you've got to put your heart and soul into it. There's no fast lane. It didn't change in one day. You have to demonstrate that the person at the top constantly conveys that they want what is really best for your children."

Lessons Learned ▶

The stories about shift leaders contained in this chapter present us with several lessons about leadership through strategic change.

Lesson #1: Leaders do not only have vision; they have peripheral vision. Shelly Lazarus led Ogilvy & Mather through a period of change—change from general advertising to integrated marketing, change from analog to digital marketing. Her explanation for how she was able to do it centered around three things: her ability to understand what was driving her customers' businesses, her ability to understand her people's capabilities, and her understanding of the culture developed by David Ogilvy.

The word *vision* doesn't adequately characterize what Shelly Lazarus brought to the table, though. Her story demonstrates something much more, which, in the corporate context, is the importance of *peripheral vision*. One of Allen's former clients, Toni Belloni, group managing director at LVMH, the well-known purveyor of fashion and luxury goods, shared a good metaphor for peripheral vision: "Think about a surfer balancing on a wave. The surfer has to be responsive to several things at once: the height of the wave, the speed of the wave, the wind, and even the currents running beneath him. He has to 'see' and be responsive to all of these forces simultaneously. He needs to make dozens of quick, almost intuitive adjustments to keep his balance. The wave is constantly moving forward, changing shape, and the ocean floor is whirling below. His ability to absorb all these inputs and react to minute changes determines success, or lack of success. Get too far behind the wave, and the surfer misses the opportunity. Too far ahead, and he's under water."

Lesson #2: Authentic credibility helps leaders through strategic change. Doug Blonsky brought a background as a landscape architect to his efforts to revive Central Park. He understood how people of all types used the park. Knowing what type of grass stood up best to foot traffic was part of his background. He, too, had peripheral vision. He reinforced the perception of authenticity with his dirty sneakers and he gained more credibility through constant contact with all park constituents, from dog walkers to the mayor.

Similarly, Bruce Rogers and the rest of the Forbes leadership team, Lewis DVorkin especially, brought a unique set of experiences in digital content creation to Forbes's shift strategy. Having founded True/Slant after working at Forbes much earlier, DVorkin had instant credibility with respect to both the magazine's heritage and original online news content development.

The Forbes story highlights an important distinction between types of authentic credibility: depth and scope. When we think of credibility, we usually think of depth in a single dimension. Nevertheless, the research literature speaks to both depth and scope.

Credibility is related to experience, and the literature exhibits significant work on the relationship between leader experience and firm performance. In a study of ninety-eight CEOs in the branded foods industry, firm performance improved steadily with tenure in the role.[11] Downturns occurred only after the CEO had served more than ten to fifteen years. On the other hand, in the computer industry, firm performance was at its highest when CEOs started their jobs.[12] This difference demonstrates that the relationship between experience and performance depends on the underlying industry. If something is brand new, perhaps experience is more constraining than informing, thereby minimizing the likelihood that a leader would possess authentic credibility.

Having authentic credibility in diverse areas seems to be a high bar to clear for a single leader. It would be easier to find in a team—such as the team that led Forbes. Nevertheless, a study of 183 CEOs of Fortune 250 firms revealed that firms led by CEOs with higher levels of career variety displayed a greater degree of resource reallocations and corporate strategic change.[13]

Lesson #3: Leaders' personal values impact how they lead a shift. In our interview, John Sexton could not have been clearer on how his personal values impacted the shift he initiated at and for New York University. His Catholic upbringing and Jesuit training led him to formulate the ecumenical underpinnings of his *ratio studiorum*. Diversity is to be embraced and even trumpeted. No place in the world is more diverse than New York. Being in and of the city of New York reflects and is the foundation of NYU's embracing of diversity, both locally and globally.

The literature presents a number of studies that empirically investigate the relationship between a leader's personal values and the decisions the leader makes. In one study, a survey of the entire population of directors and CEOs in public corporations in Sweden found that leaders' personal values play an important part in their decisions.[14] Another study examined the relationships between CEO values and organizational culture, and between organizational culture and firm performance.[15] Related to our purposes, this study concluded that CEOs with high values for self-direction were associated with innovation-oriented cultures (i.e., were more likely to shift).

Lesson #4: Shifts require bold action. A major premise of this book is that sooner or later just about every company is going to need to execute a strategic shift. Given that it's going to happen, you might as well be bold. There may be a natural tendency to play it safe, but if you do, you may become the next Kodak. So be bold. The stories about NYU, Columbia Grammar & Preparatory School, Forbes, and Ogilvy & Mather all demonstrate bold shifts.

One cannot be afraid to take a chance or make a mistake. Experimentation is the new gold standard. John Sexton realized that his chances of success were only 60 percent. James Quincey, the new CEO of Coca-Cola said, "If we're not making mistakes, we're not trying hard enough."[16]

Lesson #5: Have a purpose—instill it, communicate it, and live it. Over sixty years ago, the late great Peter Drucker wrote in his book *The Practice of Management*, "If we want to know what a business is, we have to start with its purpose. And its purpose must lie outside the business itself. In fact, it must lie in society since a business enterprise is an organ of society." How does the business make the world a better place?

John Sexton attempted to make the world a better place by building a truly global university. That is what he saw as his purpose in life. To succeed, though, the leader has to convince potential followers that the purpose is worthwhile, and worthwhile simply beyond making money.

Research has shown that a sense of purpose is a critical motivator in organizational behavior.

Wharton professor and management guru Adam Grant is often credited with shifting the thinking about job design, as the economy moved from alleviating the tedium of manufacturing jobs toward the more modern conditions of a service and knowledge economy. His work began with a study he conducted in the context of call centers when he was a twenty-two-year-old graduate student at the University of Michigan.[17] Call center jobs are repetitive and can be emotionally taxing, as callers encounter verbal abuse and rejection.

The call center manager had already tried the usual incentives (e.g., cash bonuses, contests) without great end results. Doctoral student Grant proposed a simple experiment to test a different idea. The call center he studied was involved in fundraising on the Michigan campus. Recognizing that one of the center's primary purposes was funding scholarships, Grant brought in a student who had benefited from that fundraising. The callers took a ten-minute break as the young man told them how the scholarship had changed his life and how excited he now was to be a teacher. A month after the testimonial, the workers were spending 142 percent more time on the phone and bringing in 171 percent more revenue, even though they were using the same script.

Grant's subsequent research followed up on this point and demonstrated that a sense of purpose was more motivating than even money. Highlighting positive social consequences of one's business is an obvious path. This was easy for Doug Blonsky, the landscape architect who wanted to make Central Park an environment that would improve the mental well-being and quality of life for everyone you might find on the park bench, from the senior citizen who wants to read the paper to the mother with the baby in the stroller to the woman who just lost her husband. Instilling that purpose had additional benefits. A park team with a purpose is a park team that welcomes responsibility and accountability.

Finally, instilling and communicating a purpose is often most effectively done by example. The leader has to live it. In the beginning, John Sexton flew back and forth from Abu Dhabi on a weekly basis to teach at the school there. Doug Blonsky spent countless hours in the park. Dr. Soghoian's desire to build the Columbia Grammar & Preparatory School into a modern institution with a hands-on feel could only be done by his living the purpose. As Soghoian said, "I knew I had to do it myself." He sat with parents, conveyed his excitement about the school, and built a sense of excitement about his purpose. The best way for the school to develop a family-friendly feel was for Dr. Soghoian to be friendly to the families.

8

SUCCESS STORIES: WHAT IT TAKES FOR THE LONG HAUL

We've talked about the bits and pieces of what it takes for an organi-zation to successfully shift focus to maintain relevance in a rapidly changing marketplace. We've talked about the warning signs, the leading (and lagging) indicators of a need to shift, how to prepare, pulling the trigger, and the role of leadership. Before we put all the parts and pieces together, illustrating by way of a quintessential in-market example how it's done, we want to emphasize one skill that we have not yet emphasized but that we found necessary to shift ahead.

The preeminent skill required to shift ahead in the twenty-first century is the ability to see and seize.

■

We've been discussing and dissecting the fact that the greatest challenge organizations face today is how to stay competitive and categorically relevant given the accelerating pace of change. We've made the
point that it's not change that's new. It's the *velocity* of that change that
is new. Information technology has made it possible for a company to
be launched and, three months later, have a huge valuation without
any need for raw materials, manufacturing, or packaging. Products
and services that were on the cutting edge even a year ago have fallen
off the edge today. More patents are filed with the U.S. Patent Office
than at any other time in history. A sleek home companion by the
name of Alexa can order us coffee, find us the latest episode of our
favorite podcast, and start our car on a wintry morning, all without
leaving her perch on the family room bookshelf. A car will park itself
when we get to the office. To succeed in this environment, organizations must possess the ability to see what's coming, to seize opportunities and capitalize on them, and to dodge threats at the same time—all
with speed and assurance.

And, therein, we believe, lies the preeminent shift-ahead skill required for the twenty-first century: the ability to "see and seize" while
the world spins around faster. The implications are financial, of course:
How do you maintain competitive advantage without disrupting daily
operations? You've got to deliver the numbers. But the implications for
not staying in front of marketplace dynamics are also social, cultural,
environmental, and geopolitical. Any organization that is not constantly
seeing and seizing the moment, *continuously* adjusting to changing
contexts and conflicts, is at risk for obsolescence. Yearly strategy development cycles are certainly well intentioned and still obligatory to set a
general course. But the reality is that no matter how well you plan, it's
likely you'll have to keep adjusting your plan.

This ability to "see and seize" was the central theme in the conversation we had with Steven Gardner who, with his partner Tom Nelson,
founded the ad agency Gardner Nelson & Partners, Inc.

"What's different about the age of the Internet is the *speed* at which
categories go through convulsive change," Gardner said at the beginning of our discussion. "In a rapidly changing world, the greatest skill

that a businessperson must have is the ability to see and seize an opportunity. Some people can *see* an opportunity, but they do not have the insight or executional ability to *act* on it. Most people tend to be more transactional . . . people who can implement when directed, but who lack the vision to see the opportunities inherent in change. I had the great fortune to work with Steve Jobs, who is perhaps the most extraordinary example of a single individual possessing the ability to see and seize opportunities. Steve was fond of a simple two-word saying: 'Artists ship.' What he meant by that was that you can be the greatest artist in the world, but if you don't actually *make something*—'ship it,' in manufacturing parlance—who cares? Jobs is the most profound businessperson of his generation. He fundamentally changed five or six industries, given his ability to see and act on opportunities. From computers to printing to music to phones to entertainment to film, he was able to see a market need that was not intuitively obvious to anyone else. He had the skillset to see and make it happen."

"Look at the Mac," Gardner continued. "The positioning was 'a computer for the rest of us.' The insight? Instead of making people learn programming languages to communicate with computers, why not design a computer that is easily and intuitively understandable to the average human? In the case of music, he recognized that MP3s are superior formats for listening and sharing music, but the distribution system was based primarily on piracy. The opportunity he saw was far less about the bits and bytes of technology, but more about figuring out a licensing and a distribution mechanism that would allow everyone to buy into the idea of legal MP3s. He recognized this and, in doing so, revolutionized the portable music category. Then, of course, the iPhone. Most phone manufacturers viewed their product as a phone to which they incrementally added functionality. Steve Jobs knew how to 'think different.' To him, the opportunity was to make a very small computer that had a myriad of functionality . . . including the ability to make telephone calls."

Gardner went on to suggest that the way business leaders should approach a repositioning project is to actively *look for change*. Look for the most dynamic factor in a given category, a critical change in the consumer, the world, or the culture, as that will enable the marketer to leapfrog and redefine the category. It requires the mental discipline to see opportunity versus current reality. "Look at Uber," he said. "Someone at Uber was smart enough to say, 'Gee, we could use the combination of mobile communications and GPS technology to reinvent the stale old business of taxis and car services.' That insight enabled them to rethink the taxi business based on private vehicles and on-demand availability. It's a great case of someone looking at a business model—the taxi business in New York City—and asking how to make it better."

Gardner went on to suggest that the way business leaders should look at the marketplace is to ask the question, "If you knew your company was going to start over, how would you reinvent it?" What would you do differently? What is changing about society and what impact does that have on your product and your brand? The companies that succeed today are those whose managers are actively trying to understand what is changeable in their business and get to it before others do.

"There was a catchphrase a few years back: 'Dell or be Delled.' It was another way of expressing Intel founder Andy Grove's statement that 'only the paranoid survive,' relative to the chip industry," Gardner said. "If you don't disrupt your category the way Michael Dell did, by doing the impossible [in Dell's case, lowering costs through customization, not standardization], someone else will. I don't like to think of it as paranoia, but as opportunity.

"I have always told our clients that there is actually a very simple definition of market leadership: You must figure out what the most people want the most, and then deliver it better than anyone else," he continued. "Sometimes the best way to take on an entrenched leader is to cause a fundamental change in the consumer's benefit hierarchy; to redefine what is most important to the consumer. And, in fact, the easiest way to do this is to take a step back and ask the big question: What is *changing* about the world, the society, the culture, the technology, attitudes . . . because it is in those changes that you have the opportunity to restructure how a consumer thinks about your category. In our work, we've come to recognize that the defining skillset a business manager needs is the ability to see and apply change. You have to be able to disrupt your own industry to stay ahead of the curve."

The ability to see and apply change opportunistically is such a simple premise, but obviously very hard to do. If it were easy, there would be no reason for business school courses in change management. In our conversation with Gardner, we also noted that it was ironic that during the period we were writing this book, Alvin Toffler, a writer who was among the first modern futurists, passed away. In his bestselling book *Future Shock*, Toffler cautioned that the accelerating pace of technological change would make us all sick. He described future shock as the "shattering stress and disorientation that we induce in individuals by subjecting them to too much change in too short a period of time." While a bit stark and apocalyptic, he also asserted, more constructively, that "you've got to think about big things while you're doing small things, so all the small things go in the right direction." To our mind, this is a much more positive way of framing the situation.

For all we've written about the need to shift to stay relevant, and the fundamentals underlying the process, victory in the charge to stay relevant will definitely belong to those organizations inherently conditioned to think about the big things while literally doing the small things. And, more than that, doing those things right and doing them quickly. Those for whom "see and seize" is simply a matter of business as usual will be those who succeed; they are the organizations whose leadership, culture, and financial wherewithal enable them to make small shifts along the way, executed brilliantly as a result of the clarity of focus on their mission. Much more effective and efficient than having to make a dramatic shift in degree or direction, it is the optimal business model for a world in which the acceleration of change—not change itself—is the key challenge.

Lest you think this business model is for the newly emerging, entrepreneurial sorts, that is not the case. This see-and-seize way of doing business is at the heart of two companies discussed in the first part of this chapter. They are iconic organizations, both long-standing category front-runners. Each was founded by an entrepreneur who excelled at the ability to see and seize opportunities. Each leader had an innovator's

DNA, which became part of the cultural DNA of the entire company. As such, each organization has been able to stay relevant over the course of many years and myriad market fluctuations without the need for a seismic shift. Rather, they have what it takes to have been able to shift as needed along the way. Here are their see-and-seize stories.

MARRIOTT INTERNATIONAL:
From Root Beer to Resorts

The spirit of invention and entrepreneurship has been part of the Marriott organization since its founding when, in 1927, J. Willard Marriott and his wife, Alice, drove from Salt Lake City, Utah, to Washington, D.C., to open one of the first A&W root beer franchises. Recognizing that people could also use a hot meal in the cold Washington winters, they started the Hot Shoppes Restaurant chain. Seeing that people who flew out of Washington's Hoover Airport would appreciate the chance to take along some food for the journey, they seized on the opportunity to start up an airline food services business offering boxed lunches to passengers. And, in 1957, seeing the Pentagon building going up across the river in Virginia, they realized that many people would be visiting, so they made their historic shift to the hotel business with a "motor hotel," which was managed by their son, J. W. "Bill" Marriott. He, in turn, saw the rise of international tourism and, in 1969, opened the company's first international hotel in Acapulco, Mexico. Marriott also saw the rise of cruising as a vacation choice and became the first lodging company to enter the cruising business through a partnership with Sun Line. Then Bill Marriott saw that business travelers had a completely different set of requirements than those traveling for fun, and he developed the Courtyard by Marriott chain in 1986, and went on to develop or acquire a host of other hotels (Ritz-Carlton, Fairfield Inn, and Residence Inn, among them) to appeal to the diverse needs of various target segments. In his more than fifty years at the helm, Bill built Marriott into a global lodging company with more than 4,300 properties in more than eighty countries. The company is now led by Arne Sorenson, just the third CEO in the company's history and, obviously, the first without a Marriott surname. That said, Sorenson has held a number of positions within the Marriott organization over the years, so is very well acquainted with the Marriott way of doing—and growing—business.

Bill Marriott inherited from his father more than just the ability to see and seize business opportunities. He inherited a set of guiding principles for *running* these businesses—principles that remain embedded in the company's culture today. In a 2013 interview with Steve Forbes (which can be seen on YouTube) about his life in the industry, Bill commented that every CEO talks about the importance of people[1]:

> My dad practiced it in a way that is revolutionary for the hotel business. For example, my dad started in a root beer stand and then a restaurant. One day the cook didn't show up, as he was sick. My dad needed a plan to keep people happy, so he put a doctor on the payroll. He took care of their healthcare. Our major belief is that if you take good care of people, they'll take good care of the customer and the customer will come back. We celebrate our people. More than 50 percent of our managers come from within our ranks. We are not an assembly line. Our people are out there meeting the guests. They have millions of interactions with our guests every year. We don't just tell them to do a good job. We give them the latitude to respond to customer needs without having to go to a general manager. We want them to create a great experience for guests by feeling good about their role in the organization. A people-first culture is the first element of our success in this business.

It is this very people-first culture that adds to the organization's ability to see and seize opportunities. That thousands of Marriott associates are tapped into what makes a great guest experience is a factor in the company's ongoing relevance in the industry. These associates are constantly on the lookout for what amenities and upgrades would enhance the Marriott experience, for situations that require upgrading or refreshing, for what makes guests happy and, conversely, what doesn't. It's a built-in course-correction, self-correction mechanism of the most personal order. It's a company of firsts because everyone is always tapped into what guests want—or don't want.

We had the opportunity to speak with Stacy Milne, who has been with Marriott for over twenty-five years, most recently as the vice president of portfolio marketing and strategy. "The strength of our company is that our associates go the extra mile for our guests because they are emotionally bought in. This is not a one-size-fits-all business," she said. "It's people-based, it's occasion-based, and our culture is built on embracing change. It's something that was passed down from J. W. Marriott to Bill Marriott, and on to all of our associates." She shared with us a phrase that people used about Bill Marriott's management style: "'His feet never touched his desk.' He was always out on the road looking at all the details that could make or break a guest experience. He has visited every single Marriott hotel, inspected more than 1,000, always talking to associates and checking to see if they are happy, if their attitude is positive, if the rooms are spotlessly clean, assessing the quality of the food, assessing the policies. He was picking up new ideas all the time."

Going back to Paco Underhill's philosophy on leadership and culture, which we wrote about in Chapter 5, Bill Marriott always kept his "desk" closest to the customers, and also to his employees. He walked the walk, and as a result he could see and sense what shifts were required along the way for staying a category leader. He could also assess where and how Marriott could play and win. As an example, Milne told us, "We're always looking for ways to combine technology with the heart of the company. We won't roll out a technological enhancement until we know it works. We stand for operational excellence in all areas. We're constantly innovating in all areas. Take our loyalty program, for example. We were the first hospitality company to form a multi-brand loyalty program," she said. "We know our guests stay across a number of hotels, so the more brands in our loyalty program, the greater the lifetime value of our guests. The Marriott app gives them a way to interact with us on a regular basis. My mother calls this new generation the 'heads-down generation.' People are always looking at their phones. We needed to figure out how to operationalize all sorts of digital experiences across our 6,000-

plus hotels. And we don't do this alone but, in the spirit of our culture, we do a lot of co-creation with our guests—taking into account their feedback and preferences along the way, so each experience can feel personalized to them. Whether it's using your phone as your room key or a vending machine filled with healthy options, we look at all the possibilities and determine what it is we can roll out that will provide the greatest benefit for the most people." In other words, Marriott is out to see and seize.

A campaign to make travel more brilliant—or as Marriott marketing puts it, "Travel brilliantly"—was launched specifically to engage a younger audience, the millennials, if you will. Its initiatives amplify the brand's dedication to leading the future of travel, reflecting a lifestyle of travelers who seamlessly blend work and play in a mobile and global world. From technological innovations such as mobile check-ins and check-outs and the At Your Service app (by which you can literally text your service requests to hotel associates) to redesigned lobbies and "Greatrooms," the campaign and its executional touchpoints are meant to disrupt the idea that a hotel is bound by its four walls. It shifts the emphasis to the traveler, bolsters dialogue with guests, and as Milne said, engages the traveler in creating the Marriott experience.

As Milne told us, "Dedication to the customer shows in everything we do. Innovation has always been part of our story. We continue to help shape the hospitality industry. We continue to challenge the status quo and anticipate our customers' needs with new brands, new global locations, and new experiences, both technology-based and otherwise. The core values of the company make us who we are. We put people first. Our founder's philosophy was that if you take care of the associates, they will take care of the customers. Giving people opportunities to grow and succeed is ingrained in our DNA."

Inherent in Milne's description of the culture is that Marriott employees are given not just permission but encouragement to call out and act on what they see as opportunities for change—for the small, ongoing shifts that can make a big difference to the guests they serve. There are as many pairs of eyes surveying and ears listening for what will enhance the guest experience as there are Marriott associates. By virtue of their principles and their own actions, J. W. and his son, Bill Marriott, embedded a simple way for the organization to focus on what's important to their customers, ensuring that they continuously remain relevant. Aware of the fact that, in an organization as large and as customer-centric as the Marriott organization, you can't rely only on the CEO to see and seize the moments for innovation, Marriott father and son built a culture around embracing the inevitability of change, at the same time empowering everyone to become part of the "see and seize" process. As Bill Marriott said to Steve Forbes during his interview, "Competitors are watching us and copying us, but we're out ahead of them. To stay in business for almost eighty-five years, you know you're doing something right."

FEDEX:
Keeping the Purple Promise

As the story goes, in 1965, as a Yale undergraduate, Fred Smith wrote a term paper outlining a system to accommodate urgent, time-sensitive shipments such as medicine, computer parts, and electronics. He received an average grade. Luckily, not being deterred by the tepid response to this paper, in 1971 Fred Smith went on to found Federal Express, the global leader in the overnight shipping industry. As noted on the company's website, on the first night of continuous operation, 389 Federal Express team members and fourteen Dassault Falcon jets delivered 186 packages overnight to twenty-five U.S. cities, giving birth to the modern air/ground express industry. By 1983, Federal Express had become the first American company to reach revenues of $1 billion within ten years of start-up without a merger or acquisition. In 1990, it became the first company to win the Malcolm Baldrige National Quality Award in the service category. In 1994, it launched Fedex.com as the first transportation website to offer online status tracking, enabling customers to conduct business via the Internet.

Then, in 1996, Federal Express became FedEx, in a well-considered shift intended to move the company away from the word "federal," which sounded almost governmental in nature, not to mention U.S.–centric. A key objective was to signal the international scope of the brand's business. FedEx did this. Perhaps more important, however, was the evocative association the faster, sleeker, more efficient-sounding FedEx name sent to people within the organization. While customers and everyone else were using the word as a generic verb to signify overnight delivery, it sent a powerful internal signal that FedEx was a company committed to leading the industry in getting things where they needed to be—reliably and on time. It refocused and clarified this core brand idea in a way every employee could understand. FedEx is a fast, super-efficient brand.

The FedEx logo has become a ubiquitous part of the global landscape: distinctive purple and green, purple and orange, or purple and red, on vans, trucks, airplanes, and sidewalk envelope drop-off bins. It's a logo that telegraphs instantly "The world on time," a line that pretty neatly sums up the brand's promise. As unmistakable as these vans, trucks, and airplanes have become, however, it is the people behind the logo that are the ultimate signal of its strength as a brand. From Fred Smith to every one of the over 300,000 employees, people drive the brand's reputation and its ongoing relevance in the marketplace.

As a service brand, FedEx relies on its people to ensure the promise of the brand is kept. Adopting the name FedEx gave it an almost intuitive way to signal to its fast-growing roster of employees that they were the keepers of the brand experience. Over more than four decades, FedEx has built a portfolio of innovative solutions connecting customers to more than 220 countries and territories. That's 99 percent of the world's global gross domestic product sources. Just as J. W. Marriott and his son saw and seized opportunities to keep their hospitality business in a perpetual state of relevance, giving employees the same charge, so, too, does Fred Smith, but in the overnight shipping industry. From the get-go, he has empowered his employees to be partners in identifying ways to keep their company ahead of the curve in the category. As he has said in more than one interview about the company's continued success, "No one can do anything by themselves at scale. You've got to be a team player."

At the March 2017 BRITE conference in New York City, FedEx vice president and CMO Rajesh Subramaniam spoke proudly about how FedEx has built a strong company culture that is consistent for all of its 400,000 worldwide employees. This culture is based on what FedEx calls "the Purple Promise," which states, as Subramaniam explained, "I will make every FedEx experience outstanding." It is a statement that represents the FedEx commitment to place customer needs at the center of everything the company does, and that prompts everyone who works at FedEx to continuously look for opportunities for shifts in initiative that will help them better meet the requirements of their customers in a fast-changing market. The Purple Promise is a mechanism, yes, but also an inherent part of the FedEx culture that vests everyone in the organization with the responsibility and privilege of making things "outstanding" on a daily basis. It prompts everyone to "see and seize" opportunities. Every employee believes in this promise and is trained to bring it to life in every customer interaction.

"From day one, our number-one employee, Fred Smith, understood the importance of our people," Subramaniam told the BRITE audience. "He understood that success starts with the people on the front lines, the drivers, the customer service agents who deliver, in equal part, every day. He knew that if you make your expectations clear, if you reward and recognize the right behavior, success will follow. It didn't matter where these people were—Toronto, Taipei, or Timbuktu—the FedEx language was the same. Our culture is the bedrock on which our brand and our company is built."

FedEx has taken a relatively simple idea—a commitment to excellent customer service—and focused on it intensely and consistently over the years to create a differentiating experience that has transferred from 186 packages to millions of packages a day, from a single visionary employee to over 400,000 worldwide. As Subramaniam put it, "What if going above and beyond was the baseline, not the exception?" He explained that all employees know that they have an active role in making each customer's experience with the company as outstanding as possible. "It's more than a package we deliver," Subramaniam said. "When we deliver medical supplies to Nepalese earthquake victims, we deliver hope. When we deliver an e-commerce package during the holiday season, we deliver joy. We all understand the powerful idea that we connect people with possibilities."

Of course, the challenge as it is for most brands is brilliant and constant execution of the promise. The larger the organization, the more difficult the executional challenge. While there have been a few instances of drivers not living "the Purple Promise," for the most part the company's culture delivers. Subramaniam could easily share the FedEx brand strategy with the BRITE audience because he knew that, while it's very easy to copy what somebody else makes and maybe even the process for making it, it's nearly impossible to copy what they are and what they believe in.

We spoke to Monica Skipper, vice president of brand experience marketing at FedEx, who leads advertising, brand, and sponsorship programs for the global document, package, and freight transportation giant. At the beginning of our conversation, she expressed her thoughts on branding, a topic that she said many people needlessly complicate. "You've got to know who you are," she said. "What is your unique value proposition? Then, whatever you say you are, you have to make [that unique value proposition] happen with actions and behaviors that support it. That's how we work to deliver on one brand promise. It requires us to constantly think what will make a customer experience better. It is our customers who define the experience, and as the world evolves the definition evolves." Skipper elaborated on the notion of needing to assess the FedEx experience through a much wider lens than ever before. "The totality of experiences in the marketplace set customer expectations. As the world of e-commerce opens up, people are comparing us to apps, which can tell me the driver is ten minutes away, or to the pizza delivery guy who texts that he'll be there in fifteen minutes, or to Amazon, which has my package on the front step the afternoon of the day I order it. There are so many more ways we have to think about how to constantly innovate in order to align with customer definitions and expectations of [service] quality. We have to continuously shift to meet a shifting marketplace. When the marketplace shifts, we have to be ahead of it. The only way to do that is to be constantly looking."

We asked Skipper how the company assesses potential. "When it's the right thing for the customer, FedEx takes the right steps. Whether it's build or buy, we have a history of doing the right thing at the right time. It starts with the chairman, Fred Smith, who has embedded in our culture a way of looking ahead in order to act on something before it's too late."

FedEx certainly has a history of revolutionary initiatives that have taken many forms: the first PC-based automated shipping system, later named FedEx PowerShip; FedEx Tracking, which allows customers to keep tabs on the status of packages in transit; and the first all-electric trucks to be used in the U.S. parcel delivery business. In another first, starting in 2017, FedEx will launch the use of alternative jet fuels that feature sustainable ingredients including algae, tree pulp, and scrub brush. As its corporate website states:

> These sorts of developments emerge naturally out of our focus on innovation. All of our team members are tasked with looking for ways to streamline operations and improve the customer experience. FedEx Innovation is a cross-disciplinary team with one mission: Develop game-changing ideas. Shipping more than 10 million packages per business day around the world offers new challenges every day. Those challenges drive us to develop better solutions—and build connections that allow people to flourish and prosper.

Proof point to our point. The ability for an organization to see what's ahead, to quickly recognize and efficiently seize game-changing opportunities that are to the advantage of all constituents, are the preeminent skills required to stay relevant in today's fast-changing environment. FedEx, like Marriott, has these skills. Both organizations have an inherent mechanism for seeing and seizing, which is what fuels their continued strength and allows them to make small shifts as required. They also have the ability to execute these shifts brilliantly while keeping a focus on their core identity, what they stand for in the marketplace. Each organization was fortunate enough to have been founded by a leader with not only (peripheral) vision, but the wisdom to ensure that vision became a driving force in the organizational culture. FedEx and Marriott come by their see and seize abilities naturally.

Of course, there is part of every success story that goes untold. When you move as quickly as you need in order to be able see and seize, you will inevitably make mistakes. Way back in 1984, before the widespread availability and use of fax services in homes and businesses, FedEx launched Zapmail, offering fax transmission to expedite delivery of documents. Despite their attempt to quickly "seize" this opportunity, the market moved faster and fax machines became so inexpensive and pervasive that any individual business could afford its own equipment.

The ability to see and seize, to shift and focus, is not the norm for most organizations, wherein these skills must be learned. As in so many initiatives in business and in life, the theory is simple to grasp. The implementation is a far more difficult task, as so many of the stories in this book demonstrate. The challenge of seeing what's ahead is hard enough, let alone having the peripheral vision required to see what may be coming from the sidelines. While throughout the book we've discussed the various tactics, both analog and digital, that organizations use for gauging the future and the implications for *their* future, one of the best and most obvious tactics of all is simply getting out and getting to really know the audience you serve. Talk to people, not in formal focus group settings, but where they live and shop and take their kids to get ice cream. Ask what interests them, what worries them, what delights them, and what daily challenges they face.

Seeing is just the first part of the challenging equation; seizing is the second. It is knowing when and if and how to take action when you see an opportunity, and being able to execute the necessary shift efficiently and effectively, and credibly. Many organizations have all the tools and resources they need to discern what the future may hold. However, they are either financially or culturally unable to do anything about it. It may also be a matter of inertia. The word "seize" is associated with passion and energy and motivation. *Carpe diem* (seize the day) is a phrase wonderfully brought to life in a scene in the movie *Dead Poets Society*, in which Robin Williams, portraying a passionate, energetic, and motivated teacher at a boys' prep school, implores his young charges to make every day extraordinary. To do this takes desire and ambition.

But let's get back to the "how" and the matter of credibility. In addition to everything else, as we've shown throughout this book, organizations that are successful at shifting have self-knowledge. They know what is fundamental to their character. They know what they stand for in the minds of consumers. And they know they must keep a sharp focus on whatever this fundamental is as they shift to stay relevant.

Dov Seidman, attorney, founder and CEO of LRN, a company that helps companies shape winning organizational cultures, and author of *HOW: Why How We Do Anything Means Everything*, told Allen, "We're living in a world that operates differently, and the winds in this world are more intense. It's hard not to get swept up in this wind and just go where it takes you. You have to do the difficult, internal work to identify what's true about yourself and keep one foot rooted in whatever this is," he said. "If you don't, you might find yourself in a place other than where you want to be. I like to think about it like a pivot in basketball. You put one foot solidly in place and literally announce where you stand, and then you can take the other foot and place it where you want to go, a direction that reflects a new appreciation for the conditions, for what's working and what is not. It's deliberate, it's intentional, and it's bold."

It's also necessary, which is especially true today, when not only are the conditions changing so quickly and intensely, but consumers can see clearly how organizations are behaving when confronted with these conditions. Transparency gives organizations no other choice than to focus on their values. You can see what's happening, you can shift with every new gust of wind, but you have to apply the internal fortitude to stand up to the winds of change and go where you know you should go, not where the winds want to take you. You must shift ahead.

Putting It All Together

There are no secrets or magic formulas. There are, however, five key dimensions against which an organization must exhibit strength, and they are critical for seizing what you see. We interviewed people representing about 100 organizations, from a wide array of categories, for this book. Some of them were successful in shifting; others were less so. Nevertheless, all could attest to the fact that these five dimensions were essential elements in being able to see and seize.

1. *Financial wherewithal.* The first dimension against which an organization must exhibit strength is having the necessary financial foundation, the basic rocket fuel to support the effort for the long haul. Many organizations start this journey with good intentions, but underestimate the financial horsepower required to get them where they want to go. It may be that they started the process early enough, in good financial health, but either didn't anticipate breakdowns or setbacks along the way that would require additional funding, or that the process would go on much longer than originally thought. In addition, many organizations cannot manage investor expectations or establish realistic goals, making it necessary for them to reevaluate objectives, which affects credibility and eventual outcomes.

2. *Cultural disposition.* The second dimension against which an organization must exhibit strength is having a culture with a can-do attitude, or at the very least a leader who can institute and maintain a positive cultural vibe. In all success stories in this book, the organization was *primed* to succeed. Everyone knew his or her role in making it happen and was given the tools and the appropriate support. While it is always easy to get discouraged, cultural optimism is essential to overcome obstacles. In all cases in which success was achieved, there was a sense that everyone in the organization was "in this together."

3. *Clarity of focus.* Your organization can have an abundance of both cash and optimism, but it needs to be laser-focused on where it wants to go and why. Most organizations cannot make multiple bets or hedge their bets on the future. The

goal must be simple and clear and memorable, and it must be more than to make money. Everyone must understand what the goal is and understand how a given action aligns— or doesn't—with bringing it to life.

4. *Executional excellence.* All organizations that successfully seized what they saw were able to take their concept and turn it into reality in a way that met, or exceeded, the expectations of all stakeholders. Their efforts were seen as credible and game-changing, from both inside and outside the organization. The road may be paved with good intentions, but there is no partial credit, no almost there, when it comes to a successfully executed shift of focus. If you can't make it happen, it doesn't matter.

5. *Leadership.* Finally, we have discussed the critical nature of leadership extensively throughout this book, allocating an entire chapter to the topic. To undertake a successful shift, there must be a leader at the helm who is not just forward-looking but has peripheral vision. Such an individual does not just see down the road, but can see from multiple directions. This person must be able to simplify and crystalize the mission and communicate it to the many stakeholders involved. This leader must be able to exemplify the mission in a credible fashion, not just give it lip service. The leader must be able to tolerate uncertainty and keep the troops in a positive frame of mind throughout the process. To borrow from *Star Trek*, this person must have what it takes to "boldly go where no man has gone before," at least no man (or woman) in the organization, and demonstrate a personal commitment to driving the endeavor forward.

To more fully bring these summary comments to life, we present an example of an organization that absolutely exhibited strength against the five dimensions required for a successful shift ahead. It is not a large publicly traded company or a small cash-infused entrepreneurial enterprise, but rather, a public library: the Greenwich Library in Greenwich,

Connecticut. A public library is a fitting concluding example because, for many of us, it represents the repository of all knowledge acquired in our formative years. Like all libraries around the world, the Greenwich Library faced the challenge of how to stay relevant in the digital age, given the impact of technological disruption in media, scholarship, and education, along with the challenge of modernizing in the face of on-going budgetary constraints. That it had multiple constituents was also a challenge: the public it served, the librarians and other staff, the state-funding agencies, the local donors, and the board members. The focus of its efforts was to activate an extension of the traditional services and programming that libraries have always offered, by responding to the needs of the community.

GREENWICH PUBLIC LIBRARY:
Successfully Shifting Ahead in the Age of Digital Information

We believe that free communication is essential to the preservation of a free society and a creative culture.
—American Library Association

What are your most memorable experiences with a library? Depending on your age, it might be when you were given your own library card, along with permission to take out new books every week. Maybe it was in high school or college, when you took refuge amid the stacks of books, seeking a quiet place to tackle your assignments. Perhaps it was accompanying your four-year-old to the library's children's room to share in the pleasures of a favorite book being read aloud by a kind-hearted librarian. If nothing else, libraries bring to mind both books and sanctuary. While providing books—and sanctuary—was a standalone function for centuries, libraries have had to evolve with the digital age to meet the changing needs of their users.

There are over 17,000 libraries in the United States, a ubiquitous part of the American landscape serving as a resource for millions of people. But given the incredible transformations in technology and the behaviors these transformations have produced, the characterization of the library as a "resource" has shifted dramatically, relative to the evocation of books alone. Based on a Pew study, free access to computers and the Internet has become nearly as important to users as borrowing books. Beginning with the digitization of library catalogs between the 1970s and 1990s, libraries have added digital capabilities while continuing to provide book lending and literacy services. According to a 2015 American Library Association study, 97 percent of public libraries now offer Internet access in the form of free onsite Wi-Fi, 98 percent offer some form of technology training, according to the report, and around 80 percent of institutions in the U.S. provide assistance with online job hunting services.[2] A large majority use social media like Facebook or hi5 to connect with patrons. A great many of libraries offer new recreational and content creation opportunities. They lend everything from musical instruments to gaming consoles.

Today, society is in the midst of a tremendous shift in the way Americans consume literature as well as the way they access and share information. While there is romanticism attached to the traditional imagery of libraries as hallowed halls lined with books, this image is not necessarily reflected in reality. One school that Joel recently examined for his kids, the Grace Church School in Greenwich Village, touted the fact that it scarcely had any books on its library shelves. Nevertheless, one thing that has not changed is that libraries continue to play a central role in providing free access to information and ideas. They are hubs for "free communication," in all formats. For example, in place of books, the Grace Church School Library had more computer terminals than an IBM warehouse.

While many stellar libraries across the country and around the world have successfully shifted their focus to meet the challenges of staying relevant to their users, one library in particular provides a textbook example for our purposes. The Greenwich Library in Greenwich, Connecticut, undertook its shifting by exhibiting strength against the five dimensions we highlighted. To help us tell the story, we reached out to

Nancy Better, a founder of *SmartMoney* magazine and former president of the Greenwich Library's board of directors.

"Greenwich Library is over a century old and has become the hub of intellectual and cultural life in our community of 62,000 residents," Better told us at the beginning of our conversation. "We circulate 1.2 million materials annually. Greenwich Library is actually the busiest library in the state of Connecticut, outside of Yale and the other universities. If you live in Greenwich, if you work in Greenwich, if you're a student in Greenwich, you can have a library card and enjoy all of our resources for free. It's quite a substantial facility, with a main library and two physical branches along with a virtual branch, given the proliferation of digital materials. A lot of people interact with our website more than they actually come through our doors, but that's the sign of the times," she said. "The notion of what makes a great library is changing very rapidly in the twenty-first century. We know all libraries still need books, but the question of how you serve your patrons in a time of unprecedented change is complicated. If you continue to think that a library is a shop of books, then a library could seem antiquated. Our librarians are here to help people navigate the world of information, no matter what format that takes."

Relative to the process of shifting its focus to move beyond the traditional concept of what constitutes a great library in the twenty-first century, Better went on to explain that Greenwich Library leadership saw the need for a formal strategic plan, which they began to explore in 2011. Despite the library's tradition of excellence, they recognized that they couldn't be complacent. They needed to plan for the future and keep pace with technological and cultural trends in order to maintain their relevancy to the population they served. Their early-warning signals tuned them onto the advances in technology that had major impact on the continually changing dynamics of how people access information and interact with one another. More than that, an unstable economy affected the services people need from a library, challenging them to do more with existing resources and to make smart investments. The increasing diversity of the Greenwich population meant that the library had to be equipped to serve a broader community with a wider range of interests.

"Patron needs and technology only continue to change," Better said. "That this technology also changes how people *use* the library poses additional challenges. They want quiet spaces, but they also want group collaboration spaces. They want a study space where you can set up a bunch of laptops and maybe remotely work with people via Skype. We are constantly sifting through, constantly staying on top of what our patrons want and what they need—and figure out how to do it without breaking the budget. We need to identify how to hedge and place our bets in terms of investments. It's exciting work, and it's thrilling work, but it's also very demanding work. Today's technologies and global outlook are creating new kinds of interactions, and new avenues are constantly developing for collaborative learning. Through the 2012–2017 strategic plan, we aimed to preserve our legacy as a 'Community Treasure' and to give our great community the great library it deserves."

Better told us that the Greenwich Library embarked on the strategic planning process to study and respond to key issues facing the library. The plan, which established a long-term strategic framework for the library's ongoing efforts, identified five key areas for action to position the library to build on its strengths to meet the evolving needs of the community: Collections, Technology, Lifelong Learning and Enrichment, Service and Community Space, and Community and Connections. Here is what each entailed, as outlined in the strategic plan:

Collections: Continue to expand and curate collections and provide easy access to Library resources. Embrace and integrate emerging media into the collections. Use appropriate media and targeted messages to raise patron awareness of relevant Library resources.

Technology: Ensure patrons and staff have access to established and emerging technologies and the opportunity to achieve technological literacy. Provide technology training on a wide range of topics and tools; hardware and digital resources that are accessible to patrons with a wide range of special requirements.

Lifelong Learning and Enrichment: Meet the needs and interests of Greenwich residents by making strategic programming choices. Support the academic and life success of Greenwich children by promoting early literacy and a love of reading.

Service and Community Space: Reimagine our public spaces to reflect changes in technology and how people use the Library. Strengthen our focus on satisfying the questions, needs, and preferences of our patrons.

Community and Connections: Strengthen the community of readers by increasing patron connections to one another and to the Library's collections. Community [is] based [on] collaborative efforts with partners that bring people together for social, educational, and enjoyable interaction. Expand and focus on partnerships for the collective benefit of the Greenwich community.

This is a long and robust list of efforts, to be sure. They were based on copious research, strategic analysis, and not least, forward thinking. The library team started by identifying its strengths, recognizing that the ultimate measure of their success would be whether they had positioned the organization to better meet the continually changing needs and interests of the Greenwich community, both present and in the future. To determine the library's place in the community, they began with a community asset map—an inventory of the businesses, organizations, and institutions that constitute a community. The rationale was that by identifying the social, material, and intellectual assets of its community, a library discovers a local network or resources to help broaden its impact and contribution.

The Greenwich Library strategic plan was developed with a full understanding of its position in the web of community assets that strengthen and support the community, focusing the library on its role and identifying opportunities for collaboration with community partners. The plan, the catalyst for its shift focus initiative, was unanimously adopted by the library's board of trustees in June 2012, after an eighteen-month-long process that included a community-wide survey, focus groups, a trustee survey, a staff survey, and countless hours of evaluation and analysis. It was titled *Connecting Our Community*, an apt descriptor of its clear focus.

Relative to framing this story—and its outcome—around the five key dimensions against which organizations must exhibit strength in order to succeed in staying relevant, we asked Better to respond directly. Her answers:

Financial wherewithal—How did Greenwich Library assess the financial factors required to successfully shift its focus?

Greenwich Library is supported by a combination of public and private funding and must be tightly attuned to both the town's budgetary demands and local donors' needs. The library has been hailed as a model of financial stewardship for many years. The strategic plan for 2012–2017 did not require extensive new resources; it was not tied to a capital campaign, for example, but rather a deployment of existing resources.

Cultural disposition—What is the general cultural nature of the Greenwich Library and how did it help move the process forward?

Greenwich Library's culture is welcoming, open, and inclusive, consistent with its mission of connecting the community. There is an emphasis on encouraging users from every pocket of the town to feel at home. Over the past decade, the library has repeatedly earned the coveted "five-star designation" from the *Library Journal*, which is a testament to patrons' satisfaction with its facilities, staff, and services. The library's nickname—"Our Community Treasure"—speaks to the pride that Greenwich residents take in having such a wonderful institution in the center of town.

Clarity of focus—Beyond a formal mission statement, how does the Greenwich Library continue to ensure it stays aligned with its primary objective?

One of the chief goals of the 2012–2017 strategic plan was to have it be a dynamic document that would actually be implemented, rather than sit in a desk drawer. To this end, execution has been a highly iterative process. The board's planning committee has consistently benchmarked results against the plan and reported on its progress. Many of the initiatives have been achieved; others have been retooled or reexamined to ensure they are aligned with the library's direction as it may evolve throughout the execution period. Leadership clearly recognizes that libraries are continuously evolving, and Better says they are constantly evaluating the tools and resources patrons need to advance their skills and pursue their interests.

Executional excellence — How do you determine executional priorities and ensure that initiatives are brought to life in the manner expected?

As Better explained, the staff at Greenwich Library, led by Director Barbara Ormerod-Glynn (who played a critical role in developing the plan), was responsible for executing the priorities, which were determined in conjunction with the board. Early on, an outside consultant (Maureen Sullivan, a professional library consultant based in Annapolis, Maryland, and former president of the American Library Association) stressed the importance of having the staff participate and become deeply involved in the planning process so that they could "own" the outcomes and be fully invested in delivering them. This was excellent advice; in fact, the planning process served to invigorate the staff and energize them to perform even more strongly.

Leadership — Given the myriad constituents involved, what key leadership factors, or specific characteristics of the players, enabled the plan to move forward so successfully?

Greenwich Library benefited from a combination of strong leadership among the staff, the volunteers, and the board members, as well as a shared sense of the importance of collaboration. As a public-private partnership, the library aims to support the interests of the community members. The board and staff worked closely together to produce a strategic plan that could drive innovation and connect the community, yet protect the library's treasured 200-year history. Although libraries are generally considered traditional or conservative by nature, the team that developed the plan was open to change and eager to envision ways to steward a revered town institution into the future.

So, what does it look like on the other side of the Greenwich Library shift? While a number of the priority projects were launched and are being positively embraced (which we'll get to in a minute), Better emphasized, "It's a work in progress. This is not a onetime situation. We have a continuous feedback loop. Constant change makes it necessary for us to be constantly reimagining and reenvisioning. We will continue to keep our focus on 'connecting the community.' It's sort of a bold stroke, saying we see the library as the center of the community, where connections are formed. But everything we do is with the intention of enhancing the connection to resources, materials, the programs, the staff, and all that happens at the library. More than ever, people see us as a sort of community university—a center for intellectual and cultural activity, a hub for information and learning. Connecting people is a constant focus."

That said, Better also told us that, at its core, Greenwich Library is a *library*, a place for books, albeit a place for books that eyes its competition not as the library down the street, but rather Apple stores, Amazon, Netflix, Spotify, universities, and of course, Google. As all successful organizations do in a dynamic marketplace, Greenwich Library had to widen its competitive lens to meet the needs of its patrons. "The book collection is still at the center of what the library does," she said. "We have to be respectful of that. At the end of the day, people want a library to have books. What we're now doing is working at digitizing materials that aren't available digitally anywhere else, so they're unique to our library."

Beyond digitizing materials, further enhancements in technology were also among the priority initiatives implemented as a result of the strategic plan. Technology is an ever-present and evolving factor facilitating every aspect of library work, and these other priorities have ranged from relatively simple changes, such as the addition of self-check-out kiosks, to more robust initiatives like BiblioCommons. It was at the suggestion of the librarians that the Greenwich Library invested in this software (the first public library in Connecticut to do so). BiblioCommons is an online catalog that virtually transforms the library's essential online services, from website to card catalog to calendars of events that connect the community to needed information as well as each other. It has become the foundation for the patrons' online experiences at the library. It enables functions such as intuitive online searching, e-book integration, library staff recommendations, and the ability to create a community around the library collection. As Better put it, "BiblioCommons can take you way beyond the borders of your own library. It's been a game changer, enhancing the library experience to a great degree."

With the underlying purpose of "connecting the community," access to other technological resources, along with the appropriate training, is another of the short-list efforts that have been instituted at Greenwich Library, for both staff and patrons. This is to ensure that all patrons have the tools and skills they need to use technology, be it for education or for recreation or for job searching. Beyond having what librarians refer to as a "digital petting zoo," an area with an array of computers, iPads, Kindles, and other e-reading devices, the library offers ongoing technology training sessions and facilities. It even has an Apple-like genius bar for non-Apple users. In addition to the formal staff who take on the teaching responsibilities, the library has created a program so that teenagers can come in to help patrons (and older staff!) learn how to use the devices more easily and intuitively. It is among the many programs established to foster shared learning, to enable patrons to become more facile with technological resources, and to bring generations together. Greenwich Library is the only source in the community for free print and digital material, in terms of free access to the Internet and other tools, and free training in usage of this technology.

Addressing the ongoing cost of these enriched technological resources, Better said that "in terms of budgetary oversight, we have to constantly evaluate emerging technology rather than immediately adopt every leading-edge product. We figure out how to test products and services so as to ensure we are getting the most bang for the buck. We try to incorporate technology in a mindful way in response to the needs of the community, but keep our position as a good steward of financial resources."

To further meet the changing needs of the community, another of the library's immediate executional priorities was altering the interior of the library to better reflect how patrons use the spaces today, and will use them going forward. The goal has been to make spaces more flexible and readily adaptable to different activities. "We want to be as nimble and as facile as we can be relative to the physical space," said Better. "Given the fluidity of the marketplace and technology, you can't build with forever in mind. We need to embrace flexibility, even from a structural point of view." As she explained, think of the spatial requirements as a barbell. At one end, there are quiet study rooms, private traditional library spaces where people can work on the great American novel, write their big papers, or update their resumes. On the other end are great communal spaces where people can collaborate and share and work on projects with other people. The library is in the process of working with an architectural firm to reenvision the footprint.

A look at the Greenwich Library's website is indicative of the depth and breadth of its offerings. From the digital library to its extensive research resources, from programs for children, young adults, and seniors to its Oral History Project, from health information to its language and music programs, it is a stellar community asset. While always a "town jewel," the recognition that the library had to shift its focus in a substantial way to stay relevant to the community was indicative of its understanding that complacency is not an option in the face of today's ever-changing conditions, circumstances, and opportunities. For over eighteen months, the management team at the library, together with staff and patrons, endeavored to identify and understand the evolving needs of the community leading to the catalytic strategic plan.

As Better told us, "We're constantly trying to keep pace with the needs of the population. At the end of the day, it's all about relevancy.

The question we keep asking ourselves is, How can we be more relevant to the needs of the population we serve? . . . We are always learning from our patrons. Every year things shift a little bit, and we need to keep pace. We don't want to always play catch-up, but have to figure out how to stay ahead of changes." Exhibiting strength against the five key principles necessary to successfully shift focus, we'd say they will continue to give Greenwich "the great library it deserves."

The Greenwich Library reflects a successful shift ahead, but it is relatively recent. Some organizations have been able to shift over and over again as circumstances warrant.

9

SUCCESS IS NEVER FINAL

While we've made clear that there are many things that have to be done right to successfully shift ahead, our final thought is this: Success is never final. In a world that is changing as fast as this one, you can never take your foot off the gas. Concurrently, you can never take your eyes off your customers and the purpose you serve in their lives. You must constantly let the customer know that *you* know what's important to them. Not just on a transactional level, but on an emotional level. They are the ones who will decide if you continue to fit into their lives in a meaningful way. They are the ones who will determine whether you continue to effectively meet their evolving needs. Keeping the customer in your sights and your pedal to the metal will greatly increase your chances for not just successfully shifting ahead, but successfully staying ahead.

It is this story line that is at the heart of these final stories. Each of the organizations profiled has sound methodologies for assessing what's down the road and exhibits strength against the five key dimensions required to successfully shift ahead (as outlined in Chapter 8). More than this, to paraphrase the contemporary cultural expression, they know there is no other option but to "keep on keeping on." To paraphrase the Fleetwood Mac tune, they are always thinking about tomorrow. They have strategic vision, which is the ability to look ahead. They have peripheral vision, which is the ability to look around. And they have proved they can anticipate, capture, and categorically lead through one market transition after another. They create disruption before they let themselves be beaten by it and, in fact, view disruption as an opportunity. Each of these organizations has a culture that fosters innovation and a management team that is comfortable in dealing with disruptive forces as they arise.

The organizations profiled in this final chapter also take a purpose-driven approach to their businesses, not a transactional or product-driven approach. Tied to doing what is important to the consumer, purpose is the driving force behind everything they do, and it gives them greater flexibility in ensuring their actions stay aligned with what they stand for in the minds of those they serve. More important, their actions demonstrate an awareness that it is the consumer who will decide what is relevant. Being purpose-driven gives them the stability to make changes as needed, to see and seize on initiatives as they arise. While the organizations profiled in this section are altogether different from one another in form and function, they all operate on the assumption that success is never final.

IAVA:
A Clearly Focused Mission as a Compass for Veterans' Shifting Needs

We begin not with a publicly traded company, but an exceedingly public-facing group, IAVA: the Iraq and Afghanistan Veterans of America. Go to the website and the first words you see are "Be Part of The Movement." It *is* a movement, a wholly constructive one, with a clearly defined mission that serves as both compass and catalyst for its vital work. IAVA is the leading post-9/11 veteran empowerment organization with a diverse and rapidly growing membership. Its purpose is to be the voice of these veterans, and to use this voice to address the critical issues facing the veterans and their families. The organization provides resources and empowers veterans to connect with one another to foster a strong and mutually beneficial community. As the IAVA website states, "Through education, advocacy, and community building, we strive to create a country which honors and supports veterans of all generations."

IAVA serves the 2.8 million veterans of Iraq and Afghanistan, raising awareness in the media, on Capitol Hill, and among the general public about the issues that veterans face. Among these issues are mental health injuries, the challenges of working with the Veterans Administration system, inadequate healthcare for female veterans, and GI educational benefits.

IAVA is an organization founded and run by veterans, and it is strongly committed to ensuring its programs make the largest impact for as many veterans as possible. More than this, as its website asserts, its goal is to do so at the lowest cost possible. As for the proficiency of its leadership and its fiscal responsibility as an organization, the site states, "Since our founding 11 years ago, IAVA has connected more than 1.27 million veterans with resources and support while being exceptionally fiscally responsible to the thousands of individuals, foundations, and corporate partners who support our mission. And we do so on the smallest budgets."

IAVA was founded by Paul Rieckhoff, an American writer, advocate, activist, and veteran of the United States Army and the Iraq War. He served as an Army first lieutenant and infantry rifle platoon leader in Iraq from 2003 through 2004. It is in very good part due to his leadership acumen, his (peripheral) visionary skills, and his personal passion for the mission of the organization that IAVA has emerged as a key player on veterans' issues on Capitol Hill. Among the various veterans' issues in which the organization is engaged are four top priorities: combat suicide among troops and veterans; services for women veterans; government reform for veterans; and defense education budgets for veterans. With regard to CEO Rieckhoff, Senator Patty Murray from Washington State has been quoted as saying, "He's relentless. When he brings a new issue to me, I know it's what I should be fighting for."

We spoke to Rieckhoff about IAVA, its mission, and how the organization continuously shifts gears to develop new initiatives for the population it serves. "When we created IAVA," he said, "we based it on what I call a constituent empowerment model that enables a relatively small number of people to do huge things. We are built to be relevant. Our mission has remained the same: listening to our constituents' needs and representing their interests by advocating for positive change. This sounds pretty basic, but it's the most critical *part* of advocacy. Our members are an underrepresented population who feel like their voice isn't heard. The most important thing we do is create mechanisms to listen to them and amplify what they say as a catalyst for transformational change. We are able to pivot relative to what's important to them. If your mission and values are right," he said, "you will be durable. This is as true when it comes to running an ad agency or a bank as it is in running an advocacy group. Staying focused on your core mission enables you to be in a constant state of beta. If you're not evolving and changing, you're going to lose. On the battlefield the saying is 'evolve or die.' In other words, the enemy is changing, the threats are changing. If you don't change, you die."

"Keep on keeping on" is embedded in the fabric of IAVA's culture. Leadership's background and immersion in the military makes this phrase as much a part of their mindset as saying, "Look both ways when crossing the street."

It came as no surprise to us that, in terms of implementation strategies and tactics, what allows IAVA to "pivot relative to what's important" is that the group took its lessons from the brutal realities of the war zones and brought them home to Washington and Wall Street. "What we've learned from the battlefield is the need to improvise, adapt, and overcome. We're good at logistics. We're good at moving groups of people from one place to another, which is important when you work in advocacy. Over the years, policy issues have shifted, from the need for better body armor in Iraq, to the GI Bill, to 'don't ask, don't tell,' to suicide." These form the core of IAVA's DNA.

Among the organization's greatest tactical strengths, and one developed out of necessity, is its ability to leverage the media, and especially social media, to get out veterans' stories as a catalyst for the desired outcomes. "We punch way above our weight," Rieckhoff told us. "Our budget hasn't changed, but the power of our communications artillery has. There is an urgency to our work that is essential. We understand we have a short window of consciousness with the American public. We have to communicate as quickly and clearly before the window closes. Another thing we learned in the military is, keep your communication simple and focused. In our work, we have to ensure people understand our message."

A significant aspect of ensuring that people understand the message is that IAVA recognizes the value of having a person be the face of an issue, a fight, a catalyst for the legislative or policy change you are trying to implement. Even though the challenges are constantly changing, personification of the challenge provides a common way to approach them. You can throw facts and statistics at people as much as you want, but that won't have nearly as much influence as emotional impact. The Clay Hunt Suicide Prevention for American Veterans (SAV) Act is a perfect example of putting forth a story that, sadly, so many people could personally relate to.

"Our members would say, 'Hey, our friends are dying and nobody knows about it. We've got to do something about it,'" Rieckhoff said as he recounted the initiative. "Clay Hunt was a Marine from Texas. He came back from Iraq, wounded, but then redeployed to Afghanistan where he saw several of his buddies killed. After he came home, he struggled with the aftereffects of the wars and found some comfort in helping other veterans cope with their own struggles. He became very active in our organization as an advocate for mental health support. And then, he went down a rough lane and took his own life in 2011 at the age of twenty-eight. It devastated our community and our organization," said Rieckhoff. "We wanted to do something about it. It was a two-year-long campaign to explain to Washington that we were losing twenty-two of our buddies a day to suicide. But Clay became the face of that campaign. He became like a North Star for the whole community."

One of the leading causes of death for American military forces is suicide. In 2012, 349 active members of the Armed Forces took their own lives, more than died in combat. In February 2015, a year after IAVA launched the Campaign to Combat Suicide, IAVA and its partners celebrated the signing of the Clay Hunt SAV Act into law. This law makes possible improved access to high-quality, timely mental health care for service members, veterans, and their families and expanded suicide prevention efforts.

As Rieckhoff made clear, you can't *buy* media presence as influential—as sharable—as Clay Hunt's story. It was a very real and very compelling story that not only unlocked the enormous potential of social media, but exemplified IAVA's broader mission. It was a small, personal story that evolved into a bigger story as a result of its emotional resonance. "We play where we can win," said Rieckhoff. "We pick issues that we believe can have impact. What is the overall urgency of the issue? What is our capacity to make a change? Is there anyone else doing it? We want to be a true leader, and a true leader takes on things that no one else does. We're ahead of the curve. We're not afraid to throw punches, and we're always loyal to our constituents."

In addition to showing strength against the five key principles required to successfully shift gears, not as a onetime event but on an ongoing basis, IAVA recognizes that you *do* have to know where you can play and win, where you can be a leader and have influence and efficacy. It wouldn't be unfitting, in this case, to say it's knowing how to pick your battles when time and/or resources are limited. As Rieckhoff put it, "We sit down and say, What's the one thing I can move the needle on at this point that will have a major impact? The stakes are enormous for our veterans. We want to do things that change the world for the better. There is an old saying that pilots use, 'Focus on the target.' We've got planning templates that come from the military. You lay out the situation, the mission, the execution, the communication, the command and control. We always keep in mind, it's not about me. It's about the mission, the greater goal. You can't be greater than the mission. We say 'men and women before me.'"

As a result of IAVA's laser focus on its mission, along with its battle-tested strategy and tactics, it has become a trusted brand known to policy makers, the media, and Washington. It has become *the* go-to source on veterans' issues. It is, we might add, a perfect analog for this book and this chapter on the need for all organizations to relentlessly focus on issues that can make a difference; to continuously shift gears to stay relevant to the people they serve. A final and fitting comment from Rieckhoff: "To succeed, keep your compass on true north. True north may take you over a mountain or through water, but you know what direction you're going in."

To try and produce an apt segue between the IAVA story and the next one (HBO), relative to the scale of human benefit, would be off the mark. So we won't try. We can, however, draw parallels about the role that having a clear purpose plays in enabling an organization to continually and successfully "keep on keeping on" when it comes to shifting ahead. In the case of HBO, staying focused on its purpose has provided advantageous leverage in one of the most rapidly changing and mercurial business categories there is: entertainment. From the day of its inception, the folks at HBO knew what they *didn't* want to be, and in fact couldn't be, if they wanted to keep consumers voluntarily tuning in season after season. They didn't want to be a TV network. They wanted to be the entertainment network brand that provided programming you couldn't find anywhere else. It's a purpose that has driven the brand—and, ergo, its supremacy in the ratings—for decades. HBO keeps on keeping on, no matter on which screen people watch their programming.

HBO:
Always Ahead, It's *Never* Been Just TV

"We knew our business. We knew what we needed to get to, we knew what our skillset was. . . . We were able to keep growing the business without hurting it. We knew what was going on out there in terms of technology and competition. But, you can't act emotionally. If you make knee-jerk reactions, you can make some mistakes from which you might never recover. HBO continues to maintain its equity as a premium brand. It's a high-quality product, in terms of content, in terms of talent, in terms of the look of the service on the air, the production qualities, and the technology. HBO spares no expense to make sure it looks different, and that it *is* different from everything else. This is the philosophy that has carried through."

Eric Kessler, former president and chief operating officer at HBO, offered these comments completely unprompted in response to our query about how the company has continuously shifted to keep its position on top of the category leader board. If anyone should know what's required to shift, and what to focus on to stay relevant to consumers, it's someone who, for decades, has been associated with the hyper-changing entertainment business. It was during the span of Kessler's twenty-seven years with the company that the industry itself shifted dramatically (no pun intended) its content model, given the expanding range of competitors, as well as its content distribution model, given the evolution of technology. It was under Kessler's leadership that HBO had innumerable accomplishments, including the launch of the network's signature "It's Not TV. It's HBO" marketing campaign.

To be sure, HBO was unique coming out of the gate, and it has stayed fully attuned to the requirements of staying ahead in the entertainment-technology marathon—a marathon with very fickle spectators. Perhaps the most critical factor in HBO's continued success as it has shifted to meet the demands of these very fickle spectators is its philosophy. The core essence of the HBO brand, what it strives to stand for in the minds of consumers, is "groundbreaking entertainment." It is groundbreaking in the programming and in the manner in which consumers *consume* this entertainment. For an entertainment brand to win over the long term, it means constantly finding ways to reinvent itself. HBO has always been a forward-looking company and has consistently been ready for what it saw coming.

As Kessler told us, "There had been very few significant changes in the way people watched television since 1946 until just a few years ago. There was the introduction of color in 1951, and the introduction of HD in 2000. The box itself changed from that big clunky set sitting on a table to being a sleek screen mounted on a wall. Regardless, [for] the first fifty years of television, people were tethered to their living rooms if they wanted to watch their favorite shows. Over the course of just the last decade, we've seen multiple devices hit the market on which people can get entertainment, including television shows. Computers, iPads, and smartphones have fundamentally changed the way people think about watching television," Kessler said. Expanding distribution opportunities brought an expanding set of competitive players. In addition to networks, HBO was also competing against an emerging list of direct-to-consumer streaming services like Netflix, Hulu, and Amazon Prime.

In response to the changing technology, HBO modified its distribution model, which was based on paid subscriptions, the staple of cable television. Kessler explained that they had to implement this change at an appropriate pace. HBO couldn't afford to harm its relationships with Comcast and Direct TV, among others, whose thousands of representatives were selling HBO's channels to millions of viewers. Much as they did everything else, it was a well-thought-out process. HBO GO, launched in 2010, was a partial answer to this challenge. HBO GO allows subscribers to watch HBO shows anytime and anywhere it's convenient for them. "HBO GO was the integration of delivery and content through technology created specifically to meet audience needs," Kessler said. "The concept is simple. An HBO subscriber should have the ability to watch whatever they want, whenever they want, at no extra cost. They've paid for the content. They should be able to watch it on their terms. If you take this further, as HBO has, it changed the whole competitive set for television, and for HBO. You had the consumer sitting at home on the couch watching HBO or another network. To move ahead, we had to evaluate this experience within the context of both programming and technology. Beyond individual networks, for example, you had content aggregators gaining on us, including the growth of over-the-top services such as Hulu, Netflix, and Amazon. The key for HBO was, and continues to be, to look at the competitive set and see it as inclusive of technology and myriad new content options."

Getting HBO GO as part of an HBO cable bundle was the first step in shifting the distribution model. It was more likely that users would keep renewing their subscriptions if they could watch what they wanted, when they wanted. By increasing access, HBO, like any other premium cable channel, would increase customer satisfaction with the brand experience, thereby making subscribers more loyal. Next, in 2014, after years of saying it didn't make sense to sell an online-only version of HBO because the economics of the pay-TV bundle were too good and the size of the broadband-only market was too small, Richard Plepler, the current CEO of HBO, decided to launch HBO Now to target the "cord-cutters," or people without pay-TV subscriptions. This decision was in response to the need to compete for the ever-growing audience of people who consume programming online from Netflix, Amazon, and Hulu, among others. As the Internet remakes the television landscape, targeting cord-cutters becomes a growth imperative. HBO Now, among the latest online pushes for HBO and Time Warner, is a service that lets broadband users watch new episodes of popular HBO shows like *Game of Thrones*, *Veep*, and *Silicon Valley* without a traditional cable subscription.

HBO continues to be a crowd pleaser for Time Warner with its non-stop creation of groundbreaking offerings, from big-ticket dramas to comedy specials, brilliantly produced documentaries to sports-related programming. Its obvious challenge is the proliferation of home-based entertainment choices, and the fact that it has to prove on a regular basis that its programming is worth the price of admission. "The genesis of 'It's Not TV. It's HBO' was that if it was the type of program you could see on a regular TV network, we wouldn't do it," Kessler told us. "Basic cable? Let's do it differently. We needed to take a position that was different and we needed to deliver on it. The simple statement captured the essence of the brand idea at the time and became the driving force behind everything we did. If you make a claim like that, you've got to develop programming to support it. We needed to *transcend* the category. Once we latched onto the idea, the programming took on a life of its own."

The key thing to notice in HBO's story is that the shift in technology went hand in hand with the shifting in programming in the late 1990s and early 2000s. HBO used to simply have first-film licensing agreements until the company decided to create and own original content. It served as a major differentiator that separated HBO from other premium services, but it also redefined the network's competition as not just other premium networks but other basic cable and broadcast networks. The creative minds at HBO used that as a touchstone for its programming. They developed an intuitive feel for what was—and wasn't—HBO quality. Beginning in the 1990s with *The Sopranos*, followed by *The Wire, Band of Brothers, The Pacific, Six Feet Under, Entourage, Sex and the City, Curb Your Enthusiasm, Big Love, Game of Thrones, Boardwalk Empire, Silicon Valley*, and *Westworld*, HBO continued to break new ground. The network has aired more than 100 series and twenty miniseries in its history, ushering in, along with AMC, what some have called a new golden age of television entertainment.[1]

HBO also continues to be a crowd pleaser due to its ability to see what's coming in terms of technology and shift as needed. HBO Now, its stand-alone streaming service, has surpassed 2 million domestic subscribers. More than this, HBO has lined up a host of A-list players in the digital arena to help distribute and market the service, partnerships that include Amazon, Microsoft's Xbox, Samsung, and PlayStation Vue. All this may at first glance seem counterproductive in that HBO is cannibalizing its own traditional cable TV–based service. However, the cord-cutters are coming, and if HBO doesn't cannibalize them, someone else will take them away.

As a critically acclaimed innovator, ratings-breaker, and multiple Emmy and Golden Globe winner in the cable industry, HBO creates the programs that everyone talks about, driving conversations online and off. Its original series, miniseries, documentaries, comedy specials, and films draw ratings numbers its competitors covet. With streaming video now among the competitors in the television space, HBO has invested heavily in technology to expand its own streaming service and to build new applications to support its content.

"HBO and all networks have to get continuously better at technology," Kessler said. "Not the technology required to take a signal, send it to a satellite, and have it beam back content. Rather, the development of software and use of analytics that make for the best customer experience possible. HBO has had to evolve and bring in different types of talent in recognition of the fact that things are changing and companies in the category need to improve and broaden their skillsets. That said, HBO has kept the culture intact. It's always had the right people for the job at the right time. They're no longer competing with other cable networks, but with Facebook and YouTube and Apple. It's always had a culture of wanting to try new things. We've brought in interns not to learn from us, but to *teach* us what the next generation wants. If you're not keeping pace in this industry," said Kessler, "you're quickly falling behind to the extent that you can *never* catch up. It requires constant investment, in software and in people. Success in this industry demands that you continuously make adjustments; that you are constantly in beta mode." One has to "keep on keeping on."

Kessler oversaw the distribution of both the HBO and Cinemax networks in both domestic and international markets, along with the worldwide sale of HBO's programming through licensing, DVD products, and digital distribution. An early seer of the digital future, he was instrumental in the exploration of mobile experiences and, ultimately, the launch of HBO GO and HBO Now, HBO's first direct-to-consumer service in northern territories. Today, HBO continues to make the shifts necessary to help keep HBO a leader in its category with a laser focus on keeping up with content and the latest in technology.

Perhaps no business is as prone to dramatic changes as the entertainment business is today. Taking home the awards is equally dependent on leveraging evolving technology and perfectly forecasting mercurial consumer tastes. HBO's tagline has morphed from "It's Not TV. It's HBO" to simply, "It's HBO." This is in recognition of the fact that the category is not just about TV anymore. That said, HBO has not deviated from its "true north," providing groundbreaking programming with only the highest levels of production values, from the writing to the acting and directing. As Kessler said, "One thing is for sure. In this business, doing what you did before rarely leads to success. It's good to be first out of the box and have that advantage, but what matters most is to get it right. It's more important to differentiate your product and to spend the time to really get it right and be sure you're visionary. HBO has always been visionary, [able] to look for the new and to try different things. You can't survive in entertainment if you just rely on the tried and true."

As we've said in a number of ways throughout this book, there are few, if any, industries in which you can survive, let alone shift ahead, by relying on the tried and true. This is especially true of industries in which technology plays a pivotal role. General Electric, a huge multi-faceted, multinational organization with thousands of employees and hundreds of products, absolutely gets it. The company has boiled down what it stands for into a simple, emotional idea—a statement of purpose—that everyone can connect with, inside and outside the company: *imagination at work*. It defines the culture and it's believable because coming from GE, imagination is credible. As this final story illustrates, from the get-go, GE has used its imagination to powerfully fuel its way forward in a rapidly changing world.

GE:
Reinvention at Work for over 125 Years

"Imagine a world where we treat great female scientists like celebrities." General Electric (GE) is in the perfect position to not only imagine this, but to do something about it. In the sixty-second TV spot that poses this idea, Millie Dresselhaus, the first woman to win the National Medal of Science in Engineering, is treated like a paparazzi favorite— photographed, celebrated, thronged by crowds of admirers. The spot is part of GE's campaign to raise awareness that it plans to employ 20,000 women in STEM (science, technology, engineering, and mathematics) roles by the year 2020 and have a 50/50 gender representation in its technical entry-level programs by the same time. The campaign shows how celebrating female scientists could inspire girls to become scientists and help GE find its recruits to meet its 2020 deadline.

In a press release in *Adweek* following the launch of the campaign, GE's chief marketing officer, Linda Boff, said:

> We think celebrating people, in this case women, who have had great achievements is far more important than celebrating people who are famous for fame's sake. There are people out there— Millie Dresselhaus is the one we've chosen to highlight—who have done remarkable things and deserve admiration and adulation, and holding up these women as role models is a really fun way to shine a light on what we're calling balancing the equation and addressing what is an industry-wide challenge of getting more women in STEM. The data show that women are still underrepresented in IT and engineering roles—that's not a GE number, that's just global—so the fact that we can help inject urgency into this conversation, that's something we're super proud to be part of.[2]

GE has been injecting urgency into conversations—and actions— for over 125 years. In our conversation with Boff about the company's ability to continuously shift gears to stay relevant, she said, "Progress is part of our constant. Progress and solving tough problems for the world. You don't get to be 125 years old without continually reinventing. Our ongoing pivot points reflect the advantage we can bring our customers. We are continuously defining what a superb customer experience will be for GE customers. Increasingly, our offerings are digital in nature and we want to make sure that the experience we are delivering is simple and frictionless. We want the best possible outcomes for our customers," Boff said, "be it productivity or efficiency. Our marketing is a reflection of how iterative our business is. It's reflected in the storytelling. That said, our core is constant. It's rooted in our DNA. We are and always have been about imagination and reinvention. We know who we are. Our ethos has never changed. I like to say 'embrace your own interesting-ness.' How can we be relevant? What moments can be ours?"

This is very much reminiscent of the IBM story in Chapter 6. Iconic companies become iconic for a reason. They change, they adapt, all the while staying true to who they are.

Boff went on to explain that, unlike having a core mission that is focused on products—the things a company makes—existing to solve problems is an "evergreen idea." Problem solving requires reimagination according to which specific problems need solving at different points in time, as the marketplace changes. Having purpose, not product, as its laser focus gives GE the freedom to experiment, to take risks. "You have to invent and to market in the year in which you live," Boff said. "Our DNA doesn't change. How we bring things to life changes. You have to look in real time at the world you live in. You have to try new things and go outside of your comfort zone. You have to spend time out of the conference rooms to see and assess what changes are coming and how to deal with them. The risk is not in experimenting with new things, but in *not* experimenting. Our teams are organized to experiment. Embracing your inner geek is something we take pride in."

There have been many successful pivotal moments that have belonged to GE in its history, all the result of the company's core DNA *and* its can-do culture: its built-in ability to shift as the marketplace conditions evolve and a new set of challenges emerge to be solved.

As a crash course in the history of science and GE, 1876 was the year Thomas Alva Edison opened a laboratory in Menlo Park, New Jersey, where he could explore the possibilities of electricity. Out of his tinkering was to come one of the greatest inventions of the age—a successful incandescent light bulb. By 1890 Edison established the Edison General Electric Company, bringing together its various businesses. This was, in GE's history, the beginning of its industrial age. It was a company of tinkerers, proud to celebrate its "inner geek" and even prouder to be able to develop and manufacture products that would enhance life for generations of people around the world. They "brought good things to life."

This worked as an inspiring tagline—and driving force—for the company's mission until around twenty years ago. As if the pace of change were not fast enough, there was no question that competition was increasing at a "Moore's Law" pace, most significantly in the technology space. Globalization was no longer a concept hovering on the horizon, but a requisite way of doing business. GE's business model was shifting year by year in response to these new conditions, yes, encompassing not just the production of light bulbs and refrigerators, but extending to the areas of transportation, health services, consumer finance, and entertainment, with digital experiences underlying many of these competencies. It was evident that this sweep of newer and newer offerings called for a different rallying cry, a new way to communicate its continued relevance and significance to the world market.

To achieve this, led by then CEO Jeffrey Immelt, GE went back to its genesis, Thomas Edison. From day one, GE had been able to imagine things that other companies couldn't and make them real. As Immelt put it, they could do things that made people go "wow!" Within this framework, the company rallied its more than 300,000 employees around an idea: "What we can imagine, we can make happen." Or as the tagline stated, "Imagination at work."

Imagination continues to be very much at work at GE. Also at work, however, is the ever-quickening pace of change in the world, specifically in the technology realm, from big data to artificial intelligence. The explosion of the "Internet of Things" or the "Industrial Internet," as it's sometimes called, has been the stimulus for GE's latest series of necessary shifts to stay relevantly differentiated: industrial company to imaginative company to digital industrial company. As Boff explained to us, by staying focused on its core mission of invention, GE has been able to stay ahead of others in this category. It realized, before many of its competitors, that the current economy depends on the swift, silent transmission of information. As such, in its work, GE is looking to turn jet engines, locomotives, and other giant machines into data-churning computers. It is putting additional effort into healthcare solutions and on various forms of energy. As a company, GE is at the leading edge of the intersection of the physical and the analytical, a very different portfolio than even just twenty years ago.

To raise awareness of this shift in its history, along with its proud focus on its geekiness, in early 2016, GE introduced an advertising campaign that featured Owen, an earnest young software developer who had just been hired by the company. In a series of ads and online platforms, in his charmingly befuddled way Owen has to explain to his friends and family that their preconceived notions about GE are no longer valid. Rather than design light bulbs, he has been hired to write the code that runs transportation systems, industrial equipment, and power grids. This campaign was produced to help clarify consumer perceptions about the company. GE doesn't make things; it solves problems. Owen was also meant to be a recruiting mechanism, reaching out to millennials who had never associated this traditional company with dominance in the technology arena. The twofold approach to the campaign was to reinforce GE's presence as a digital industrial company, a leader in the space of merging digital and industrial. The second was to recruit software developers.

And this brings us back to the beginning of this story—and the beginning of GE—with just a minor detour for recent news from the company's website. As part of the next phase in its ongoing shift to brilliantly implement its digital industrial strategy, the company announced the formation of GE Digital, a business unit that will provide customers with the best industrial solutions and the software needed to solve real-world problems. It has also launched Predix, an operating system for the "Industrial Internet of Things." Overall there are 20,000 developers working on Predix. In 2017, GE is expecting to grow the platform to 35,000 developers and continue to expand its digital capabilities. In addition, the company has acquired software companies such as Meridium, Servicemax, and Wise.io that bring together sensors, cloud-based algorithms, and advanced field technology to help transform the way engineers and coders work together. And—yes— imagine if at least 50 percent of this population of technology experts could be women?

As GE says and continues to do in so very many cases, what they can imagine, they can make happen. The public commitment to hire more women in STEM positions is an ambitious one. And although plenty of companies introduce goals for narrowing the gender gap in technology positions, GE is among the first to take a tangible step in achieving this goal. The beautifully produced ad campaign was created to raise awareness of this goal. Among the tactics to "make it happen," GE is expanding recruitment efforts at colleges and universities that have greater proportions of women in technical majors and enhancing efforts to retain and promote women who are current employees. As Boff told *Adweek*, "While we're really proud of the nearly 15,000 women that we currently have in technical roles, we're talking about adding 36 percent more. I would like to highlight that while I'm thrilled at how this ad will hopefully capture people's attention, the heart of this will be more women working in technical roles."

To repeat what Boff told us, "Our marketing is a reflection of how iterative our business is. How can we be relevant? What moments can be ours?" Well, from Thomas Edison and an incandescent light bulb to the one billion terabytes of information Predix will process by 2020, from your grandmother's refrigerator to a host of transformational medical technologies, from wind turbines to more energy-efficient airplane engines, GE has had a lot of moments. Its visionary leadership has certainly made this possible, as has its laser focus on using its imagination to solve tough problems for the world. GE has been shifting for over 125 years, and given its strength against the five dimensions required for successful shifting (presented in Chapter 8), we can only imagine that the company will keep it up for the next 125 years, making changes that will continue to reflect "the world in which we live."

Lest you think that we are groundbreaking in our belief that success is never final, we openly admit otherwise. Recall from Chapter 4, Gary Briggs told us about Facebook's credo of being one percent done. If you look at the Marriott organization's list of core values, for example, key among them is that "success is never final." Bill Marriott, son of the company's founder, has been quoted as saying:

> When my father was alive, we would discuss the progress the company was achieving. With each great success, he would tell me to stop patting myself on the back and would remind me of one of his favorite sayings, "Success is never final," which I think he read in a book by Winston Churchill. From then on, I realized there

are still great hills to climb, new markets to conquer, and more guests to satisfy.[3]

At the risk of being too obvious, no matter the organization, whether public or private, for profit or not, there will always be more "guests" to satisfy. As demographics, markets, technology, and global forces continue to rapidly change, so, too, will the needs and expectations of these guests. For organizations to meet these needs and expectations, for organizations to maintain their relevance in a fast-changing world, they must possess both the skills and the attitude required to shift ahead. The skills, detailed in this book, can be learned and applied. The attitude is in your court.

That said, in addition to the lesson that "success is never final," we'd like to end with two personal stories from our own "shift ahead" experiences—lessons we continue to find valuable and hope you will, too.

CONCLUDING REMARKS

As we stated at the outset, a primary objective in writing this book was to share the many lessons we have learned along the way about what it takes to successfully shift ahead to stay relevant in a fast-changing society—Joel from his academic perspective and Allen from his in-the-trenches perspective. While there were many places throughout this book we could have inserted our favorite personal stories, we decided to save them for the end.

ALLEN ADAMSON

It was, perhaps, the most important piece of wisdom I received during my many years working as a marketing executive, given to me by Ken Roman, the CEO of Ogilvy, in the very early days of my career. And it continues to have an impact on how I approach business—and life, for that matter.

This advice was not handed to me before or after a particularly challenging assignment but, rather, during my job interview with Ken. It was actually my *first* job interview after graduate school, with Ogilvy & Mather, a still much-venerated communications firm. Suffice it to say,

I was somewhat nervous. I knew that I knew my stuff, but I was going to have to convince the people who would be paying me that I knew my stuff. After a full day answering questions from a host of managers about marketing segmentation, media analytics, and other areas of functional process and procedure, I was told to stop by Ken Roman's office for the ultimate thumbs-up, thumbs-down meeting. Gearing myself up for yet more questions on marketing strategy, I was surprised when after the initial exchange of pleasantries, Ken asked me to tell him about the last book I had read and the last movie I had seen, and how they had affected me. Thankfully, after a moment of fumbling, I was able to pull together a pretty decent response, after which Ken explained the reason for his question. It was that, as a client representative, among my most important responsibilities was to stay in touch with what was going on in the world, far outside the boundaries of any specific marketing initiative. I had to be the social barometer, the cultural point person, the ears and the eyes for our clients. I could be as diligent as possible in knowing my marketing stuff. However, if I wasn't intellectually curious and creatively aware of contemporary trends and social issues, I would not be able to serve my clients well. I would not succeed in the business.

I took this advice to heart both as a newbie account guy and, as I ascended into positions of higher authority, the supervisor of class after class of newbie account and creative people. In my role as a manager, I counseled that, to best serve clients, it was essential to get out of the "bubble." I encouraged my employees—and my colleagues—to get real, to make oneself aware of what was happening in the real world, beyond strategy documents and research reports. To not let themselves get consumed by the emails and spreadsheets, the trade publications, the industry conferences, and the general information overload on whatever it is they were supposed to be selling. To not be so consumed by the "busyness syndrome" to which so many of us fall victim. We forget to look up. We forget to look around. Consumers don't live in a vacuum. As marketing professionals, we can't operate in one.

Many of the people we interviewed for this book talked, in one way or another, about this need to get out of the bubble in order to be credible and to be genuinely valuable to consumers. It was a common theme, with good reason. Those who are successful at shifting ahead know that staying in touch with the cultural zeitgeist is critical to their success. All these many years later, I want to thank my first boss for his sage advice. Ken, while I've been extremely diligent in keeping up with my marketing skills, I have been equally diligent in ensuring I would be able to provide more than a pretty decent response to your original question. I know what's going on out there in the market beyond my assignments, and I know why it matters. Your advice has served me, and hundreds of other marketing people, very well.

JOEL STECKEL

I am a relatively successful marketing professor at the Leonard N. Stern School of Business at New York University. Forty years ago, I was a math and physics major at Columbia University. Although I did not wear a pocket protector or horn-rimmed glasses, I would certainly have qualified as a geek. My "shift ahead" from geek to marketing professor was a process—a process that involved answering the door when opportunity knocked while respecting my own DNA.

In the late 1970s, when I was in college, kids went straight to graduate school. They did not take time off the way most students do today. As a senior, after realizing that I didn't have the type of mind that would enable me to reach what was then my dream—a Ph.D. in math and a career as a math professor at a prestigious university—I had to find something else to do. Given the environment, it was going to involve school, not work. Not wanting to endure medical school or law school, I decided to make a last-minute application to business school and was admitted to the Wharton School's MBA program. In retrospect, the reason I went was that I didn't really have anything better to do.

Not surprisingly, I hated business school. I was a young twenty-one, not motivated for a career in commerce or happy with the material in the courses I was taking. After four years of advanced mathematics and physics, an MBA program seemed easy at the time. The most boring course? Ironically, it was marketing.

To alleviate the boredom of MBA courses, I took mathematically based Ph.D. courses as substitutes. It was easier and more entertaining to solve equations using calculus in economics than it was to shift supply and demand curves to the right or left to find a new equilibrium. Through those courses, I became acquainted with three men that would change my life. The first was Abba Krieger, a statistics professor. Abba needed a teaching assistant for his statistics course and I needed to make a little money, so this former math major got the job being Abba's teaching assistant. Abba took me under his wing. He introduced me to a professor of marketing, Len Lodish, whose research was on mathematical models in marketing. I had barely gotten a B in my introductory marketing course (while being totally bored). I did not even know that mathematical models in marketing existed. Then Abba introduced me to Len over lunch one day and at that lunch, Len explained what he did. I then worked as Len's research assistant. It was the first intellectually appealing thing I did in business school. Len advised me to stay at Wharton beyond my MBA and get a Ph.D. What a great idea.

Abba then introduced me to Professor Jerry Wind, the man who would become my dissertation adviser. I began my dissertation research and the rest is history.

I often think back and wonder what would have happened back at Wharton if I didn't take Ph.D. courses as an MBA student. What would have happened if I assisted a professor other than Abba Krieger? I might never have met Len or Jerry. The initial lunch I had with Len Lodish was a turning point in my life. A door opened, and I entered. Opportunity knocked and I answered. I entered the world of marketing. I shifted ahead into an intellectually appealing field for which I had some aptitude.

Oh yes, that aptitude is in my DNA. I was able to build a successful career by applying my mathematical skills. My career has focused on building mathematical marketing models, using statistics to analyze marketing data, and teaching students how to do the same. I have been president of an important professional organization and the editor of one of our journals. Most ironically, I now teach the course that bored me almost forty years ago. I guess my students will now know that I only got a "B" in it when I was in business school. Well, they should know, too, that the course they are getting is very different from the one I got.

NOTES

CHAPTER 1

1   Vincent P. Barabba and Gerald Zaltman, *Hearing the Voice of the Market* (Boston: Harvard Business School Press, 1990), 52.

2   BAV Consulting, "Industry Leading Brand Insights," accessed February 18, 2016, http://bavconsulting.com/insights/reports/.

3   http://www.economist.com/news/briefing/21679448-pace-business-really-getting-quicker-creed-speed.

CHAPTER 2

1   Catharine Smith, "Website Lets You Opt-Out of Yellow Pages Delivery," *HuffingtonPost.com*, updated May 25, 2011, http://www.huffingtonpost.com/2011/02/03/yellow-pages-opt-out-website_n_818050.html?ir.

2   *Reinventing Adobe*, Harvard Business School Case 9-514-066, Sunil Gupta & Lauren Barley, 3.

3   Chunka Mui, "Five Dangerous Lessons to Learn From Steve Jobs," Forbes.com, updated October 17, 2011, https://www.forbes.com/sites/chunkamui/2011/10/17/five-dangerous-lessons-to-learn-from-steve-jobs/#f9c95263a95c.

4   Russell L. Ackoff, "Management Misinformation Systems," *Management Science*, Vol. 14, No. 4 (December) B147–56.

5   https://www.youtube.com/watch?v=VQ9nhDUXTsk.

CHAPTER 3

1   Hal Arkes and Catherine Blumer, "The Psychology of Sunk Cost," *Organizational Behavior and Human Decision Process*, Vol. 35 (1985), 124–140.

2   Barry M. Staw, "The escalation of commitment: An update and appraisal," in Zur Shapira, ed. *Organizational Decision Making* (New York, Cambridge University Press, 1997), 191–215.

3   Ian Austen, "Blackberry Abandons Its Phone," accessed August 6, 2017, https://www.nytimes.com/2016/09/29/technology/blackberry-phones-earnings-q2.html.

4   Theodore Levitt, "Marketing Myopia," *Harvard Business Review*, July–August 1960, 45–56.

5   http://www.bain.com/publications/articles/get-your-mojo-back-with-the-founders-mentality.-video.aspx.

6   http://www.economist.com/node/13760551; https://www.youtube.com/watch?v=UUddgE8rI0E.

7   Theodore Levitt, "Marketing Myopia," *Harvard Business Review*, July–August 1960, 45–56.

8   Daniel Kahneman, Jack Knetsch, and Richard H. Thaler, "Anomalies: The Endowment Effect, Loss Aversion, and Status Quo Bias," *Journal of Economic Perspectives*, Vol. 5, No. 1, 1991, 193–206.

CHAPTER 4

1   Jim Taylor, "Business: Ten Laws of Prime Business Preparation," *Psychology Today*, September 5, 2010, https://www.psychologytoday.com/blog/the-power-prime/201009/business-ten-laws-prime-business-preparation.

2   Peter Drucker, *Management: Tasks, Responsibilities, Practices* (New York: Harper & Row, 1973), 39.

3   http://trueviralnews.com/clayton-christensen-has-a-new-theory/.

4   Frances Frei and Anne Morriss, "Culture Takes Over When the CEO Leaves the Room," *Harvard Business Review* (blog), posted May 12, 2012, https://hbr.org/2012/05/culture-takes-over-when-the-ce.

5   James Heskett, *The Culture Cycle: How to Shape the Unseen Force That Transforms Performance* (Upper Saddle River, NJ: FT Press, 2012).

6   Eric C. Sinoway, "When to Fire a Top Performer Who Hurts Your Company Culture," *Harvard Business Review* (blog), posted October 15, 2012, https://hbr.org/2012/10/beware-of-the-cultural-vampire. See also https://hbr.org/2011/12/what-great-companies-know-abou.

CHAPTER 5

1   Christopher Mims, "How Self-Driving Cars Could Wipe Out Uber," *Wall Street Journal*, May 8, 2017, B1, B4.

2   Amy Webb, *The Signals Are Talking: Why Today's Fringe Is Tomorrow's Main-stream* (New York: Public Affairs, 2016), 97.

CHAPTER 6

1   Robert Klara, "Why 74-Year-Old Cheerios Is Still America's No. 1 Cereal," *Adweek.com*, September 9, 2015, http://www.adweek.com/brand-marketing/why-74-year-old-cheerios-still-america-s-no-1-cereal-166715/.

2   Ibid.

3   Bali Sunset, *Marketing Campaign Case Studies* (blog), posted January 12, 2009, http://marketing-case-studies.blogspot.com/search/label/General%20Mills%20Inc.

4   Nathalie Tadena, "Cheerios Is King of Commercial Spending Among Cereal Brands," *Wall Street Journal*, July 17, 2014, https://blogs.wsj.com/cmo/2014/07/17/cheerios-is-king-of-commercial-spending-among-cereal-brands/.

5   Hasbro Corporate, "Brief Overview of Hasbro's History," https://corporate.hasbro.com/images/2013_HasbroHistory.pdf.

6   Megan Wilde, "Evolution of Mr. Potato Head," *Mental Floss* (blog), posted March 18, 2011, http://www.cnn.com/2011/LIVING/03/18/mf.mr.potato.evolution/.

7   "Hasbro, Inc.," International Directory of Company Histories, *Encyclopedia.com*, accessed June 21, 2017, http://www.encyclopedia.com/social-sciences-and-law/economics-business-and-labor/businesses-and-occupations/hasbro-inc.

8   "Hasbro, Inc. History," *International Directory of Company Histories*, Vol. 16 (Detroit: St. James Press, 1997), cited at FundingUniverse.com, http://www.fundinguniverse.com/company-histories/hasbro-inc-history/.

9   Ibid.

10 Ibid.

11 "Hasbro Outlines Growth Strategy Rooted in Licensing and with an Emphasis on International Sales," *Intellectual Property News* (blog), posted October 24, 2013, https://www.bvresources.com/blogs/intellectual-property-news/2013/10/24/hasbro-outlines-growth-strategy-rooted-in-licensing-and-with-an-emphasis-on-international-sales.

12 Harold L. Erickson, "Cable News Network (CNN)," *Encyclopædia Britannica*, last updated May 5, 2017, https://www.britannica.com/topic/Cable-News-Network.

13 Kathryn Rudie Harrigan, *Joint Ventures, Alliances, and Corporate Strategy* (Washington, DC: Beard Books, 2003), 169, https://books.google.com/books?id=JeY_afXHSnEC&pg=PA167&lpg=PA167#v=snippet&q=satellite%20news&f=false.

14 Erickson, "Cable News Network (CNN)."

15 Pew Research Center, "State of the News Media 2016," June 2016, http://www. journalism.org/2016/06/15/cable-news-fact-sheet/.

16 Associated Press-NORC Center for Public Affairs Research and American Press Institute, "How Millennials Get News: Inside the Habits of America's First Digital Generation," March 2015, https://www.americanpressinstitute. org/publications/reports/survey-research/millennials-news/.

17 Gerry Smith, "Comcast CEO Prepares His Netflix Killer For An Olympics Showcase," Bloomberg.com, accessed August 7, 2017.

18 Darcy Frey, "How Green Is BP?" *New York Times Magazine*, December 8, 2002, http://www.nytimes.com/2002/12/08/magazine/how-green-is-bp.html; and Terry Macalister and Eleanor Cross, "BP Rebrands on a Global Scale," *The Guardian*, July 24, 2000, https://www.theguardian.com/business/2000/ jul/25/bp.

19 John Browne, Robin Nuttall, and Tommy Stadlen, *Connect: How Companies Succeed by Engaging Radically with Society* (New York: Public Affairs, 2015), 67, 68, 71.

20 Browne, Nuttall, and Stadlen, *Connect: How Companies Succeed by Engaging Radically with Society*, 71–72.

21 "CNBC Transcript: Facebook COO Sheryl Sandberg Speaks with CNBC's Julia Boorstin on 'Squawk Alley' Today," news release, September 27, 2016, http://www.cnbc.com/2016/09/27/cnbc-transcript-facebook-coo-sheryl-sandberg-speaks-with-cnbcs-julia-boorstin-on-squawk-alley-today.html.

22 David E. Bell and Jason Riis, *"Red Lobster," Harvard Business School* Case 511-052, September 2010. (Revised February 2011).

CHAPTER 7

1 Daan Stam, Robert G. Lord, Daan van Knippenberg, and Barbara Wise, "An Image of Who We Might Become: Vision Communication, Possible Selves, and Vision Pursuit," *Organization Science* 25, no. 4 (July–August 2014), 1172–1194 at 1173; Eric Van den Steen, "Organizational Beliefs and Managerial Vision," *Journal of Law, Economics, and Organization* 21, no. 1 (2004), 256–283 at 257.

2 Daan van Knippenberg and Sim B. Sitkin, "A Critical Assessment of Charismatic-Transformational Leadership Research: Back to the Drawing Board?," *Academy of Management Annals* 13 (February 2013), 1–60.

3 Ibid.

4 Warren Boeker, "Strategic Change: The Influence of Managerial Characteristics and Organizational Growth," *Academy of Management Journal* 50, no. 1 (February 1997), 152–170.

5   Bruce J. Avolio, Fred O. Walumbwa, and Todd J. Weber, "Leadership: Current Theories, Research, and Future Directions," *Annual Review of Psychology* 60 (2009), 421–449.

6   Stam et al., "An Image of Who We Might Become."

7   Central Park Conservancy, "Central Park: A Research Guide," accessed June 23, 2017, http://www.centralparknyc.org/assets/pdfs/institute/Central-Park-Conservancy-Research-Guide.pdf.

8   Pew Project for Excellence in Journalism, "The State of the News Media 2009," http://www.stateofthemedia.org/2009/network-tv-intro/audience/; and Pew Research Center, "State of the News Media 2016." See also http://assets.pewresearch.org/wp-content/uploads/sites/13/2016/06/30143308/state-of-the-news-media-report-2016-final.pdf.

9   Kathy Haley, "Forbes' DVorkin Shares Lessons Learned," *NetNewsCheck*, October 2, 2014, http://www.netnewscheck.com/article/36306/forbes-dvorkin-shares-lessons-learned.

10 Lisa O'Carroll, "Forbes Media's Lewis DVorkin, 'I'm not a geek, I just like doing new things,'" *The Guardian*, April 21, 2013, https://www.theguardian.com/media/2013/apr/21/forbes-media-lewis-dvorkin.

11 A. Henderson, D. Miller, and D. Hambrick, "How Quickly Do CEOs Become Obsolete? Industry Dynamism, CEO Tenure, and Company Performance," *Strategic Management Journal* 27, no. 5 (2006), 447–460.

12 Ibid.

13 C. Crossland, J. Zyung, N. Hiller, and D. Hambrick, "CEO Career Variety: Effects on Firm-Level Strategic and Social Novelty," *Academy of Management Journal* 57, no. 3 (2014), 652–674.

14 R. Adams, A. Licht, and L. Sagiv, "Shareholders and Stakeholders: How Do Directors Decide?," *Strategic Management Journal* 32 (December 2011), 1331–1355.

15 Y. Berson, S. Oreg, and T. Dvir, "CEO Values, Organizational Culture, and Firm Outcomes," *Journal of Organizational Behavior* 29, no. 5 (2008), 615–633.

16 Jennifer Maloney, "Coke's New CEO James Quincey to Staff: Make Mistakes," *Wall Street Journal*, May 9, 2017, https://www.wsj.com/articles/cokes-new-ceo-james-quincey-to-staff-make-mistakes-1494356502.

17 Adam M. Grant, Elizabeth M. Campbell, Grace Chen, Keenan Cottone, David Lapedis, Karen Lee, "Impact and the Art of Motivation Maintenance: The Effects of Contact with Beneficiaries on Persistence Behavior," *Organizational Behavior and Human Decision Processes*, Vol. 103 (2007), 53–67.

CHAPTER 8

1   "Marriott: From Root Beer Stand to Ritz-Carlton," Forbes YouTube Channel video, 24:12, December 18, 2013, https://www.youtube.com/watch?v=FRRBDaNxLLQ.

2   http://www.govtech.com/network/Wi-Fi-Hot-Spots-for-Rent-How-Public-Libraries-Are-Changing-with-the-Times.html.

CHAPTER 9

1   Mark R. Leffler, "The New Golden Age of TV Drama: How HBO and AMC Became the New NBC and CBS," *Review Magazine*, 2009, https://review-mag.com/archive/680-689/689/captain_video.htm.

2   Kristina Monllos. "GE Imagines A World Where We Treat Female Scientists Like Celebrities," accessed August 6, 2017, http://www.adweek.com/brand-marketing/ge-imagines-a-world-where-we-treat-female-scientists-like-celebrities/.

3   Bill Marriott, "Success Is Never Final—Marriott On The Move," http://www.blogs.marriott.com/marriott-on-the-move/2014/06/success-is-never-final.html.

INDEX